Contemporary Library Architecture

Focusing on the practical issues that need to be addressed by anyone involved in library design, Ken Worpole offers his renowned expertise to architects, planners, library professionals, students, local government officers and members interested in creating and sustaining successful library buildings and services.

Contemporary Library Architecture features:

- a brief history of library architecture

- an account of some of the most distinctive library designs of the twentieth and twenty-first centuries

- an outline of the process for developing a successful brief and establishing a project management team

- a delineation of the commissioning process

- practical advice on how to deal with vital elements such as public accessibility, stock-holding, ICT, back office functions, children's services, co-location with other services such as learning centres and tourist and information services, and sustainability

- in-depth case studies from around the world, including public and academic libraries from the UK, Europe and the USA

- full colour illustrations throughout, showing technical details and photographs.

This book is the ultimate guide for anyone approaching library design.

Ken Worpole is Emeritus Professor at the Cities Institute, London Metropolitan University, and adviser on public policy to the UK government, the Commission for Architecture and the Built Environment, and the Heritage Lottery Fund. He is also the author of many books and studies on architecture, landscape and urban design. *The Independent* newspaper wrote that 'for many years Ken Worpole has been one of the shrewdest and sharpest observers of the English social landscape.'

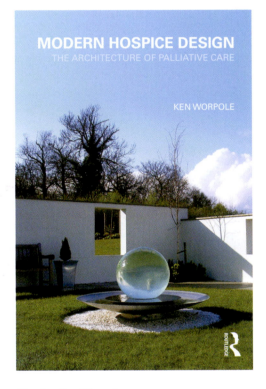

Also by Ken Worpole

Modern Hospice Design: The Architecture of Palliative Care
(Routledge 2009)

Contemporary Library Architecture

A PLANNING AND DESIGN GUIDE

Ken Worpole

Routledge
Taylor & Francis Group

LONDON AND NEW YORK

First published 2013
by Routledge
2 Park Square, Milton Park, Abingdon, Oxon OX14 4RN

Simultaneously published in the USA and Canada
by Routledge
711 Third Avenue, New York, NY 10017

Routledge is an imprint of the Taylor & Francis Group, an informa business

British Library Cataloguing in Publication Data
A catalogue record for this book is available from the British Library

Library of Congress Cataloging in Publication Data
Worpole, Ken.
Contemporary library architecture : a planning and design guide / Ken
Worpole.
pages cm
Includes bibliographical references and index.
1. Library architecture. 2. Library buildings--Design and construction. I.
Title.
Z679.W83 2013
727'.8--dc23
2012036229

ISBN: 978-0-415-59229-1 (hbk)
ISBN: 978-0-415-59230-7 (pbk)
ISBN: 978-0-203-58403-3 (ebk)

Typeset in ITC Officina Sans Std 9/12.5 pt
by Fakenham Prepress Solutions, Fakenham, Norfolk NR21 8NN
Printed in Great Britain by Ashford Colour Press Ltd, Gosport, Hants

There is nothing natural about the public domain. It is a gift of history, and of fairly recent history at that. It is literally a priceless gift. The goods of the public domain cannot be valued by market criteria, but they are no less precious for that. They include fair trials, welcoming public spaces, free public libraries, subsidised opera, mutual building societies, safe food, the broadcasts of the BBC World Service, the lobbying of Amnesty International, clean water, impartial public administration, disinterested scholarship, blood donors, magistrates, the minimum wage, the Pennine Way and the rulings of the Health and Safety Executive.

David Marquand, *Decline of the Public: The Hollowing-out of Citizenship*, 2004

A library is a very specific sort of building. A building where you collectively do something individual. With a theatre it's the other way round. There you look individually at something collective. The interesting thing about the phenomenon of the library is that everyone wants to create a private domain, even if only for ten minutes. You see also that visitors nearly always consciously choose a place. I don't think there's any other building where the tension between the individual and working in a collective space is so emphatically present as in a library. That's why we also said – discovered actually – that as soon as you enter a library, you're also involved with other people. Just like in a park for instance. Individual versus collective plays a strong part in a library.

Wiel Arets, architect of Utrecht University Library, *Living Library*, 2005

Designers of these turn-of-the-twenty-first-century library buildings have rejected architectural precedents; they have, for the most part, done away with the notion of type and developed highly individualised schemes, many of which call into question tried and true ways of organising a library. And they have reconsidered what it means to reflect a sense of place and how to respond to the building's site and its urban and regional contexts. These new public libraries have taken on forms and characters that support the libraries' fundamental goals: to promote easy access to information, to provide a legible layout and effective circulation, to permit the effective deployment of staff, to allow for flexibility and relatively easy expansion, to enhance the interior environments for the myriad activities that go on inside, and to respond to their urban and regional contexts. The balance of these responsibilities is different in each city, and the design that achieves that balance is different in each case. Hence we have the great diversity among the great contemporary libraries.

Shannon Mattern, *The New Downtown Library*, 2007

Contents

Acronyms **viii**
List of illustrations **ix**
Acknowledgements **1**

PART 1 THE LIBRARY IN THE CITY   2

CHAPTER 1 A city with a great library is a great city   4

PART 2 THE LIBRARYNESS OF LIBRARIES   30

CHAPTER 2 Libraries: the 'sacred' spaces of modernity   32

CHAPTER 3 What you see is what you get: key elements of library architecture   42

CHAPTER 4 A new wave of library architecture   52

PART 3 PLANNING AND DESIGN PROCESSES   58

CHAPTER 5 Developing the brief and establishing a project management team   60

CHAPTER 6 Places and partners   76

CHAPTER 7 Programmes and people: the changing library programme   88

CHAPTER 8 A vital space for children and young people   98

PART 4 SELECTED CASE STUDIES   102

CHAPTER 9 Public library case studies   104

CHAPTER 10 Academic library case studies   146

PART 5 LESSONS FOR THE FUTURE   164

CHAPTER 11 Lessons from the case studies and post-occupancy evaluation   166

CHAPTER 12 Twenty-first century libraries: changing forms, changing functions   186

Bibliography **190**
Further acknowledgements **193**

Acronyms

AIA   American Institute of Architects (USA)

ALA   American Libraries Association (USA)

ARCLIB   Architectural Librarians Group (UK)

BREEAM Building Research Establishment Environmental Assessment Method (UK)

CABE   Commission for Architecture & the Built Environment (UK)

CILIP   Chartered Institute of Library & Information Professionals (UK)

DCMS   Department for Culture, Media and Sport (UK)

DDA   Disability Discrimination Act (UK)

ICT   Information & Communications Technology

IFLA   International Federation of Library Associations

MLA   Museums, Libraries, Archives (UK)

MOA   Mass Observation Archive (UK)

OPAC   Online Public Access Catalogue (UK)

PFI   Private Finance Initiative (UK)

POE   Post-Occupancy Evaluation

RIBA   Royal Institute of British Architects (UK)

RFID   Radio Frequency Identification

SCONUL Society of College, National and University Libraries Librarians (UK)

List of Illustrations

Entrance to Brighton Library and piazza foreground   2

Figure 1.1 Seattle Public Library: Fourth Avenue Plan (Copyright OMA)   5

Figure 1.2 Seattle Public Library: Dewey Decimal System - organised book spiral (Copyright OMA)   6

Figure 1.3 Seattle Public Library by Rem Koolhaas & OMA (Photo: Graeme Evans)   6

Figure 1.4 Ground floor reading lounge of Seattle Public Library (Photo: Graeme Evans)   7

Figure 1.5 Entrance to Bibliothèque Nationale. Architect: Dominique Perrault   8

Figure 1.6 Public piazza at British Library. Architect: Colin St John Wilson; sculpture by Eduardo Paolozzi   9

Figure 1.7 Hot-desking in British Library café   9

Figure 1.8 Aberdeen University Library, designed by schmidt/hammer/lassen, opened in 2011   10

Figure 1.9 The library as a 'third place' between home and work: first floor reading area of Jaume Fuster Library, Barcelona, designed by Josep Llinàs, and opened in 2005   12

Figure 1.10 Mixture of informal reading armchairs and study tables on ground floor of Norwich Library, designed by Michael Hopkins & Partners, and opened in 2001   12

Figure 1.11 Central Library, Birmingham, by architect John Madin, opened in 1974, now due for demolition   15

Figure 1.12 Library of Birmingham: image of front elevation at night (Credit: Hayes Davidson)   15

Figure 1.13 Computer-generated image of the new Library of Birmingham in its Centenary Square setting (Credit: Hayes Davidson)   15

Figure 1.14 Library of Birmingham: image of bookwall rotunda (Credit: Hayes Davidson)   18

Figure 1.15 Library of Birmingham: image of public amphitheatre (Credit: Hayes Davidson)   18

Figure 1.16 Main eastern entrance of Mitchell Library, Glasgow, designed by William B. White, opened in 1911   19

Figure 1.17 Ground floor fiction section of refurbished Mitchell Library, Glasgow   20

Figure 1.18 Busy ground floor café and reading area of Mitchell Library, Glasgow, re-designed and refurbished in 2004   20

Figure 1.19 The heroic facade of what was once St Andrew's Hall, designed by James Sellars and opened in 1877, now forming the western entrance of Mitchell Library, Glasgow   20

Figure 1.20 Canada Water Library, Southwark, London, designed by Piers Gough of CZWG, opened in 2011, integrating Docklands and Underground railway connections   21

Figure 1.21 Exterior of Clapham Library by Studio Egret West, opened 2012, combining apartments, health centre and public library   22

Figure 1.22 C. L. R. James Library, Dalston, London Borough of Hackney, designed by Earle Architects, opened in 2012   22

Figure 1.23 Dagenham Library, London Borough of Barking & Dagenham, designed by ArchitecturePLB, opened in 2010   22

Figure 1.24 Extension to Enfield Library, London Borough of Enfield, designed by Shepheard Epstein Hunter   23

Figure 1.25 Shepherd's Bush Library, London Borough of Hammersmith & Fulham, part-designed by FaulknerBrowns, opened in 2009   23

Figure 1.26 Clapham Library street level entrance, fronted by public sculpture by Andrew Logan spelling out LIBRARY in free-standing sculpted letters   24

Figure 1.27 Drawing by architect Christophe Egret of proposed main atrium hall at Clapham Library   25

Figure 1.28 Interior of new Clapham Library, opened 2012; bold massing on a busy thoroughfare, combining apartments, health centre and public library. Designed by Studio Egret West   25

Figure 1.29 Krystalgade Library, Copenhagen, an early example of the grand library atrium   26

Figure 1.30 Deep plan interior of Flushing Library (Queens Public Library) designed by Polsheck Partnership. (Photo: Nick Darton)   26

Figure 1.31 The multi-level atrium at Aberdeen University Library, designed by schmidt/hammer/lassen   27

Figure 1.32 Interior of Rotterdam Library   28

Figure 1.33 Library of Birmingham: image of section (Credit: Hayes Davidson)   29

Impressive entrance to Passmore Edwards Free Library in Shoreditch, London, designed by architect H.T. Hare, and opened in 1897   31

Figure 2.1 Capital figure on former Cardiff Central Library   33

Figure 2.2 Sailors' Reading Room at Southwold, Suffolk   34

Figure 2.3 Stockholm City Library, designed by architect Erik Asplund   34

Figure 2.4 Ceremonial staircase at Swiss Cottage Central Library, designed by Sir Basil Spence, opened in 1964 and refurbished by John McAslan & Partners in 2003   35

Figure 2.5 Ceremonial staircase at Sheffield Western Library, designed by Gollins Melvin Ward and Partners, restored by Avanti Architects   35

Figure 2.6 Ceremonial staircase at Cranfield University Library, designed by Foster + Partners   36

Figure 2.7 Canada Water Library, Southwark, London, designed by Piers Gough of CZWG, occupying a key waterside site in former docklands   37

Figure 2.8 The 'Black Diamond' city library, an extension to the Royal Library of Copenhagen, designed by schmidt/hammer/lassen   38

Figure 2.9 Bold LIBRARY sign at Boscombe Library, Bournemouth, a development by Hawkins Brown, including apartments   39

Figure 2.10 Children's section at Sutton Library, London (All rights reserved – London Borough of Sutton Library Services)   41

Figure 3.1 Steps of New York Public Library, one of the city's great meeting places   43

Figure 3.2 Peckham Library designed by Alsop & Störmer, winner of 2000 Stirling Prize   44

Figure 3.3 Rotunda of the former British Library Reading Room in Bloomsbury, now vacated and used by the British Museum   44

Figure 3.4 Imposing presence of The Picton Library, Liverpool   45

Figure 3.5 Great Rotunda of Manchester Central Library, designed by E. Vincent Harris and opened in 1934   45

Figure 3.6 Imposing entrance of Stockholm Library   45

Figure 3.7 Circular facade of Bourne Hall Library, Ewell, in Surrey, designed by A.G.Sheppard Fidler and Associates, opened in 1970   46

Figure 3.8 Circular stairwell at LSE Library, London, designed by Foster + Partners   47

Figure 3.9 Circular stairwell at Canada Water Library, Southwark, London, designed by Piers Gough of CZWG   47

Figure 3.10 Public atrium of Norwich Forum leading to Norwich Central Library, designed by Michael Hopkins & Partners, and opened in 2001   48

Figure 3.11 Entrance and facade of Carnegie Library, London Borough of Enfield   49

Figure 3.12 Entrance and facade of Carnegie Library, London Borough of Enfield (detail)   49

Figure 3.13 Interior of Uppsala Public Library   50

Figure 3.14 Striking design of the prow end of the modernist Swiss Cottage Library, designed by Basil Spence, opened in 1964   51

Figure 3.15 Southend on Sea Central Library opened in 1974   51

Figure 4.1 Idea Store reception desk, London Borough of Tower Hamlets   54

Passers-by stop to look at site hoardings with plans for new Library of Birmingham, displayed by Mecanoo architect, Francine Houben   58

Figure 5.1 People, programmes, partners and places: the virtuous circle (CABE & RIBA, 2004)   64

Figure 5.2 Pop-up library: Seven Kings Library, London Borough of Redbridge, converted from a vacant discount store   65

Figure 5.3 Interior of Seven Kings Library, London Borough of Redbridge, converted from a vacant discount store   65

Figure 5.4 Amsterdam Public Library designed by Jo Coenen & Co Architecten, opened in 2008, and much visited by librarians from around the world. (Photos: Mike Llewellyn)   69

Figure 5.5 Interior of new public library and community centre in former mining community of Houghton Le Spring, near Sunderland   70

Figure 5.6 New art gallery in refurbished public library at Bishop Auckland by Ainsworth Spark Associates   70

Figure 5.7 Site plan of March Library, Cambridgeshire, designed by Bernard Stillwell Architects   71

Figure 5.8 Cross-section of March Library, Cambridgeshire, designed by Bernard Stillwell Architects   72

Figure 5.9 March Library   72

Figure 5.10 March Library interior   73

Figure 5.11 Corner entrance to Apeldoorn Cultural Centre in The Netherlands, designed by Herman Hertzberger   74

Figure 5.12 Facade of existing Apeldoorn Library   75

Figure 5.13 Café and gallery at Apeldoorn Cultural Centre and Library   75

Figure 6.1 Shepherd's Bush Library occupies a corner site, much to its advantage   78

Figure 6.2 Uppsala Library Reading Room   80

Figure 6.3 Cardiff Central Library designed by BDP: connecting views   81

Figure 6.4 Aberdeen University Library: the view from above of the café-foyer area   82

Figure 6.5 Mediathèque Jean-Pierre Melville in Paris, with strong visual connections between library and street   84

Figure 6.6 Library & Health Centre at Cambourne in Cambridge, designed by West Hart Partnership (Practice)   85

Figure 6.7 Interior of Library & Health Centre at Cambourne in Cambridge, showing common foyer, waiting area and reading room   85

Figure 6.8 Boscombe Library, Bournemouth, a development by Hawkins Brown, including apartments   87

Figure 6.9 Gallery and art workshop at Winchester Discovery Centre   87

Figure 7.1 Floor plan of West Derby Carnegie Library, 1905, re-drawn by Ian Worpole. Clear allocation of spaces to functions, including separate reading rooms for 'Boys' and 'Ladies'   89

Figure 7.2 Floor plan of Parkhead District Library, Glasgow (Courtesy of Gerald Blaikie, Scotcities). The children's library has its own entrance into a separate basement, as at Viipuri. Separate Ladies' Reading Room   90

Figure 7.3 Photographs of local scenes enliven ends of stand-alone shelving units at Huntingdon Library   91

Figure 7.4 The Hague Library, designed by Richard Meier, opened 1995   92

Figure 7.5 Good use of columns for clear sign-posting at Jaume Fuster Library in Barcelona   94

Figure 7.6 Open Air Library in Magdeburg, Germany, designed by Karo with Architektur + Netzwork   96

Figure 7.7 Terrace garden and entrance to new extension of Winchester Discovery Centre   97

Figure 8.1 Childrens's Zone clearly dermarcated at The Hub, Kinson, Bournemouth, designed and installed by Radford HMV Group Ltd   100

Figure 8.2 Stylish Philippe Starck chairs in Internet Zone, Ward End Library, Birmingham, designed by John Hunt Associates (Photo: Kevin Duffy)   101

Figure 9.1 Site plan, Jaume Fuster Library, Barcelona, Courtesy of Josep Llinàs   104

Figure 9.2 Ground floor plan, Jaume Fuster Library, Barcelona, courtesy of Josep Llinàs. The self-contained children's library is to the right. The cafe is bottom left, and the art gallery top left.   105

Figure 9.3 First floor plan, Jaume Fuster Library, Barcelona, courtesy of Josep Llinàs   105

Figure 9.4 Street corner view of Jaume Fuster Library, Barcelona, commanding a major intersection   106

Figure 9.5 Canopied, set-back entrance to Jaume Foster Library, drawing visitors in   106

Figure 9.6 First floor, Bournemouth Library. Courtesy of BDP   107

Figure 9.7 Elevation, Bournemouth Library. Courtesy of BDP   108

Figure 9.8 Section, Bournemouth Library. Courtesy of BDP   108

Figure 9.9 Interior view of main first floor atrium at Bournemouth Library   109

Figure 9.10 Brightly painted angular support columns add dynamism to interior of Bournemouth Library   110

Figure 9.11 Ground floor plan, Jubilee Library, Brighton (© Bennetts Associates)   111

Figure 9.12 Section perspective, Jubilee Library, Brighton (© John Bradbury)   112

Figure 9.13 View of ground floor of Brighton Library   113

Figure 9.14 Corner view of 'floating' first floor reference library, connected by walkways and bridges   113

Figure 9.15 Ground floor plan, Canada Water Library. Performance auditorium to the left, courtesy of CZWG Architects   115

Figure 9.16 First floor library floor plan, Canada Water Library, courtesy of CZWG Architects   116

Figure 9.17 Second floor library plan, Canada Water Library, courtesy of CZWG Architects   116

Figure 9.18 View from upper tier of Canada Water Library to first floor lending library   117

Figure 9.19 The new Canada Water Library end-stops a public piazza linking bus, underground and overground rail services   117

Figure 9.20 Bold corner canopied entrance of new Dagenham Library by ArchitecturePLB, with apartments above and either side   118

Figure 9.21 Main staircase and atrium at Dagenham Library   119

Figure 9.22 Floor plan and cross section of Bourne Hall Library, Ewell, opened 1970 (Images courtesy of Surrey Libraries and held in the Epsom and Ewell Local Family History Centre)   120

Figure 9.23 Art gallery interior, connected to circular edge of public library at Bourne Hall Library, Ewell, Surrey   121

Figure 9.24 'It looked as though a space ship had landed.' Bourne Hall Library designed by A.G. Sheppard Fidler and Associates   121

Figure 9.25 The Bridge Library at Easterhouse Arts Centre: floor plan and context, courtesy of Gareth Hoskins Architects   122

Figure 9.26 The Bridge Library at Easterhouse Arts Centre: library section   123

Figure 9.27 The Bridge Library, Easterhouse, by Gareth Hoskins Architects. Internal walkway adjacent to main library space   123

Figure 9.28 The Bridge Library at Easterhouse Arts Centre at night. Photograph by Andrew Lee   124

Figure 9.29 Street frontage of Hook and Chessington Library, Royal London Borough of Kingston upon Thames, by Dunlop Haywards & Quintessential Design   125

Figure 9.30 Hook Library and Community Centre: library, café, meeting rooms, computer training and recording studio   126

Figure 9.31 Main library desk at Hook Library overlooking computer suite   126

Figure 9.32 Huntingdon Library: ground floor plan. Courtesy of CPMG Architects Limited   127

Figure 9.33 Huntingdon Library: first floor plan. Courtesy of CPMG Architects Limited   128

Figure 9.34 Pronounced corner of new Huntingdon Library and Archive, designed by Crampin Pring McCartney Gant and opened in 2009   129

Figure 9.35 Ground floor interior of Huntingdon Library and Archive   129

Figure 9.36 Level 1 Floor plan, Newcastle City Library, courtesy of Ryder Architecture   131

Figure 9.37 Level 2 Floor plan, Newcastle City Library, courtesy of Ryder Architecture   131

Figure 9.38 Ground floor of Newcastle Library by Ryder Architecture   132

Figure 9.39 Enquiry desks and quick access computer stalls on ground floor of Newcastle Library   132

Figure 9.40 Corner glazed tower of Newcastle Library   133

Figure 9.41 Norfolk and Norwich Millennium Project: The Forum Context Plan. Courtesy of Michael Hopkins & Partners   134

Figure 9.42 Norfolk and Norwich Millennium Project: Ground Floor Plan. Courtesy of Michael Hopkins & Partners   135

Figure 9.43 Norfolk and Norwich Millennium Project: The Forum Cross Section. Courtesy of Michael Hopkins & Partners   136

Figure 9.44 Glazed facade of Norwich forum, from library, looking across to main market square and city roofline   137

Figure 9.45 Norwich Library purposely mixes reference and lending stock, causal reading and study areas   138

Figure 9.46 Main public area of Norwich Forum leading to Norwich Millennium Library   138

Figure 9.47 Idea Store Whitechapel: ground floor plan with subsequent suggestions by designers, mackenzie wheeler, for adaptations and enhancements after several years of intensive use   139

Figure 9.48 Whitchapel Idea Store   141

Figure 9.49 Curving book display units and bright rubberised floors at Idea Store Whitechapel   142

Figure 9.50 Ground floor plan, Winchester Discovery Centre. Courtesy of Hampshire County Council   143

Figure 9.51 Grade I listed former Corn Exchange now refurbished as Winchester Discovery Centre (including library)   144

Figure 9.52 Well sign-posted lending library rotunda and stairs to upper library floor and gallery at Winchester Discovery Centre   145

Figure 9.53 Handsome extension to former Winchester Corn Exchange providing additional library space and café, designed by Hampshire County Council Architects   145

Figure 10.1 Aberdeen University ground floor and furnishing plan. Courtesy of HCS Business Interiors   147

Figure 10.2 Aberdeen University first floor and furnishing plan. Courtesy of HCS Business Interiors   148

Figure 10.3 Aberdeen University seventh floor and furnishing plan. Courtesy of HCS Business Interiors   148

Figure 10.4 Aberdeen University Library by schmidt/hammer/lassen, opened in 2011   149

Figure 10.5 Main raised plaza entrance to Aberdeen University Library, reflecting older buidlings   149

Figure 10.6 Sculptural atrium balconies and library areas at Aberdeen University Library   149

Figure 10.7 Cranfield University Library: Section   150

Figure 10.8 Cranfield University Library: Ground floor plan   151

Figure 10.9 Cranfield University Library: First floor plan   151

Figure 10.10 Cranfield University Library: Second floor plan   151

Figure 10.11 Scalloped overhang canopy at Cranfield University Library by Foster + Partners   152
Figure 10.12 Interior view of library atriums and galleries at Cranfield University Library   152
Figure 10.13 Library balconies and galleries at Cranfield University Library   152
Figure 10.14 University of Sheffield Information Commons: Ground floor plan. Reproduced courtesy of RMJM   153
Figure 10.15 University of Sheffield Information Commons: First floor plan. Reproduced courtesy of RMJM   154
Figure 10.16 University of Sheffield Information Commons: Section BB   155
Figure 10.17 External view of Sheffield University Information Commons by RMJM, opened in 2007   155
Figure 10.18 Informal reading room lounge at Sheffield University Information Commons   155
Figure 10.19 Western Bank Library, The University of Sheffield. Catalogue Hall & Reading Room Plan – After Works. Reproduced with kind permission of Avanti Architects   156
Figure 10.20 Western Bank Library, The University of Sheffield. Section – AA   157
Figure 10.21 Western Bank Library, the University of Sheffield. Section – BB   157
Figure 10.22 Park view of Sheffield University Western Bank Library by Gollins Melvin Ward and Partners, restored by Avanti Architects   158
Figure 10.23 Restored first floor library reception hall at Sheffield Western Bank Library   159
Figure 10.24 University of Surrey: Proposed site plan. Reproduced courtesy of RMJM   160
Figure 10.25 University of Surrey: Ground level plan. Reproduced courtesy of RMJM   161
Figure 10.26 University of Surrey: Level 1 plan. Reproduced courtesy of RMJM   161
Figure 10.27 University of Surrey: Section 2-2. Reproduced courtesy of RMJM   162
Figure 10.28 New extension of Surrey University Library and Learning Centre by RMJM   162
Figure 10.29 Stairwell and study areas at Surrey University Library and Learning Centre   163
Walkways, bridges, galleries and light-wells at the new Cardiff Central Library   165
Figure 11.1 Corner prow of Flushing Library, New York (Photo: Nick Darton)   168
Figure 11.2 Corner prow of Bournemouth Library providing a bold end-stop to the urban edge   169
Figure 11.3 The library at night: Barking Learning Centre (Library & Art Gallery)   169
Figure 11.4 The library at night: The Bridge Arts Centre, Easterhouse, Glasgow (Photo: Andrew Lee)   170
Figure 11.5 Lewisham Library at night   170
Figure 11.6 The Whitechapel Idea Store is firmly rooted in the street life of the busy market area   171
Figure 11.7 Bold corner presence of C.L.R. James Library, London Borough of Hackney, but entrance poorly evident   172
Figure 11.8 Confused arrangement and sign-posting of entrance and exit doors at Boscombe Library, Bournemouth   173
Figure 11.9 The amphitheatre stairs outside Birmingham Central Library – a popular meeting place   174
Figure 11.10 Clear, well sign-posted entrance to the Library, Cirencester, new extension opened in 2008   174
Figure 11.11 Principal first floor library area at Bournemouth Library   175
Figure 11.12 Good connectivity between ground and first floors of Lewes Library   175
Figure 11.13 Bright glazed entrance vestibule to underground library at Essen in Germany   176
Figure 11.14 Interior of public library, Essen, Germany   176
Figure 11.15 Oval atrium with ceremonial staircase at Winchester Discovery Centre with excellent signage of shelving   177
Figure 11.16 Group Study Room at Surrey University Library: maximum transparency   178
Figure 11.17 Forest Gate interior   178
Figure 11.18 Café at the Library, Huntingdon Library, Cambridgeshire   180
Figure 11.19 Café and browsing area at Newcastle Central Library   180
Figure 11.20 Ground floor foyer and café area at Aberdeen University Library   181
Figure 11.21 Informal meeting area for library users and local voluntary groups at The Bridge Arts Centre, Easterhouse, Glasgow   182
Figure 11.22 Colour can create a sense of luxury and fun: Cardiff Central Library   183
Figure 11.23 Transparency and interplay between indoor and outdoor spaces at Norwich Forum Library   183
Figure 11.24 Restored spiral staircase at Swiss Cottage Library   184
Figure 11.25 Open-plan and approachable staff area at Cranfield University Library   185

Acknowledgements

I am very grateful to colleagues at the Cities Institute, London Metropolitan University, for support in many ways during the researching and writing of this book, in particular Professors Graeme Evans and Leonie Kellaher, along with Sue Bagwell, Jo Foord, Clare Redwood and Antje Witting. Many thanks also to Caroline Mallinder, and to Laura Williamson at Routledge. As always, an enormous debt of gratitude is due to Larraine Worpole, who shares in everything.

Unless otherwise credited, all photographs are by Larraine Worpole and Ken Worpole.

PART 1

The library in

Entrance to Brighton Library and piazza foreground

he city

CHAPTER 1

A city with a great library is a great city

The public library building is enjoying a new era of prestige across the world, with considerable architectural innovation during the past twenty years. Today, however, libraries are as much about creating places where people meet, read, discuss and explore ideas, as they are about the collection and administration of books in an ordered form. The idea of the modern public library as a 'living room in the city' is becoming a vital feature of modern urban culture, and architects are having to respond to this change of role. Towards the end of this chapter a schema is proposed which compares and contrasts the distinctive attributes of the traditional public library and the modern public library architectural paradigms. Such changes necessitate a major shift in the way these new building projects are developed and commissioned, and these highly political procurement and development processes are discussed.

Against expectations, the public library building is enjoying a new era of prestige across the world. So too are many other forms of library design and architecture, as higher education expands to meet a global demand for better educated populations capable of attending to their own intellectual self-development and professional expertise. No modern town or city is truly complete without a confident central library functioning as a meeting place and intellectual heart of civic life, echoing the sentiment of the inscription above the door of the grand reading room of the modern Nashville Library which opened in the summer of 2001: 'A city with a great library is a great city.'

The core functions of these new libraries are not simply more of the same (and bigger and bolder) – they are different in very many ways from what has gone before. As architect and critic Brian Edwards has observed, 'Libraries have seen more change in the past twenty years than at any time in the past hundred' (Edwards, 2009: xiii). Edwards is one of an admirable group of contemporary library historians, architectural critics and practitioners, whose advocacy of the new library movement has been especially helpful in the writing of this book, along with Alistair Black, Kaye Bagshaw, Biddy Fisher, Shannon Mattern,

Ayub Khan, Simon Pepper and Romero Santi. I also learned much from the study into new library buildings conducted at Sheffield University by Jared Bryson, Bob Usherwood and Richard Proctor. Many other researchers and writers are acknowledged at the end. Likewise the bibliography will, I hope, provide some idea of the scale and range of writing now available which regards the library building as central to the improved life chances and well-being of people in modern democratic societies.

In a special edition of the journal *Architectural Review*, devoted to 'The Library and the City', architectural critic Trevor Boddy (2006) expressed some scepticism about the so-called 'Bilbao Effect', which suggested that only iconic museums designed by world-famous architects could rescue failing cities from oblivion. He noted that, 'It seems evident that the building that will come to emblematise the beginning of a new century of public architecture is not the latest Kunsthalle by Hadid, Holl or Herzog & de Meuron, but rather Rem Koolhaas' Seattle Central Public Library.' In this I concur, noting that in several of the most audacious designs for new world-status museums there is actually nowhere for people to sit or engage with each other. Who are these buildings really being designed for, and what is the nature of civic entitlement and democratic exchange embodied within them? Such questions are now being asked around the world as a generation of 'iconic' cultural buildings struggle to find revenue funding and audiences. For a devastating critique of the baleful influence and final implosion of the 'Bilbao Effect', few can better Deyan Sudjic's acerbic essay on 'The Uses of Culture' in his book *The Edifice Complex* (2006), where Sudjic itemises the overblown rhetoric and spiralling costs of many of these grand self-referential museum projects, and their early demise or slow foundering.

The reason why libraries still have a clear civic edge over the proliferation of art galleries and museums of recent years – in the name of urban regeneration – is because they continue to provide a much richer range of public spaces than these other forms of cultural provision, public or private. It was Seattle Library's 'trailblazing take on public space' that excited Boddy. He enthused that its 'levels provide niches for scholars, corporate researchers, bibliomanes, teen-daters and even the homeless seeking refuge from the rain' (Boddy, 2006: 45). This universal welcome and reach he stated, were 'shared by most of the libraries gathered in these pages.' Economic historian Edward Glaeser urges all those involved in future urban regeneration programmes to invest in people, and in projects such as public libraries which encourage learning, participation and the development of social capital, not *grands projets* providing consumer spectacle for those lucky enough to have time and money to spare (Glaeser, 2011).

Seattle Public Library

Now probably the most famous newly designed and completed public library in the world, Seattle's Public Library opened on 23 May 2004. Designed by Rem Koolhaas and his Dutch firm, Office for Metropolitan Architecture (OMA), along with LMN Architects in Seattle, its gigantic, deconstructed irregular mass now dominates one area of the city, and has

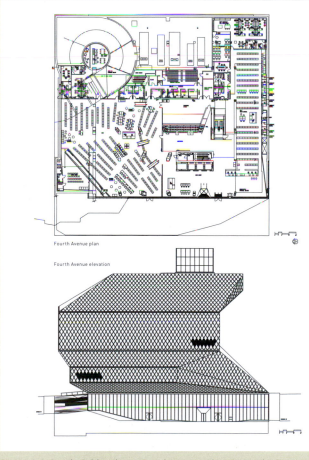

Fourth Avenue plan

Fourth Avenue elevation

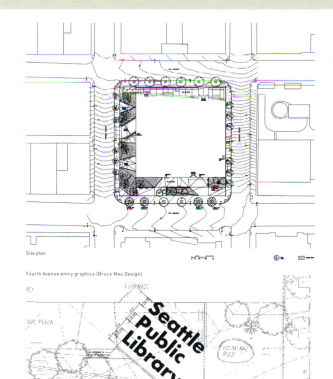

Site plan

Fourth Avenue entry graphics (Bruce Mau Design)

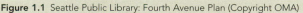

Figure 1.1 Seattle Public Library: Fourth Avenue Plan (Copyright OMA)

clearly been designed to express the shock of the new, whilst simultaneously challenging every accepted cliché of what a public library should look like. It is said that Koolhaas refuses to accept architectural concepts such as 'type' and 'generic style', and believes that architecture should be based on a research-based approach to the design process that takes nothing as given but always starts with a *tabula rasa*. In his own words, the library is 'a physical expression of the struggle to maintain the sanctity of public space and build an efficient, technological machine in a world that is in a constant state of flux' (Mattern, 2007: 75).

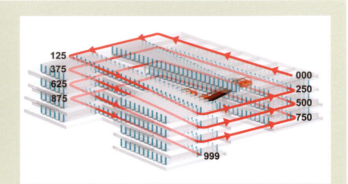

Figure 1.2 Seattle Public Library: Dewey Decimal System - organised book spiral (Copyright OMA)

The building's strikingly unconventional shape – basically a series of five boxes (one below ground) stacked irregularly on top of each other, producing a set of cantilevered overhangs as well as deep insets – is said to make it more resistant to wind and earthquakes, reinforced by an exoskeleton of diamond-patterned steel mesh. Seattle journalist Regina Hackett aptly suggests that 'the building has a split personality. All the brutal chic is on the outside, its diamond-shaped steel and glass skin stretched over muscle ... Inside, the library appears to change its character, starting with the assymetrical steel skin, which internally is painted a luscious and lulling baby blue.' The deeply indented or extended edges on all four sides produced a range of lighting conditions inside which offer both shade and direct sunlight, all mediated by the steel mesh skin.

The internal spaces are located across eleven different levels, with the first five levels given over to children's and teen library areas, auditoria, language centre, fiction, living room, café and meeting rooms, with the 'mixing chamber', described by one writer as a 'trading floor for information' taking up most of level 5. Above that the famous Books Spiral works its way up through levels 6, 7, 8 and 9 – where the main non-fiction stock is to be found in one continuous thread of shelving following an internal ramp which slopes continuously upwards at an angle of two degrees. At level 10 there is a large reading room with views out across the city, and, finally, level 11 is wholly allocated to administration. This schema or division of space is based on the programme being divided into five main compartments: Administration, Books, Meeting,

Figure 1.3 Seattle Public Library by Rem Koolhaas & OMA (Photo: Graeme Evans)

Information and Parking. Those using the reading room to study, browsing for non-fiction, and thus likely to stay longer will need to rise further up the building. Those coming to attend language classes, to borrow a novel, or accompany children, or meet friends will find most of their needs met closer to the ground. Each floor is connected to the next by escalators as well as elevators.

To European eyes the building appears to become its own biosphere, almost entirely separate from the street or any kind of meaningful public landscape or street culture. It is its own world. But this is true of almost every steel and glass high-rise building surrounding it in downtown Seattle – each one a self-contained universe cut adrift from life at ground level. Unsurprisingly the building is served by its own

underground car park with 143 spaces. Apparently during the consultation process the City Librarian, Deborah Jacobs, said that more car parking was one of the biggest issues raised at public meetings. There are street level entrances at Level 1 on Fourth Avenue and at Level 3 on Fifth Avenue.

The new library cost $165 million and offers 363,000 square feet of library space and 49,000 square feet of underground parking. In its first year of use the library was attracting 15,000 visitors a day. The library has the capacity to hold more than 1.4 million books. It has been awarded Silver Rating by the U.S. Green Building Council as well as a 2005 Honor Award for Outstanding Architecture given by the American Institute of Architects (AIA).

Figure 1.4 Ground floor reading lounge of Seattle Public Library (Photo: Graeme Evans)

Certainly in North America, today's civic boosters no longer demand a new convention centre but, rather, want a splendid new city-centre library. Shannon Mattern has detailed this precipitate rise of interest in her account of the development of new libraries in Brooklyn, Cincinnati, Chicago, Denver, Nashville, Queens, Salt Lake City, Seattle and many other US cities. In Europe, and most certainly in the UK, the story is the same, with a writer for the Daily Telegraph declaring that today 'the library is becoming a must-have element in prominent town-planning schemes'. However, the excitement for the new needs to be tempered with

the knowledge that in other parts of the social landscape the branch library or the community library is facing real problems of survival, as neighbourhood economies wilt under the macro-economic pressures of centralising goods and services in towns and cities across the world.

Nevertheless, these new libraries are winning architectural prizes for their bold imaginative response to the changing public library programme. In 2000 the relatively small library in Peckham, south London, designed by Alsop & Störmer won the highly prestigious

Stirling Prize. In 2003 Bournemouth Library designed by Building Design Partnership won The Prime Minister's Better Public Building Award, which Brighton's Jubilee Library designed by Bennetts Associates & Lomax Cassidy Edwards went on to win in 2005 (along with thirteen other awards), in a highly competitive field on both occasions.

PUBLIC AND CAMPUS LIBRARIES IN PARTICULAR

This guide to the planning and design of libraries focuses specifically on public libraries and libraries serving higher education campuses, principally in the UK. Though there are many things to be admired in the design of national libraries, for example, there are major generic differences which make it impossible to 'scale down' from a single, national institution to a widely disseminated local one. While today's public and college libraries have to function successfully as meeting places, this is not necessarily true of national libraries. For example the Bibliothèque Nationale in Paris is not only located away from the city centre, but is raised on a forbidding plinth, after which one descends via narrow escalators down to a basement entrance. This design renders it almost determinedly resistant to informal or casual use. Dutch library administrator Bas Savenije is similarly critical of Colin St John

Wilson's British Library, whose café spaces and other gathering areas are too tucked away he feels – though there's no doubt that the piazza in front of the British Library works well in good weather for library users and visitors, it is not felt to be a public space in its own right. Meanwhile, more and more British Library users now make use of every available space, including the stairs and floors, to work or meet, so there is a sense that they themselves have created spaces, even if they were not originally planned.

Furthermore national libraries generally have restricted conditions of use and serve people coming from very long distances, including other countries. By contrast, the public library and the campus library have to provide a convivial setting for all those living and working close by, and thus have a universal remit to be welcoming and open to everybody. The astonishing new campus library at the University of Aberdeen, designed by architects schmidt/hammer/lassen, embraces this wider remit as a beacon for the city, the region and the nation beyond. As its prospectus notes:

> The largest cultural project in Scotland for many years, our library will be a symbol that beckons to the future as much as it showcases the past. It will stand as an international beacon that challenges us to defy stagnation and rethink what our region is capable of, to embrace the belief that education must be inspirational, not merely pragmatic.

Figure 1.5 Entrance to Bibliothèque Nationale. Architect: Dominique Perrault

Figure 1.6 Public piazza at British Library. Architect: Colin St John Wilson; sculpture by Eduardo Paolozzi

Figure 1.7 Hot-desking in British Library café

Figure 1.8 Aberdeen University Library, designed by schmidt/hammer/lassen, opened in 2011

Even so, some of those with much to say about the role of the library in society remain unhappy at this expansion of the core library remit – which is now to serve as a place in the city for people to meet, as much as it is a space where books are collected for public reference and use. In the summer of 2011 there was a heated exchange of letters in the *Times Literary Supplement* in response to a columnist ridiculing a local authority policy statement which suggested that today libraries are as much about people as they are about books. A similarly charged debate erupted in early 2012 surrounding the proposal to re-configure the lower floors of the New York Public Library – in a design by Foster + Partners – and to replace storage space with circulating library space and new space for readers and writers, including easy access public borrowing, along with, inevitably, a coffee bar (Darnton, 2012). The proposal actually intends to increase and widen public use of the library, yet has been denounced by critics as an attack on the historic democracy of public library space. 'A

vast Internet café', is the nightmare vision of the old guard, even though the design is intended to increase book borrowings.

This otherwise unremarkable creed remains a heresy in some literary and academic quarters, though one suspects it exists most strongly amongst people who, in fact, rarely use public libraries in the course of their busy opinionated lives. As someone who has visited public libraries inside the Arctic Circle, behind the Iron Curtain, in the Australian outback and in small-town America, along with Brian Edwards I remain completely relaxed about the contemporary public library ethos which shares its attention equally between the collection of books and providing a meeting place for the people who use them. As Edwards cogently argues: 'The library would be needed even if we abandoned the book merely because it brings people together in the pursuit of knowledge' (Edwards, 2009: xii). The books provide the focus of the library ideal, and always will, but it is the meeting of minds, the conversations and the interchanges, the everyday humanity of sharing a common intellectual space with other people, that matters equally. It is for these reasons that one agrees with Danish and international library consultant, Hellen Niegaard, that 'The library universe is growing' (Niegaard, 2011: 177).

Make no mistake, the libraries detailed in this book are attracting large numbers of people. Brighton now gets nearly 1 million visits a year, Newcastle and Norwich 1.5 million each per annum, and even smaller libraries such as the Idea Store in Whitechapel or the new library at Shepherd's Bush, both in poorer London neighbourhoods, are getting up to 1,500 visitors a day. Mecanoo's new library for Birmingham, now under construction, anticipates attracting up to 15,000 visitors a day, in the same league as Seattle. Moreover the range of people using libraries continues to expand, with many of the newer libraries reporting much higher levels of use by young people. While having reservations about David Adjaye's original design for Whitechapel's Idea Store (and continuing uncertainties about this new generic 'brand' name), every time I visit the building it is buzzing from top to bottom, from the penthouse art gallery and café area to the ground floor lending stock – as busy as a department store at sale time, and certainly more socially and culturally uplifting.

In this regard the library continues to function successfully as what sociologists such as Ray Oldenburg have termed a 'third place' – a vital place distinct from the two other main sites of human existence, the home and the place of work. These 'third places' are where both conviviality and sanctuary are offered in a range of highly public as well as more intimate forms and configurations. Given that 34 per cent of UK households now consist of a single person (by comparison, in Sweden it is an astonishing 47 per cent and in India just 3 per cent), then such meeting places become ever more vital (Klinenberg: 2012). The growing phenomenon of the 'single-person' city – both Amsterdam and Paris have single-person households now in a majority according to the *New York Times* of 5 February 2012 – provides new opportunities for public libraries to become centres of a new urban sociability.

This is equally true of the campus library as it is of the neighbourhood or city centre public library. Indeed the case studies provided later clearly emphasise the social role that academic libraries play in student life, even when not strictly needed by those who could get all the information they need online. The campus library is today a great meeting place where social identities are formed, as well as being a place of research and private study. The expansion of higher education in the UK and in many other parts of the world has led to a boom in library construction and, according to Karen Latimer, as a result of the 1993 Follett Report, 'some one hundred new academic library

building projects were initiated in the late twentieth and early twenty-first centuries in the UK' (Latimer, 2011: 117).

However, there is a principal difference between the campus library and the public library, notably that the former is usually restricted to a known and immediate constituency of users – accredited students – and the need to be quite so open and transparent to the outside world is not required. For this reason even the newer academic libraries evince a higher degree of introversion in their design than the new public libraries. They are still places where people can hide away for a day in quiet study, oblivious to the world outside. A design for a new university library in Katowice in Poland, by HS99 architects, has an almost entirely solid facade of sandstone panels and looks to all appearances like two large brick boxes joined together – almost a mausoleum. Conversely, large areas of glazing and transparency are dominant features of many new public libraries, keen to entice passers-by inside by day and night.

Of particular interest in this regard has been some scenario planning by the 'Academic Libraries of the Future' project in the UK, designed to describe possible futures for teaching and research libraries in Higher Education, given the economic, social and political pressures they are currently experiencing. They outline three distinct scenarios, each with its own opportunities and drawbacks:

- the 'Wild West' library
- the 'Beehive' library
- the 'Walled Garden' library.

In the first case, the library becomes an entirely 'customer-focused' service, funded from a mixture of public, private and voluntary sources, whose central ethos is simply giving users what they want from a range of largely self-directed programmes of learning materials and modular courses. It espouses little connection to traditional university values of study for its own sake, or even specialist strengths associated with particular departments. It is a pick and mix world of highly individualised, retail learning. One might adduce – though architectural implications are not discussed in these scenarios – that a library building serving this 'Wild West' would be rather like an educational mall, where study 'product' is attractively displayed, and which can easily be accessed via customised packages, all supported by coffee shops, technology outlets and other commercial support services.

Second, the 'Beehive' scenario envisages a library which is principally state-funded, hierarchical and ordered, and leans more towards training a skilled workforce and intellectual sector

Figure 1.9 The library as a 'third place' between home and work: first floor reading area of Jaume Fuster Library, Barcelona, designed by Josep Llinàs, and opened in 2005

Figure 1.10 Mixture of informal reading armchairs and study tables on ground floor of Norwich Library, designed by Michael Hopkins & Partners, and opened in 2001

than supporting a consumer-based free-for-all. It elides with a top-down notion of state planning for economic success, and is highly vocational. Designing the ideal building for this model would emphasise mass production, efficiency, high turnover and fast circulation, all supported by state of the art timetabling of rooms, lecture theatres and computer suites. Modular buildings would be ideal, pre-fabricated offsite and assembled quickly.

Finally, the 'Walled Garden' library cleaves to the traditional notion of the academic library as a place apart from the press of everyday life, a sanctuary of quiet and disinterested intellectual values, remote from either commercial interests or public policy agendas, and a place where the imagination – but also and including scientific innovation and discovery – might flourish, which itself would ultimately benefit the wider society. Here the architectural imagination could take wing, providing an inward-looking collection of large and small spaces, cloistered possibly around a central courtyard, with strict rules of entry, but liberal freedom of movement allowed inside: access all areas to the *illuminati*!

Clearly, none of these scenarios is like to take shape entirely within any single library, and one can see how a number of new campus libraries already contain clear elements of each, though in different proportions. But the scenario planning is a good *aide-memoire* when discussing the programme for a new academic library, and should be appreciated and valued as such for all those involved in current and future academic library provision and planning.

With regard to the public library, a similarly dramatic programmatic transformation from a building designed almost exclusively to house a collection of books and other research materials for public access, to a building which emphasises its social role as a hub of self-learning and enquiry (and as a meeting places for groups and individuals, and as a venue for talks and discussions about literature, ideas, professional development and even job opportunities), has enormous architectural implications. Many of these new libraries are no longer foursquare neo-classical buildings with an imposing facade and entrance hall, but are sequences of brightly lit spaces, some highly public, others discreet and personal. As Shannon Mattern has noted:

> Libraries continue to be relevant – vital – public institutions. And this vitality is now encoded in new physical forms. Unlike their turn-of-the-twentieth-century and mid-century predecessors, today's libraries do no fit a mould. In fact,

many of them don't even 'look like libraries'. In rejecting an obligation to conform to an architectural type, today's public libraries are free to choose shapes and styles that speak to the cities and populations they serve.

(Mattern, 2007: ix)

These sentiments are also echoed in Finland, where library architecture enjoys a very high status, with one commentator noting that today 'the public library building has come to be regarded as highly complex with multiple social and cultural functions; and no longer is any single model for it considered plausible' (Mehtonen, 2011: 164).

LIBRARIES, OLD AND NEW

The evolution of library architecture is one of the most fascinating stories in the wider history of architectural adaptation and change. Such a story could be told at length – and has been – but it can also be represented schematically (see Table 1.1). When I first proposed this schema, as a mildly provocative *aide-memoire*, I assumed that people would not take it as being literal. Alas some did. It was intended to be suggestive and ideal-typical, not definitively true.

The new libraries and radical refurbishments detailed in this book all contain elements of this major shift to a wholly new way of thinking about library design and the services it is seeking to achieve. Nevertheless, every decade or so a new library exerts a particular hold on the imagination of all of those who love libraries, wherever they live in the world, and in recent decades the King's Norton Library at Cranfield University by Sir Norman Foster + Partners (UK, 1992), the new extension to Malmö Library by Danish architect, Henning Larsen (Sweden, 1997), Delft's Technical University Library by Mecanoo (Netherlands, 1997), Peckham Library by Alsop & Störmer (UK, 2000), Norwich Public Library by Michael Hopkins & Partners (UK, 2001), the Seattle Central Library by Rem Koolhaas & OMA (USA, 2004), J.M.Coenen's Amsterdam Library (Netherlands, 2007) and most recently Aberdeen University Library by schmidt/hammer/lassen (Scotland, 2011) have all set new benchmarks for design and understanding how libraries must now work to meet the demands of students and citizens today. I believe that Piers Gough's Canada Water Library and Studio Egret West's Clapham Library will also enjoy similar prestige and acclaim. Shortly to come are major new libraries in Aarhus (Denmark), Birmingham (UK), Oslo (Norway), Caen (France) and Helsinki (Finland).

Table 1.1 Traditional library architecture and contemporary library architecture

Traditional Library Architecture	Modern Library Architecture
Neo-Classical pattern-book	Modern free-style
Imposing steps and entrance halls	Street-level, retail entrances
Needs of disabled people unmet	Good disability access
Domes and rotunda	Atria and ground-floor cafés
Galleries and mezzanines	Escalators & lifts
Clerestory light	Atrium light
Restricted access to books	Open access to books & other materials
Bookshelves requiring ladders	Bookshelves at human scale
Temple of knowledge	The 'living room in the city'
Institutional furniture	Domestic or 'club' furniture
Stand alone service	Shared space with other services
Hierarchical design & circulation	Open-plan design & circulation
Canonical stock-holding	Contemporary cultural market-place
Individual study carrels	Seminar rooms and computer suites
Defensive space	Networked space
Librarians as knowledge custodians	Librarians as knowledge navigators
The rule of silence	A culture of mutual respect

Brian Edwards has proposed a briefer but no less helpful and suggestive schema for understanding the history of library design, in Table 1.2.

Edwards concludes:

> More recent library designs have almost reversed the principles upon which earlier generations of buildings were based. The question of orientation and legibility on the one hand, and access to natural light, view and ventilation on the other, has allowed library typology to go through a profound change. Most recent libraries are shallow (as against deep) in plan, have a variety of types of space inside, have daylight throughout (and often sunlight in

selected areas too), have clearly identified routes with their own architectural language, have distant views as well as close desk ones and, as a consequence, more organic configuration. Functionally, the computing and book material is integrated so the reader can move readily between both types of information.

(Edwards, 2009: 253)

Table 1.2 Changing environmental strategies in the design of libraries

Time period	Daylight	Ventilation
18th century	Natural light, shallow plan	Natural ventilation, perimeter windows
19th century	Natural light, roof-lit deep plan	Natural ventilation, perimeter & roof cross-ventil
20th century	Artificial light, deep plan	Air-conditioning & mechanical ventilation
21st century	Natural light, roof-lit, light-shelves	Nat vent, mixed-mode, solar chimneys

(Edwards, 2009: 85)

Not only are the external appearances of the new libraries changing. The internal layout of the library is also being reconfigured, from a highly compartmentalised and differentially regulated set of discrete spaces, towards a more open-plan, exploratory set of 'zones and hubs'. As a result the working practices and skills of those working in libraries are changing too. The introduction of self-service machines enables staff to come out from behind the issues and returns desk and meet and greet visitors, guiding them towards the services they require. The role and status of the library user is changing too, and in the course of researching this book, one architect told me that he quickly learned that 'there is no typical library user any more'.

In the 1980s it seemed necessary to describe those who used libraries as 'customers', representing the introduction of market disciplines and relationships into public services. Today there is some move to altering the terminology yet again, perhaps more positively. Brian Gambles, who has spearheaded the development of the new library in Birmingham, likely to become the largest public library in Europe, prefers to think of those who will use it as 'members'. The library of the future will act more as a club, he claims, bringing both a sense of belonging and benefits of membership to the relationship, rather than the instrumental transactionalism of the 'customer-provider' relationship. He says he wants the new library to 'foster that sense of community ownership of the physical space'. It thus becomes a destination building as much as a service centre.

Birmingham: Library of Birmingham

Opening date: Summer 2013
Client: Birmingham City Council
Architect: Mecanoo Architecten
Project description: Public library, exhibition and performance space.
Library size: 31,000 square metres
Cost: £189 million
Stock: 2 million books, 3m photographic images and 6,000 archive collections
Visitor numbers expected: up to 15,000 per day.

The present building

The present Birmingham Central Library was designed by architect John Madin in a monumental and consciously 'brutalist' style, and opened in 1974 as part of a development called Paradise Circus, close to the other major civic buildings. At the time it was said to be the largest civic library in Europe. The building dominated what was then an under-developed site, with much later development (1990s) enclosing within its interior courtyard a shopping

Figure 1.11 Central Library, Birmingham, by architect John Madin, opened in 1974, now due for demolition

Figure 1.12 Library of Birmingham: image of front elevation at night (Credit: Hayes Davidson)

Figure 1.13 Computer-generated image of the new Library of Birmingham in its Centenary Square setting (Credit: Hayes Davidson)

mall mostly occupied by pubs, cafés and fast-food outlets. The main entrance faces across a stepped public amphitheatre in Chamberlain Square to the former Town Hall (designed to imitate a Roman temple by J.A. Hansom and Edward Welch in the 1830s), and to the Birmingham Museum & Art Gallery. These south-facing steps have always provided a popular meeting place and sitting out area in the city centre.

Though not always loved by the public, the unusual and memorable style of the building, principally a vast, four-square, upturned ziggurat, dominated the skyline from the west, and the curved entrance pavilion also gave it a distinctive look when approached from the south – where the main entrance is located. Both English Heritage and the Twentieth Century Society fought long and hard to have the building listed for its singular contribution to twentieth century British architecture, but without success, and the old library is due to be demolished after 2013, once the new building opens close by.

Despite its severe appearance and modest front entrance, the old library was one of the busiest in the UK, attracting up to 5,000 visits a day. Lending library services were spread over several floors, with the reference sections to the west of the building, looking inwards, and creating a rather cloistered – and appropriately secluded and reflective – space according to many of its users. A series of semi-enclosed escalators took library users from one floor to the next. This large complex also housed a 250 seat library theatre, a pioneering 'Centre of the Child' on the ground floor (created to make up for the fact that in the original design the children's library in the basement had been something of an afterthought), extensive photographic and document archives, business library and a large number of specialist book collections.

A number of factors contributed to the decision by Birmingham City Council to develop a new library. One was that the existing library building was in dire need of repair, and valuable collections were being slowly damaged by inappropriate environmental conservation conditions within; it was estimated that repairing the building might well have cost as much as building anew. Of equal importance was that the original Paradise Circus development itself now blocked the vital connectivity of a wholly new and free-flowing quarter encompassing the historic buildings of the Cathedral, Council House, former Town Hall, Museum & Art Gallery, with the refurbishment of the Birmingham

Repertory Theatre, the National Convention Centre and Brindleyplace to the west of Centenary Square. A new library – or 'people's palace' as its architect, Francine Houben, calls it – would complete the major regeneration of this area, creating one of the largest cultural districts of any major European city.

The new building

Seven architectural practices were selected through a competitive process to discuss how they might approach the question of designing an exemplary building on a difficult site. These firms were short-listed on the basis of a detailed submission including their track record – whether in library or related architectural achievement (including public realm projects) – and a number of different practices' earlier projects were visited by politicians and city council officers. The Dutch firm, Mecanoo, were selected for their ability to fully understand what the Council wanted to achieve, and in their imaginative response to the final brief.

Central to the design is the wish to relate the library interior to the popular public life of Centenary Square itself. 'Bringing the outside in' and 'Bringing the inside out' were proposed in the brief. This idea was allied to the very strong aspiration that anyone entering the library must feel that they are embarking on a journey, in which events, places and experiences unfold as visitors move through the building, along with a sense of delight and surprise. The traditional spatial and regulatory divide between 'lending' and 'reference' functions is now abandoned – as increasingly happens in most new public libraries today – in favour of 'broad thematic subject groupings or zones and hubs'. Self-service for checking in and out lending materials is now the norm, and library staff will adopt a much more inter-active role with visitors, 'offering advice, support, mentoring and guidance; this will influence the design of floor layouts.' In short, the former, highly compartmentalised library with its fixed service points and highly regulated staff/visitor relationship is clearly giving way to a much more flexible series of spaces where the visitor is now largely responsible for his or her own use of the facilities, in a more exploratory and informal way.

However, it is recognised that this flexibility needs to be tempered by the fact that 'parts of the building may need to be open 24 hours a day, for example loan returns and some study space'. Furthermore there are security issues which also require clear boundaries:

> All visitors leaving the Library of Birmingham must cross a security line that screens for items not authorised to be removed from the building. The provision of security screening will be complicated by movement between areas within the development including the lending and reference areas, the archive and heritage centre, front and back of house, the library, the theatre and the shared facilities. Differing levels of security will be required in different parts of the building. For example, in the archives and heritage centre, access to rare and fragile materials must be in a controlled and secure manner. Dealing with security issues effectively yet sensitively will be fundamental to the overall appeal of the Library of Birmingham.

The differentiation of space, both for security but also for programmatic reasons, raises a major issue of architectural philosophy, which was expressed in the design brief:

> At the heart of this challenge also lies the key architectural issue about whether it is possible or even desirable to create 'universal' library space, unifying material into a comprehensive whole, or whether modern demands require ever more specific and fragmented environments.

In short, is the new library to be experienced as an integrated whole, or is it to be experienced as an assembly of different elements? Will 'the libraryness of library buildings' disappear?

The library will hold some 2 million book items, 150,000 of which will be available for loan, and another 250,000 reference items on public accessible shelves. There are a number of other distinct collections which have to be treated with special regard, including the Shakespeare Library, Rare Books, the photography collection, amongst others. Then of course there is a separate children's library which will need to have its own ethos and security protocols. In addition there will be shared auditorium and conference facilities, open access computer suites and work-stations, meeting rooms, exhibition areas and non-public offices. The library will include a British Film Institute Mediatheque. Whether these can all be wrapped up in a single 'universal' design code, remains to be seen.

The library will become a central element in a cluster of nearby cultural facilities, including the International Convention Centre, the Symphony Hall, Birmingham Town Hall (now a Grade I listed concert and meeting venue), the Birmingham Museum and Art Gallery, the Birmingham Repertory Theatre and the Ikon Gallery. In a way the library also has to act as a gateway and information service for all these other facilities and their programmes.

MAJOR ELEMENTS OF THE NEW BUILDING DESIGN

The new library will occupy 10 floors, including a lower ground floor which extends into an underground amphitheatre in Centenary Square – open to spectators through a large viewing area at ground level. The children's library will be here, though as a result of the roofless amphitheatre close by and light from the triple-height floor-to-ceiling-glazing, will still have a lot of natural lighting. A set of soft-furnished terraced steps end-stop one end of the children's library providing a large, but highly individualised reading area. The top floor consists of the Shakespeare Memorial Library housed in a rotunda. Most of these floors are visually connected to each other through sight-lines across balconies, large atrium spaces, escalators (some suspended across open voids), so the whole is certainly a dynamic public experience.

The building has a prominent entrance on Centenary Square – served by wide revolving glass doors – and there is a hall on the intermediate floor which serves as a connecting gallery between the library and the adjacent Birmingham Repertory Theatre. Two floors are being designed as the 'golden box' where the most valuable archives are securely held and protected, but including an exhibition space where a changing display of archive material will be made available to the public.

The dramatic external appearance of the library is enhanced by the use of an aluminium frieze in black and white covering most of the exterior cladding. At levels five and six this is complemented by a gold-coloured anodised rainscreen system which contributes to the climatically controlled environment within for the archive collections. The ground floor, double-height facade is transparent glazing.

The library will feature two external terraces: a full-width 12-metre deep terrace at third floor level overlooking

Centenary Square and a smaller rear terrace at seventh floor level. The top floor will have a public viewing gallery. All these help bring the city and the library together as a continuous experience, as, it is hoped, will the roofless amphitheatre located at basement level which can be viewed by passers-by looking down from Centenary Square. This is a bold move and will require careful management, as traditionally open voids in large public areas have sometimes been badly misused.

The Library of Birmingham is due to open in 2013, and is currently on target. The building was 'topped out' on 14 September 2011, by the Leader of the Council, and a performance was given in the amphitheatre. This is almost certainly the most eagerly awaited new public library building in the UK, and beyond, for many years, and in some ways upon its success depends the continuing relevance of the city library as a central feature of urban life and democracy.

Figure 1.14 Library of Birmingham: image of bookwall rotunda (Credit: Hayes Davidson)

Figure 1.15 Library of Birmingham: image of public amphitheatre (Credit: Hayes Davidson)

THE LAST GOOD PLACE?

The space of the library therefore gains even greater symbolic value. Once embodying enlightenment values and the spirit of self-improvement, it now also represents shared or collective values too. In some ways it is 'the last good place' in an overwhelmingly commercialised urban environment, and is increasingly seen and appreciated as such. For Brian Edwards:

> The shifting politics of power in the library has been to the advantage of architectural space. As the importance of the reader has grown under the influences of falling book prices, and the ever-lowering cost of information technology, so there has been a growing recognition of the value of space as the medium of interchange. Space allows staff and readers to exchange, readers to interface with books and digital systems, the public to experience the democratic ideals of the public library and students to engage in the pedagogical value of the university library. Space, and how it is variously treated, is as important as the book.
>
> (Edwards, 2009: 7)

The current project to transform the interior of Manchester's famous 1930s circular library is 'to increase the amount of public space,' according to the Head of Libraries, Information and Archives. 'We have created a new ground floor and added an additional 2,200 square metres in the lower ground floor of the Town Hall Extension. The new design is more focused on how individuals will use the space, rather than where we put the books' (Raven, 2011: 35). This creation of a new kind of public *agora* has been very successfully achieved on the ground floor of Glasgow's historic Mitchell Library.

Glasgow: The Mitchell Library

Opened 1911 & refurbished 2004
Client: Glasgow City Council
Architect: Glasgow City Council
Project description: Major refurbishment of ground floor
  library plaza

Glasgow's famous Mitchell Library – the largest public reference library in Europe – occupies a whole block of a major urban grid, though it is a composite of different buildings from different eras. The principal entrance of the original library building faces east, with a distinctive copper dome surmounting a classical facade. This was designed by William B. White and opened in 1911. Alas this entrance area is somewhat truncated and reduced in space by a dual carriageway which passes close by. At the rear of the block is the heroic facade of what was once St Andrew's Hall, designed by James Sellars and opened in 1877. This now operates as the main entrance of the building and, together with the large intermediate extension created between 1972 and 1980, is now fully incorporated into the Mitchell Library proper. Including various mezzanines, the building consists of 13 floors.

In the life of the city the Mitchell Library played a grand but declining role. Along with many other Glasgow public libraries, the service was reaching fewer and fewer people, and in the 1990s the city council decided to review the library service, seeking to renew its appeal to the wider public and arrest the decline in user numbers. Senior library management realised the appeal of the new wave of 'lifestyle bookshops',

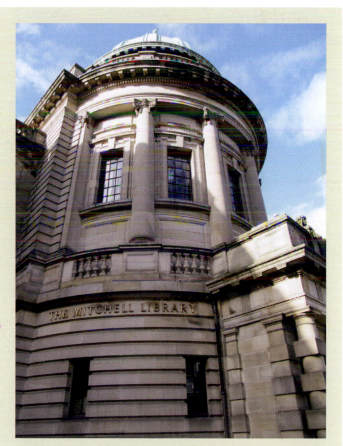

Figure 1.16 Main eastern entrance of Mitchell Library, Glasgow, designed by William B. White, opened in 1911

and sought to learn from their design appeal. They also realised they had to offer much greater public access to ICT, particularly for those who could not afford their own personal computers.

The major refurbishment of the ground floor of the entire building was undertaken by the Forward Planning & Major Projects Team of Glasgow City Council, with some design consultancy advice. The effect has been dramatic. A dark, deep, monumental interior has been re-designed as a brightly-lit indoor street and plaza, with a stylish café-restaurant, extensive computer suite & learning centre, lending library and art gallery, artfully negotiating three different ground floor levels as it leads from east to west.

Re-opened in 2004, the ground floor of the library has become another example of a very successful 'living room in the city', as well as a popular meeting place, exhibition gallery and arts venue. Only the best materials were used in the refurbishment, including beautiful parquet floors, elegant staircases and galleries, fine modern lighting. Most importantly, the once solid southern wall has been replaced by a continuous floor to ceiling glazed facade which provides light and movement to the great public interior.

Figure 1.17 Ground floor fiction section of refurbished Mitchell Library, Glasgow

Figure 1.18 Busy ground floor café and reading area of Mitchell Library, Glasgow, re-designed and refurbished in 2004

Figure 1.19 The heroic facade of what was once St Andrew's Hall, designed by James Sellars and opened in 1877, now forming the western entrance of Mitchell Library, Glasgow

Library space is always more than just Cartesian volume or empty air. It is imbued with values that have taken centuries to develop and sustain – particularly free speech and the belief that knowledge is itself powerful – and is especially precious. Those who have visited Hans Scharoun's State Library in Berlin may well agree with Peter Blundell Jones' statement that 'the library interior will be marvelled at as the work of one of the greatest spatial conceptions the world has yet seen' (Jones, 1979: 334). The sequencing of reading spaces, open floors, mezzanine floors, ceremonial staircases, is breathtaking, even in photographs (or, equally memorably, in Wim Wenders' film, 'Wings of Desire').

As is now realised, space itself is an agent of change – which is not the same thing as subscribing to a belief in architectural determinism – and in modern urban conditions the space constructed by the public library is becoming even more vital as a public setting. Some critics assume that because modern libraries devote so much space to non-book items and amenities, this is directly due to a major reduction in book stock. In most cases this is not true; rather it is that additional space is now required for other services, including IT training centres, classrooms, cafés, exhibition spaces, and so on. According to the Seattle design team, the library book stock took up just 28 per cent of the overall space – leaving room for many other activities and services.

Despite publicity given to stories of cuts to library services and library closures in many parts of the UK – especially amongst the smaller village or community libraries – it is still the case that in the UK 40 per cent of all adults continue to use public libraries as do 78 per cent of children aged 5–10. While it is true that the smaller branch libraries are struggling for funds, with a number facing closure, the modernisation or re-building of the town or city centre library is still at the centre of much urban thinking. In the course of writing this book, at least six new libraries have opened in London alone, most of them of considerable architectural ingenuity:

- Canada Water, Southwark (CZWG Architects)
- Clapham One (Studio Egret West)
- Dagenham (ArchitecturePLB)
- C.L.R.James Library, Dalston, Hackney (Earle Architects)
- Enfield (Shepheard Epstein Hunter)
- Shepherd's Bush, Hammersmith & Fulham (FaulknerBrowns).

While it is right to defend the network of older libraries against arbitrary local authority cost-cutting exercises, it is also equally important to promote and celebrate these new models of library provision.

Figure 1.20 Canada Water Library, Southwark, London, designed by Piers Gough of CZWG, opened in 2011, integrating Docklands and Underground railway connections

Figure 1.21 Exterior of Clapham Library by Studio Egret West, opened 2012, combining apartments, health centre and public library

Figure 1.22 C. L. R. James Library, Dalston, London Borough of Hackney, designed by Earle Architects, opened in 2012

Figure 1.23 Dagenham Library, London Borough of Barking & Dagenham, designed by ArchitecturePLB, opened in 2010

Figure 1.24 Extension to Enfield Library, London Borough of Enfield, designed by Shepheard Epstein Hunter

Figure 1.25 Shepherd's Bush Library, London Borough of Hammersmith & Fulham, part-designed by FaulknerBrowns, opened in 2009

Clapham Library, Lambeth

Opened: 2012
Client: London Borough of Lambeth
Architect: Studio Egret West
Project description: public library & meeting rooms within a larger development including housing and health centre
Library size: 1,900 square metres
Cost: £4 million

Clapham Library is part of a larger mixed use development designed by architects Studio Egret West, consisting of a high street public library, café, health centre and 136 apartments in a striking high rise assembly of moulded structures which brings a new energy to Clapham High Street. Development and funding came from the partnership of Lambeth Council and developers Cathedral (Clapham) Ltd.

The interior of the library consists of a large three-storey oval atrium – basement to first floor – around which slowly rises a ramp taking library users along the book-lined spiral.

The basement floor, which is essentially the public *agora*, is principally to be used as the children's library, though it can quickly be adapted for other uses. This is vital, for the key motif of the design is the library as a kind of Shakespearian globe theatre – a performance space as well as a stock-holding public library. This is a very bold design, highly dynamic, and it will be interesting to see how people adapt to its innovative shape and structure.

The wall of the drum is opened up at frequent intervals by large, irregularly shaped apertures, and some of these cut-out shapes are reproduced as suspended ceiling features, also echoed in the constructivist configuration of the mobile book units in the children's library on the drum floor. Throughout the building sight-lines are kaleidoscopic, as one moves through a series of irregular openings. A large white concrete spiral staircase occupies one edge of the interior atrium, adding yet another element of high energy to what is a very

Figure 1.26 Clapham Library street level entrance, fronted by public sculpture by Andrew Logan spelling out LIBRARY in free-standing sculpted letters

dramatic re-interpretation of the library as a public arena. All interior walls are white, and floors are polished wood.

There are also a number of breakout areas, side-rooms and sanctuary spaces, where people can read quietly, work on computers, have a coffee and read the newspapers, or retreat to their own bookish or private worlds. Principal architect, Christophe Egret, has worked on libraries before, and was centrally involved in the design of Peckham Library when he worked at Alsop & Störmer.

The public library fronts directly on to the busy Clapham High Street. It presents an attractive set of sliding glazed doors to visitors who, once inside the entrance hall can also choose to go into the health centre which shares the same entrance. Some people will want to use both facilities on the same visit, which they can easily do, while having a coffee in between.

The design has achieved an 'Excellent' rating in the Building for Life assessment process, and a BREEAM rating of 'Very Good'.

Figure 1.27 Drawing by architect Christophe Egret of proposed main atrium hall at Clapham Library

Figure 1.28 Interior of new Clapham Library, opened 2012; bold massing on a busy thoroughfare, combining apartments, health centre and public library. Designed by Studio Egret West

DO THE RIGHT THING

The decision to embark upon the design and construction of a new public library is a major public decision. The purpose of this book is to help those involved in such decisions to get it right – or as right as it can ever be. The easiest choice is to build something very similar to the old library, but bigger and brighter, or engage a famous architect and hope for the best. More rewarding for all concerned – funding bodies, politicians, library staff, library users, architects and designers – is to find a way of working together to create something very special which could only be done on that particular site in that particular town or city. Only a reflexive, problem-solving approach can achieve this. In North America, where big-budget civic libraries have

been being built over the past decade in something of a national mania, there has been a default approach which says that, if in doubt, hire a brand-name architect to do the job. This does not always work:

> Choosing a star architect, which a large number of (US) library committees have done over the years, will not solve a library's or a city's problems, of course. An architect cannot correct for poor management, a paltry collection, or lack of financial support, not can he or she promise to lead an urban renaissance, to bring patrons to an unsafe downtown with no parking and poor public transit. Particularly when an architect insists on working hermetically or interacting only superficially with the library planners, the building is bound

to be more of a homage to the designer than an important civic structure or a well functioning library. A public library is far too important a building and it has far too complex a program to ask an architect to work his or her magic without the benefit of regular interaction with a strong client.

(Mattern 2007: 24)

Increasing numbers of senior library professional and local politicians in the UK are raising their sights, and travelling abroad to see a range of new library buildings which will help them focus on what it is they need and want to do back at home. The traditional architectural competition approach to selecting the design team is changing too, becoming a more negotiated arrangement, with more emphasis on the shared vision which both client and architect are seeking to achieve rather than picking out a 'winning' design from a set of pre-arranged drawings and templates, and then sitting back and waiting until construction is finished.

Most new libraries are open-plan, often occupying several floors connected by lifts and escalators, built around an atrium which allows as much natural light into the interior as is possible – though Flushing Library in Queens, New York sticks to a deep floor plan. Krystalgade Library in Copenhagen is a classic early example of this configuration. Neon lighting and ceiling tiles are out, brightly coloured armchairs and individualised task lighting are in. The temple of learning is becoming the living room in the city, as well as 'the living lab', according to the 2011 Helsinki conference on 'The Future Library'. This latter term now seems

Figure 1.29 Krystalgade Library, Copenhagen, an early example of the grand library atrium

Figure 1.30 Deep plan interior of Flushing Library (Queens Public Library) designed by Polsheck Partnership (Photo: Nick Darton)

to be gaining ground amongst library professionals across the world, as they seek a concise way of summarising what the multi-media, exploratory nature of modern technology now demands of its public setting. The proposal for a new library in Aarhus in Denmark, to be completed by 2015 and designed by schmidt/hammer/lassen architects, is to be called Urban Mediaspace Aarhus, of which the library is just one component of an assembly of different spaces and activities.

One design principle which can work against this idea of the library space – or part of it at least – as an urban living room, is an equally powerful tendency to design the interior spaces around an atrium. While this can produce stunning and highly transparent interiors, in which users can at a glance see all the floors and the escalators and lifts to access them – as it most sensationally does at schmidt/hammer/lassen's University Library in Aberdeen – it can render the idea of sanctuary space

Figure 1.31 The multi-level atrium at Aberdeen University Library, designed by schmidt/hammer/lassen

problematic. Certainly the ground floor becomes a public arena rather than a public lounge or quiet place. Rem Koolhaas has been highly critical of the cult of the atrium in recent years, referring to them as 'voided panopticons', but there is no doubt that in some libraries they work very well to continue the life and vitality of the street – as in Newcastle-upon-Tyne's new building, or in Rotterdam's main library – but in other places, there can be a feeling of wasted space or emptiness when the library is not busy – along with the transmission of too much extraneous noise (or catering odours) from one floor to the next.

An additional reason why libraries are enjoying an increasing urban profile is because they provide a crucial space for that most important requirement of the modern town or city – the need for people to update their knowledge and keep abreast of ideas and information. Apart from the growing percentage of the population now engaged in some form of higher or continuing education (as well as professional development), white-collar work is what most urban dwellers do these days, and they will always 'hanker after public spaces to enrich the task' (Boddy, 2006: 45). The public library is now a quintessential work-space for many people, and thus has vital economic importance, even though this has yet to be realised by many local and national politicians.

Modern libraries are not only changing the patterns of library use – along with attracting a much younger audience – but are also radically changing the way staff have to work. Large formal reception desks or issue desks are disappearing, replaced by satellite information kiosks or 'hot desks' which library staff can use as and when needed, and when they are not circulating amongst users or re-filling shelves and answering reader queries. Dutch architect Wiel Arets makes the point that in the new library 'the staff should be able to see that they are working in a library, not just any old office building.' Too often in the past staff have been confined to dark basement rooms or attic rooms where they process books or undertake administrative tasks wholly cut off from the ethos of the public building.

As we shall shortly discover, surveys of library staff attitudes reveal that the quality of the building is a key factor conditioning their attitude to their work. New library architecture not only attracts a younger audience to this vital form of public provision, but also brings added status and self-esteem to those working in these new settings. This in turn can only improve the service for the public while contributing to the ideal that not only has the library a distinguished past it also has a dynamic and economically productive future.

Figure 1.32 Interior of Rotterdam Library

Figure 1.33 Library of Birmingham: image of section (Credit: Hayes Davidson)

PART 2

The librarynes of libraries

Impressive entrance to Passmore Edwards Free Library in Shoreditch, London, designed by architect H.T. Hare, and opened in 1897

CHAPTER 2

Libraries: the 'sacred' spaces of modernity

The development of the library as a public building is almost as old as writing itself. The early libraries in Alexandria and the Ancient Near East were not only storehouses of books, but were attached to museums and meeting places, and acted as cultural centres in the cities. The rise of the large civic libraries in the second half of the nineteenth century across Europe and beyond became symbolic of the enlightenment and the desire to spread knowledge to all sections of society. They were part of an improving and moralising culture which found architectural form in imposing neo-classical buildings replete with historical references. For many thinkers and writers, public libraries were the new cathedrals of the city. From their formation they were regarded as safe and quiet places, distinct and separate from the pressures of daily life, where self-improvement and study could flourish. In this world capturing the loyalty of children to the library ethos was often central to their mission.

The library is one of the oldest and most distinctive architectural types in history. Many date the building type back to the famous library at Alexandria, said to contain over 700,000 books (scrolls in fact) before it was destroyed by fire in 48 BC. However, libraries existed in a number of other places in the 'Ancient Near East' before even then. What is worth remembering about the library at Alexandria – which has continued to influence the way we think about these places today – was that the building itself (*biblion*, a place of books) was attached to a museum (*mouseion*, a place dedicated to the Muses). This cultural precinct, in today's terminology, offered, according to one historian, 'a composite model – part "think tank", part graduate school; part observatory and part laboratory' (MacLeod, 2004: 9). In short the library was not just a place where scrolls and other artefacts were collected, but was a meeting place and centre of intellectual life for the city and well beyond. In 2002 a new library was completed in Alexandria, the Bibliotheca Alexandrina, designed by the Norwegian architectural firm of Snøhetta, which has had the effect of re-connecting the library tradition in that part of the world back to its world-historical origins. The new complex

contains six specialist libraries, four museums, eight academic research centres, fifteen permanent exhibitions, a planetarium and other facilities. The historic tradition was renewed, demonstrating the power of the library ideal.

Not only is the library a distinctive building type, it is also an 'archetype' and 'prototype' for the storing of knowledge and a progenitor of an amazing range of architectural forms (Markus, 2004: 172). Yet today, as the book's dominant position as the principal format for the dissemination of human knowledge is challenged by the digital world of the Internet, so the library too faces related challenges to prove its relevance and assure its future.

While digital forms of production and dissemination are to be welcomed and embraced enthusiastically, the book as a popular cultural artefact and emblem of an educated and free society is not going to disappear in the foreseeable future, if ever at all. Nor will the traditional role of libraries as centres of information-gathering and cultural dissemination disappear either. Of their many vital roles one is to act as an archive of historical memory: a place where, as the writer John Berger once said in a radio discussion, 'we keep company with those who have lived before'. Indeed the design brief for the new Library of Birmingham specifically identifies one of its key functions is acting as a 'Memory Bank': 'It will gather, preserve, present and help interpret the collective memory and identity of the city and its communities and surroundings.'

It is a public space where past, present and future fruitfully meet. To fulfil this role, buildings are needed as much as books and other cultural records and materials. Nowhere is this critical function more beautifully captured than in a short film by Alain Resnais, *Tout la mémoire du monde*, made in 1956, where the internal workings and architecture of the Bibliothèque National in Paris are explored in all their labyrinthine detail: the 60 miles of shelving, the basement stacks connected to each other by a Piranesian network of steel galleries and bridges, the many and various reading rooms and specialist collections, in which each individual reader gathers together exactly those books and documents needed to produce that blissful state of personal 'bonheur': the happiness of the reader in a library with everything to hand and in perfect order.

THE LIBRARY ARK

The relationship between books and buildings is more complex than it looks at first sight. The French writer Victor Hugo once suggested that the book had displaced the cathedral as the source of belief and authority in society. It thus rendered one of the principal functions of architecture – as a symbolic representation of ideas – obsolete. Hugo's splendid chapter on the relationship between architecture and printing in *The Hunchback of Notre Dame*, called ominously, 'This will kill that', noted that 'the book of stone, so solid and so durable, was about to make way for the book of paper, more solid and still more durable.'

Hugo's argument was that until the invention of moveable type and the printing press, churches and cathedrals had embodied the great myths and religious stories in stone, frescoes, stained glass – along with sacred scrolls and texts retained in the hands of the priests – all contributing to 'the constant bending of all the forms of men and of nature to the incomprehensible caprices of the symbol.' Gutenburg's invention changed all that, allowing many different schools of thought to emerge and many new stories to be told. While Hugo welcomed this liberation from the old forms, he also understood just how powerful architecture had been in symbolising different belief systems and in creating structures of space that embodied ways of thinking and feeling about the

world and people's relation to it. He honoured the power of architecture by seeing it as intellectually rich in public meaning, as well as socially cohesive.

Yet he was surely wrong in thinking that printing would supplant architecture's distinctive ability to embody ideas. In fact many of the new ideas about belief, power, social relations and democracy – exemplified in what came to be regarded as the condition of modernity – equally required a new architecture to express them. The rise of architectural modernism cannot be separated from the emergence of social democracy and the welfare state, especially in Europe. The public library is today as much a symbol of civil society and democracy as the medieval monastic library was a symbol of a religious elite, and the eighteenth century private library a symbol of privilege and personal wealth. Those who question the public library's place in the civic domain, or declare it redundant or superseded, are challenging the great achievements of collective provision, public goods and the vocabulary of citizenship too.

Insofar as the book failed to displace architecture, as Hugo predicted, it is equally reasonable to assume that the Internet will not supplant the library either. Nevertheless, the changes

Figure 2.1 Capital figure on former Cardiff Central Library

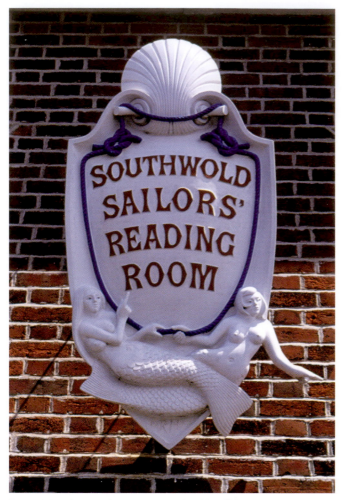

Figure 2.2 Sailors' Reading Room at Southwold, Suffolk

Figure 2.3 Stockholm City Library, designed by architect Erik Asplund

produced by the 'networked society' will require the library and the library building to be reconfigured architecturally and culturally in this new era of global information and digital culture. The irony is that in the late nineteenth and twentieth centuries public libraries became, in effect, the new cathedrals or 'sacred spaces' of the modern world, as gathering places for the culture of enlightenment and popular democracy. The Danish librarian, Jens Thorhauge, recently wrote that 'The Nordic public library system was characterised by a close interplay between the libraries and public enlightenment, along with a strong political commitment both locally and nationally to public libraries' (Thorhauge, 2002: 7). The public library thus emerged as both symbol and emblem of a new political world.

In architectural terms there were often many similarities between the old cathedrals and these new monumental civic halls: imposing Gothic or Neo-Classical entrances, with facades often displaying a frieze of symbolic figures, or niches containing busts or sculptures of great literary of cultural figures, large atria or domed halls with clerestory lighting, works of art

emblazoned on the walls, as well as public sculptures. Think of the great Stockholm City Library designed by Gunnar Asplund and completed in 1928: a long sweep of steps leads from the street up to the entrance doors, within which even steeper steps rise within marble halls decorated with scenes from the Iliad in relief designed by Ivar Johnsson, as if leading into an inner temple. The two door handles to the main entrance consisted of sculpted figures of Adam and Eve, suggesting Eden. On the exterior of the building an extended frieze displays scenes from human history, ideographs, representations of work-tools and a range of motifs and symbols offering a moral lesson to those passing by. The inner ceremonial staircase leading upwards towards the light at Stockholm is echoed in the grand staircases at Swiss Cottage Library (Sir Basil Spence), Sheffield Western (Gollins Melvin Ward and Partners, restored by Avanti Architects) and even to a degree the library at Cranfield University (Foster + Partners).

On the other hand, developing the analogy between the great library and the cathedral means that it may also simultanously function as a mausoleum, an idea proposed

Figure 2.4 Ceremonial staircase at Swiss Cottage Central Library, designed by Sir Basil Spence, opened in 1964 and refurbished by John McAslan & Partners in 2003

Figure 2.5 Ceremonial staircase at Sheffield Western Library, designed by Gollins Melvin Ward and Partners, restored by Avanti Architects

Figure 2.6 Ceremonial staircase at Cranfield University Library, designed by Foster + Partners

by Roger Stonehouse in an essay on The British Library at St Pancras, London, designed by Colin St John Wilson. Stonehouse wrote that, 'The library is in one sense a tomb, a quasi-sacred repository for the safe keeping of its contents in perpetuity, but it is also an ark, saving its contents for the use and enlightenment of future generations' (Stonehouse & Stromberg 2004: 49). Interestingly, the new public library at Canada Water, designed by Piers Gough and his CZWG practice, looks exactly like an ark, moored serenely beside the dockland waters. While unreservedly admiring the Canada Water building, there are some elements of the outward appearance of the British Library that err towards producing a mausoleum effect, notably the entrance doors. These heavy, darkened glass doors mounted in brass, and set in the monumental red-brick facade too readily bring to mind the Lenin Mausoleum in Moscow. Fortunately the effect dissipates immediately once inside the soaring public hall.

The solid wall facades of the new Bibliotheca Alexandrina are also imprinted with letters, symbols and ideographs from different cultures. Thus in many towns and cities throughout the world one of the most imposing public buildings to be found is the public library, whether old or new. The former public library in San Francisco, opened in 1917 and designed by architect George Kelham, was famous for its 24 large inscriptions in the main entrance hall. These quotations were from many literary and historical sources – though they were unattributed and gave much work for literary detectives in subsequent generations – and were commissioned by the library's major patron, Edward Robeson Taylor, whose own personal motto was a saying by Seneca: VITA SINE LITERIS MORS EST (Life without letters is death). A recent monograph on this unique library building rightly draws connections between architecture and lettering, which characterised some of the most important works of Roman architecture, and whose alphabetic script remains unimproved (Stauffacher, 2003).

Many libraries tell a similar story. Islington Central Library, designed in 1907 by architect Henry T. Hare, displays sculptures of Francis Bacon and Edmund Spenser in niches on its main facade, which is also decorated with carved stone wreathes, banners and other festive features. Hammersmith Public Library, also in London, is a Grade II listed building also designed by H.T. Hare, with statues of Shakespeare and Milton adorning the outside, alongside stained glass windows depicting Bacon, Chaucer, Spenser and Erasmus. On one of the interior walls of the main lending library at Bethnal Green Library in east London, a beautiful red-brick building converted in 1921 by architect A.E. Darby from the 1896 Bethnal House Asylum, are large plaster medallions of Karl Marx, William Morris, Charles Darwin and Richard Wagner, symbolising the great cultural heroes of an earlier period, rather like secular saints. The library also contains a fine stained glass window memorialising the dead of the First and Second World Wars, and is set in its own grounds, now a public park. In a range of library buildings from the late nineteenth and early twentieth centuries, many facades were decorated with motifs, friezes and carvings representing great literary and intellectual figures, as well as uplifting maxims such as 'Knowledge is Power' and 'Let there be Light'. Few can doubt the moral impress of these Victorian buildings.

Thus there is some truth in the assertion that the public library in many ways displaced the role of the church as a space and centre of public memory throughout Europe in the late nineteenth and twentieth centuries, as secularism and a culture of auto-didacticism took hold. Indeed these new trends became part of mainstream political culture in many new democracies. According to cultural historian, Graeme Evans, cultural provision became a key engine for civic development (and most certainly inter-city rivalry) in the Victorian era (Evans, 2001). Matthew Arnold was only one of many eminent Victorian thinkers who argued that by the end of the nineteenth century, literature had replaced religion as the source of many people's spiritual beliefs. In the 2012 public airing of views about proposals to re-design the lower floors of New York Public Library, already mentioned, Library Trustee, Robert Darnton, actually referred to the 'sacred' space of the building and his wish to uphold its role as 'the soul of the city' (Darnton, 2012).

When the Danish architect Morten Schmidt gave a lecture on library architecture at The Royal Academy in London in April 2010, discussing his practice's designs for The Royal Danish National Library in Copenhagen (completed in 1999, and more commonly known as 'The Black Diamond'), he observed that in

Figure 2.7 Canada Water Library, Southwark, London, designed by Piers Gough of CZWG, occupying a key waterside site in former docklands

Figure 2.8 The 'Black Diamond' city library, an extension to the Royal Library of Copenhagen, designed by schmidt/hammer/lassen

today's society, 'Young people are not going to church – they are going to the library' (Schmidt, 2010). He also spoke of a 'certain quiet authority' required by all library architecture as a part of its enduring identity. In Barcelona, architect Josep Llinàs, designer of the highly regarded Jaume Fuster Library in the northern part of the city, has drawn 'parallels between the library type and the nature of sacred buildings...when shaping this sequence of spaces (at Jaume Fuster) he recalls how light and sound were prioritised to control sound transmission between places of silence and interchange, balancing light levels with both natural and artificial sources' (Gregory, 2006: 64).

THE 'LIBRARYNESS' OF LIBRARY BUILDINGS

Indeed this long-standing tradition of a distinct library aura – or what was once termed 'the libraryness of libraries' (Greenhalgh *et al.*, 1995) – is something all architects and designers need to acknowledge from the outset. For libraries operate on the boundary between the secular and the sacred, between the archival and the exploratory, and between upholding the

irreplaceable tradition of the book whilst embracing the new media and digital technology. All these traditions and trajectories have to be embodied in a single building or linked set of spaces, which makes the library as a building type increasingly complex. Furthermore it is the quintessential *public* building, 'open to all' by prescript. Its design has to actively welcome people in through its doors, and offer them the possibility of new directions in life and widening intellectual opportunities. Whereas many other historic building types develop clear spatial functionalities over time for strictly demarcated constituencies of users, the library has to imbue all its spaces both with a sense of pluralism as well as universality. This is no small order.

What then is this 'libraryness' which continues to inform the design, use and public understanding of these unique places? The foundations of the concept derive from the large-scale collection of books arranged in order, in a building dedicated to their secure storage, conservation and accessibility – the very presence of books being sufficient enough to produce a contemplative or spiritual aura. Three of the great religions of the world – Judaism, Christianity and Islam – are all known as 'religions of the Book', where textual exegesis has constituted one of the principal means of sustaining religious belief. This exegetical role is something the library always refers back to. We go in to look for one thing and in the process find another. Everything, ultimately, is connected to everything else.

The architectural critic and academic, Brian Lawson, picks out libraries as the quintessential settings for public life and understanding of the rules established by design and history:

> Settings, whether they are parts of special territories or not, are important to us as ways of generating security. When we enter a library, the scene is set, as we say. Even though we may never have been in this particular library before, we recognise the setting as a library. Along with that setting comes a sense of social norms that are not so much attached to a particular group as to the setting itself. In plain simple terms, we know how to behave in a library. Without such properties of space and settings, life would be unbearably stressful.

> (Lawson, 2001: 23)

Again we return to this notion that space itself is an agent of change and civic identity. Books and libraries also imply a life of contemplation and study, and the burning of books or libraries has always been regarded as a monstrous attack on people's most deeply held beliefs and values, as Robert Bevan graphically illustrated in his study of architectural vandalism, *The Destruction of Memory* (Bevan, 2006). One of the examples he discusses was the deliberate Serbian bombing of the National and University Library of Bosnia-Herzegovina in August 1992 which destroyed the building and more than two million books and documents, many of them dating back to the fifteenth century and irreplaceable. In the aftermath of the bombing, he writes, 'Sarajevans dodged snipers to form a human chain to rescue books from the library' (Bevan, 2006: 37). In 2000 a UNESCO delegation to Kosovo found that 'three central libraries were destroyed, with 261,000 books burned; 62 provincial libraries destroyed, with 638,000 books burned' (Báez: 2008). Battlefield wars have often been accompanied by architectural and cultural wars, with religious buildings, schools and libraries deliberately targeted and destroyed in order to erase the cultural memory of a community or of a people. Even an aesthetic avant-garde such as the Italian Futurists in 1910 'published a manifesto in which they called for the destruction of all libraries' (Báez: 2008). Such future-oriented ideologies are always dangerous when they seek to throw a blanket of darkness over the past, or seek to induce forms of public amnesia in the interests of a new political trajectory.

Thus library buildings themselves are frequently held to be sacrosanct or precious, because of this memory-keeping role. Some years ago, during a series of visits to libraries in County

Durham, it was soon evident that many branch libraries also incorporated a local war memorial into their design, either as an entrance chamber commemorating the dead of past wars, or with a memorial feature in one of the reading rooms. In the new Norwich Millennium Library, a room has been provided to hold the Second Air Division Memorial Library, which honours the American forces personnel based in East Anglia during the Second World War who lost their lives in the conflict. This deeply affecting collection of books and artefacts is still visited in large numbers.

At the other end of the spectrum, there is a long tradition in which retiring American presidents commission library buildings to house their personal collections of artefacts, books and archives, continuing this role, though to less memorable effect. They are invariably exercises in self-justification and also highly partisan, which is not what one expects from a library. Architectural critic Deyan Sudjic,

Figure 2.9 Bold LIBRARY sign at Boscombe Library, Bournemouth, a development by Hawkins Brown, including apartments

who has visited many, found them to be inherently self-aggrandising and lacking in intellectual honesty or objectivity (Sudjic, 2006).

The word LIBRARY has often been emblematically engraved or carved into the stonework of a building not only as a decorative feature, but also as a means of evoking a very long civic tradition, with all that the word symbolises and embodies in eliciting public memory, a matter which is dealt with again later. Yet there are a number of other attributes of libraries which contribute to their atmosphere of inviolability, and which those commissioning, planning, designing or constructing them should not overlook, including a general presumption of public quiet within (if no longer silence). For reading is still regarded as principally a silent activity, easily disrupted by extraneous noise, as are other forms of individual study. Though many public libraries have become more relaxed about this rule it is still regarded as part of the *modus operandi* of the reference library, and those other parts of the library made available for private study. Even in the busiest of towns and cities the library continues to provide this role as a (relative) haven of quietness and retreat, and here again we see some overlap with the historic role of the church as a place of quiet and sanctuary. In the modern, highly commercialised town or city centre, the importance of such spaces cannot be overstated. Thus, in the words of Brian Edwards, 'Those who design libraries have a responsibility to convey "libraryness" through the manipulation of form, space and light. A library fails in its social discourse if, no matter how functionally efficient, it does not evoke library character' (Edwards, 2009: 246).

The public library also embodies in built form the principle of the freedom of knowledge as a universal aspiration, and thus is open to everybody and trusted to be free of censorship or political intrusion. It was a defining moment in the USA, in the aftermath of the 9/11 atrocity, when public librarians refused federal security requests to provide details of individual book borrowings, a request which was regarded by the library profession as an over-reaching by government security interests. In Northern Ireland in the mid-1990s, at a particularly fraught time during 'The Troubles', it was the public library alone of all the major community institutions – churches, schools, clubs, pubs, sports organisations, and even cemeteries – which remained free of sectional pressures and interests, and became revered for this precious role. Nor could anyone who visited Belfast during those times – as I often did – remain unaware of the role that the Linen Hall Library played in that city's life. Established in 1788 in the era of the Enlightenment, it continues to this day to act as a collecting centre and reference library for materials of all shades of opinion in the life of the city, and as neutral meeting place for all those interested in its history. The poet Seamus Heaney wrote that, 'In our cultural and in our historical understanding,

the very words "the Linen Hall Library" represent not just books, but better hopes for the way we live. For a just, civilised and inclusive society' (Morrison, 2002: 12). Another writer said that it 'has gained an almost sacred status in the history of Northern Ireland's capital city' (Morrison, 2002: 12).

While in the past librarians have exercised a degree of censorship or selectivity, especially on matters of sexual or religious sensitivity, there is today a common assumption that they are there to provide access to the widest possible range of views, beliefs and materials, as demonstrated by the story of the Linen Hall Library. This slow change from being in some sense moral missionaries of the word to becoming enablers of self-development has its counterpart in Finnish library culture, where after the Second World War, 'there was a gradual adjustment in the professional identity of librarians, who started to see their work more neutrally as the administration of resources, rather than as part of public education with moral aspirations' (Mehtonen, 2011: 162).

Librarians are regarded as being non-judgemental, unlike their counterparts in other cultural or commercial institutions, where partisan artistic positions are often adopted as a matter of principle. In this the public library's principles of selection differ from those of the commercial cultural market-place, which is geared to the rapid turnover of stock, with little room made available for the back catalogue or specialist interests. However, in the age of the Internet, the use of public funds to provide the space and facilities to create unfettered access to all kinds of unregulated material – pornography, extremist literature, abusive social networking sites – has brought some forms of online monitoring and filtering into play. In the UK this has not provoked any great libertarian outrage, though in the USA questions of public 'censorship' are still fraught with difficulty.

The public library also largely operates on the principle that access to such materials is for the most part free of charge, certainly for all materials accessed within the library. While there may be charges for CDs and DVDs on loan, and in the future may be for downloading digital material on licence, the vast majority of the stock and the services offered – access to archives, historical records, family history materials, specialist collections – remains free to users. It was for this reason that many pioneering public libraries were specifically named 'Free Libraries'. This principle thus also sets them against the increasingly commercialised environment within which they find themselves operating in city centres, and they are therefore one of the few places which can be used and inhabited by anybody at no cost. This is particularly important for children and their families, as well as young people, who remain amongst the public library's key users.

It is often said that the acquisition of a library card is a child's first induction into civil society. The importance of libraries to children's early interest in books and story-telling is incalculable, with research claiming that 'children who were taken to libraries as a child had significantly higher recent attendance rates than those who were not taken as a child' (Hodge, 2010: 21). The children's library has been of enormous symbolic importance to children and their families, providing a safe, second 'domestic sphere' outside of the home, as is evident from the presence of carpets, toys, story-telling adults, and child-sized furniture. For immigrant families and their children, the public library is one of the first places outside of home that they feel secure in using (Greenhalgh et al., 1995). However, in an age in which 'child protection' issues have become paramount, the architectural problems associated with the design and management of the children's library – whether integrated into the larger adult library or designed as a separate space – have become increasingly complex, as is discussed later.

If the public library is seen as a safe place for children, it is also a place in which women early on found a new home in the city, and some early public libraries had separate male and female reading rooms. Glasgow's magnificent Mitchell Library still conserves the original décor of the Women's Reading Room, though the interior has been adapted for other uses today.

With the rise of the branch library in the 1920s and onwards, smaller libraries emphasised their 'domesticity' through the use of potted plants, picture-hangings, armchairs and a stock-list that reflected the rise of suburban life and interests – in cookery, home-furnishings, romantic novels, as well as the classic literary tradition. This inflection is now being lost as the once extensive network of branch libraries is whittled away, and priority again returns to the larger, city centre libraries with their emphasis on information technology, archives, reference functions and the general stock list.

Even so, there is one area in which the public library has found a thriving new 'domestic' role – as a home for book-reading groups. It was recently claimed that the number of library-led reading groups in England and Wales nearly trebled to 10,000 between 2004 and 2008, and 100,000 people now belong to a reading group convened in a library. (Hodge, 2010) Thus the public library demonstrates an ability to change to meet new 'public good' obligations, with regard to the dissemination of information, literacy and culture, as and when new needs and technologies arise. When it comes to planning space in the new library, then flexibility is vital in order to accommodate these changing opportunities.

Figure 2.10 Children's section at Sutton Library, London (All rights reserved – London Borough of Sutton Library Services)

CHAPTER 3

What you see is what you get: key elements of library architecture

The first Victorian public libraries were monuments to the ideal of municipal reform and the rise of civic culture. In the great cities they often took the form of monumental, neo-classical buildings, with flights of steps leading up to imposing entrance doors, with highly regulated spaces within. Reading rooms were often circular in design, allowing the world of human knowledge to be taken in one long sweep, as well as making surveillance of the library easier from a central control desk. The very word 'LIBRARY' was regarded as an emblem of a universal ideal, and of a building type that was central to the idea of democracy and an educated citizenry. Over time library design went through a number of distinct phases, from the early Victorian 'Civic' buildings to the 'Welfare State' library, with other key moments in between. Today we are seeing emerge a new kind of civic building, a meeting place for global technology, citizenship and cultural democracy.

WHAT'S IN A NAME? THE PUBLIC FACE OF THE LIBRARY

It was the Public Libraries Act of 1850 (extended to Scotland and Ireland in 1853) which first paved the way for the great library movement of the late Victorian era in Britain. Though the new movement was slow to take off, when it did so this was accomplished in style: monumental style. The reasons for this are explained by library historians Alistair Black, Simon Pepper and Kaye Bagshawe:

> The monumentality of early public library buildings was not a mistake (although, to be sure, it is easy to find some examples of truly astonishing and bizarre buildings). The highly artistic treatment of the vast majority of libraries – in a wide variety of styles and freestyle concoctions – reflected a burning belief in the value of learning, culture, information and imaginative literature. This belief was also underwritten by a high degree of ornamentation, which also paid homage, through sculpture and heraldry, to national and imperial greatness.
>
> (Black *et al.*, 2009: 344)

The impulse to create these new powerhouses of knowledge was closely related to the new ideal of civic culture espoused by the Utilitarians and Philosophic Radicals, usually associated with the figures of William Ewart and John Stuart Mill. These earnest radicals envisioned a newly enfranchised (male) working class in urgent need of education and elevation if a more moral and self-disciplined society was to be achieved. This was not without a degree of utilitarian cost-benefit analysis. As the economist W.S. Jevons argued at the time, the provision of free public libraries (along with public museums, art galleries, parks, municipal clocks, *et al.*) could and should ultimately achieve a great deal of 'utility' at a very small cost (Black *et al.*, 2009: 31). Such arguments continue to recur, even today, whereby advocates justify the support of public funding of arts and cultural provision in terms of much larger civic and social benefits, especially in the form of urban regeneration.

While many Neo-Classical libraries and museums were entered up a flight of monumental steps, their architects never envisaged that these steps would one day become a favourite meeting and 'hanging out space' as they have so often become. Arrange to meet anybody in New York and it is likely that they will suggest meeting on the steps of the New York Public Library, a popular gathering place guarded by the two stone lions, Patience and Fortitude. The same is just as true in Birmingham where, on a fine day, it is still almost impossible at times to thread one's way through the crowds of people sitting on the steps outside the main library taking a break by watching the world go by. Somewhat unanticipated, the design for the Norwich Millennium Library has also brought a new element to Norwich life, as the then Head of Library Services noted:

On a lovely summer day the steps are just full of people, and it looks like a scene in Paris. There are these public spaces, but in Norwich there has never been that sort of public space. I think it takes time for people to realise the potential of a space like that.

(cited in Bryson *et al.*, 2003: 33)

Emphasis was also placed on the prominent display of the word 'Library' above the entrance facade, a key motif of library exterior design, already noted. The architects Alsop & Störmer made great play with this, when they erected a very large 'LIBRARY' sign in bright, light-catching steel, on the roof of their highly regarded library in Peckham, south London. ArchitecturePLB have done something similar at their new Dagenham Library, where the exterior library signage is strongly pronounced. Even more dramatic is the use of the word BIBLIOTHEEK, almost as a structural device, above the corner entrance of a new library in Helmond, near Eindhoven in the Netherlands, designed by Bolles+Wilson, which opened in 2010. It is as if to say, if you've got this powerful word, flaunt it. And few words in the Western lexicons carry as many rich associations as LIBRARY, BIBLIOTHEQUE, BUCHEREI and their linguistic variants. This is a

Figure 3.1 Steps of New York Public Library, one of the city's great meeting places

Figure 3.2 Peckham Library designed by Alsop & Störmer, winner of 2000 Stirling Prize

Figure 3.3 Rotunda of the former British Library Reading Room in Bloomsbury, now vacated and used by the British Museum

cause for optimism about the future of the public library. For as Jens Thorhauge, Director-General of the Danish National Library Authority wrote in 2006:

> The library's real and symbolic value is still strong, even if public debate has predicted that libraries will stagnate and die, as dissemination of information becomes digital and is taken over by other suppliers. The library's real and symbolic value is seen both in relation to the still very high circulation figures and the fact that new and spectacular libraries are still being built all over the world – as well as in the North.
>
> (Thorhauge, 2006: 8)

It is true that there have been experiments in the UK with re-branding libraries under a different name: Idea Stores in the London Borough of Tower Hamlets, or Discovery Centres in Hampshire. Both have been effective in attracting and retaining new users, but once inside many people still refer to them as 'the library'. There is no doubt the new Library of Birmingham will be called precisely that, though it may look radically different from the conventional building style we associate with libraries. When I interviewed the principal librarian responsible for overseeing the new development, he told me that 'We took the view early on that what we were trying to do is to redefine the word and concept of library, rather than declare it redundant and invent another term which might turn out to be highly localised and transient.'

THE DOME OF KNOWLEDGE

A common plan for many of the larger municipal libraries centred on a great circular reading room, clearly echoing the Reading Room at the British Library commissioned by Anthony Panizzi, designed by Sydney Smirke, and opened in 1857. This has been described as embodying 'universal knowledge held in a universal space'. The Great Hall in Manchester Central Library, designed by E. Vincent Harris and opened in 1934 clearly does this, as did The Picton Library in Liverpool already mentioned, though Gunnar Asplund was the first to adapt and develop this idea in the twentieth century with the Stockholm City Library opened in 1928. As Edwards has pointed out, citing A.Whittick, 'of the 600 new public libraries built in the UK between 1885 and 1920, the main element was provided by a central, often circular, space' (Edwards, 2009: 12). This was predominantly the central reading room.

Yet even before Smirke's great reading room, the domed rotunda was already established in a number of European aristocratic

private libraries as the principal form of the library, as well as in James Gibbs' Radcliffe Camera in Oxford, exemplifying in Thomas A Markus's words, 'important metaphors for universal knowledge' (Markus, 2004: 178). Thus in the circular library all knowledge

Figure 3.4 Imposing presence of The Picton Library, Liverpool

Figure 3.5 Great Rotunda of Manchester Central Library, designed by E. Vincent Harris and opened in 1934

Figure 3.6 Imposing entrance of Stockholm Library

seemed to be visibly available in a single sweep of the eyes – though those with a more conspiratorial frame of mind might also suggest that circularity provide the simplest form of surveillance on the part of the library staff at their central desk. A post-war pioneer of circularity is Bourne Hall Library at Ewell in Surrey, detailed in one of the case studies, which gives the impression of a spaceship arrived on earth.

Interestingly Rem Koolhaas and Joshua Prince-Ramus of OMA/ REX sought to develop this principle in their design for Seattle Public Library (opened 2004), with their 'Book Spiral', which presents all of the library's non-fiction in a continuous series of Dewey-classified shelves which spiral upwards along an inclined corridor and can be perused by library users without using stairs or needing to go into another part of the building. Here we can find echoes of Frank Lloyd Wright's spiral internal staircase at the New York Guggenheim Museum. In the refurbishment of the main library at the London School of Economics by Foster + Partners, completed in 2001, the central atrium is dominated by a twin lift-shaft surrounded by a spiral staircase linking five separate floors. A similar configuration can be found at Sandton Library in Gauteng, South Africa, designed by GAPP Architects – and very striking it is too.

Even Bolles-Wilson + Partner's mould-breaking design for the Münster City Library includes a perimeter wall at the edge of the site which 'appears as a slice of a larger drum that defines and endorses the return of the books' (Sanin, 1994: 10). In the new library at Canada Water in London's former docklands, designed by CZWG, the centre of the building is dominated by a large circular staircase which rises within a dramatic, almost slightly-larger-than human-scale, wooden-slatted drum.

Either the rising spiral staircase, or the internal rotunda – or a combination of both – remain an architectural reference for many library architects. Christophe Egret, architect and founding partner of Studio Egret West, has written of the interior of his practice's combined library and health centre in Clapham, south London, which opened in 2012, that:

> inspired by Erik Gunnar Asplund's Stockholm City Library, books line the walls of a curved oval ramp, avoiding traditional rows of shelves that chop up the space. Orientation is intuitive as soon as you join reception. The building can be read as a simple spiral diagram – with neither floors nor corridors but a continuous book-lined ramp. Quiet reading and computer rooms sit like carved recesses behind the curved bookcases.
>
> (Egret, 2011: 56)

Figure 3.7 Circular facade of Bourne Hall Library, Ewell, in Surrey, designed by A.G.Sheppard Fidler and Associates, opened in 1970

Figure 3.8 Circular stairwell at LSE Library, London, designed by Foster + Partners

Figure 3.9 Circular stairwell at Canada Water Library, Southwark, London, designed by Piers Gough of CZWG

Time and again we find references to – or adaptations of – the top-lit dome and circular reading room.

Circularity in library design is similarly referenced in the design for the Norwich Millennium Library by Hopkins & Partners, which opened in 2001. When interviewed one of the project architects said that:

> You can analyse our building and say quite simply we've got a semi-circular library that you could say is half a classical reading room, literally chopped in half – around the outside of which we've got a relatively traditional construction with relatively modest window-sized openings with bay windows, with study booths, we've then got a panopticon-type radial plan which comes into a central space. And then the other half of that we've got, instead of having your complete circle of the library we've got the equivalent of a Victorian railway station, really with a large open concourse with people milling through it. So in a way the Victorians had the prototypes and we've merged various ideas that have been around…The building makes an outside space and then that connects through a big glass wall to an inside space…so that it links directly into the streetscape…
>
> We had a three-storey building and we had it at the back of a hub of this U-shaped space. And we decided to have this semi-circular form, and that had interesting aspects in terms of context on the outside of the building, but had an interesting aspect in terms of the inside of the building, in that it had very much a central space which could allow a more noisy activity, and then you could filter through that space towards the outside of the building and go towards quieter study areas. So there was a very clear idea on the plan how a circular arrangement might work architecturally.
>
> (Bryson *et al.*, 2003: 30)

This is fascinating, suggesting as it does the judicious use of two great Victorian spaces – the circular reading room and the railway station concourse. And it is true that the further the visitor penetrates into the library the quieter it becomes. What this open plan but sectionalised approach does is allow the library user to choose a particular spot where they feel most comfortable. Some people like to hide in libraries and cut themselves off from the crowd; others like to sit where there are other people. With the ubiquity of Wi-fi in libraries and the increasing use of laptops and digital notebooks, studying is now a moveable feast, and young people seem as relaxed reading a book and typing up their notes in a café or on a chair located next to the fiction section, as their predecessors felt in the studious silence of the reference library and its ranked tables.

Figure 3.10 Public atrium of Norwich Forum leading to Norwich Central Library, designed by Michael Hopkins & Partners, and opened in 2001

The larger the library the more dominant and architecturally grand the main reading room had to appear – and these became the most photographed images we have of the more historic libraries. Row upon row of long tables with elegant table lamps or ceiling lamps suspended above the desks give the effect of an almost industrial scale of individual study, in a hushed and almost forbidding atmosphere, as evoked by film-maker Alain Resnais. The great reading room has more or less disappeared in most new public libraries in Europe, though some of the larger American libraries, particularly those constructed in a neo-classical, monumental style, such as Chicago, Nashville, Phoenix and San Francisco, have retained these monumental halls. In Europe the trend has been to mix study space with browsing space, while providing the now ubiquitous laptop with its own power supply wherever there is a chair or table close to hand.

ONE WAVE AFTER ANOTHER

For the most part, however, the great wave of library-building which occurred from the 1880s onwards was the work of local architects, often influenced by some of the classic designs, as well as some of the design requirements of those two great philanthropic sponsors of libraries in the UK: Andrew Carnegie and John Passmore Edwards. Between 1850 and 1939 over 1,000 library buildings were designed and constructed in the UK, making this one of the most common building types of modern civic Britain. (Black *et al.*, 2009: xv) However, as Shannon Mattern has adroitly noted, when libraries were designed by local architects, they employed a range of styles and local references. Once Carnegie became involved, a process of standardisation ensued, which began to determine the idea that a library had to look exactly the same as other libraries (Mattern, 2007: 3).

Alistair Black and his colleagues note that:

> The public library rarely attracted interest from the heavyweights of the architectural world (Alfred Waterhouse was an exception). On the contrary, public library design was highly 'democratic' in that it was carried out by a myriad of local architects and borough engineers and surveyors. This dilution of design responsibility goes some of the way to exploring the eclecticism (and historicism) of style that characterised much of the period, even the inter-war years when modernism began to make its mark.
>
> (Black *et al.*, 2009: 345)

Having established a successful model for a public library service as part of the infrastructure of an incipient democracy, there was little else required other than to build more and more, where

Figure 3.11 Entrance and facade of Carnegie Library, London Borough of Enfield

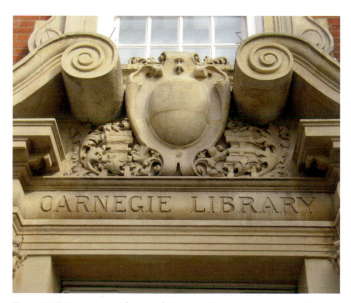

Figure 3.12 Entrance and facade of Carnegie Library, London Borough of Enfield (detail)

the only design variable tended to be size in relation to the population catchment. It was in Scandinavia – where the move to the cities occurred later – that new architectural templates for public libraries became more readily apparent and exciting. In these countries design leap-frogged the Victorian prototype and new public libraries became set-pieces or exemplars of Scandinavian modernism, with its emphasis on transparency, light, and democratic taste and civility.

In all, five distinct periods of library design have been identified in Britain since the inception of the public library movement. They are:

- the 'Civic' Public Library: 1850–83

- the 'Endowed' Public Library: 1883–1919

- the 'National Network' Public Library: 1919–39

- the 'Welfare State' Public Library: 1939–79

- the 'Post-Modern' Public Library: after 1979 (Black *et al.*, 2009: 27).

The only one of these categories which might be challenged is the last. While there are a few libraries which prioritise effect over civility – and not even the much reviewed Peckham Library

by Alsop and Störmer in reality does this, embodying as it does clear functional characteristics – the new generation of large libraries developed after 2000, not only in the UK but across the world, have resisted the post-modern call for ornamental extravagance (let alone stylistic kitsch), opting instead for architectural intelligence and public sobriety.

The reason why architecture is so important is that 'Members of the public rarely recognise a distinction between physical libraries and "the library service"' (MLA, 2010a). Behind the scenes there is a vital yet mostly invisible network of services provided by public libraries, including inter-library lending, negotiating rights, electronic networking, professional training, negotiating with authors and publishers, commissioning re-prints, operating mobile libraries, amongst others. Yet for most people the public library is a building, and a highly symbolic building at that. 'Architectural style,' Alistair Black has written, 'represents an important part of the meaning of the public library in our early twenty-first century digitally mediated world' (Black, 2011: 31). Perhaps more than ever, the buildings have to do more work in explaining and shaping the library ethos and service, in a world in which little is taken for granted or accepted without demur. How various architectural approaches to the contemporary public library chime with public regard and expectation is the subject of the next chapter.

Figure 3.13 Interior of Uppsala Public Library

Figure 3.14 Striking design of the prow end of the modernist Swiss Cottage Library, designed by Basil Spence, opened in 1964

Figure 3.15 Southend on Sea Central Library opened in 1974

CHAPTER 4

A new wave of library architecture

The new libraries are no longer places of regulated patronage in formally distinct rooms, but are increasingly open-plan – places where independent users come who 'want to solve their intellectual problems on their own'. They may even bring their own laptops, but want the space, the comfort and the associational life offered by the company of fellow citizens, to support them in their personal endeavours. The modern library is now much more than a book depository, formerly accessed by a catalogue, but is a meeting place of books, media, people and ideas (including talks, events, readings and children's activities). In this new world the external appearance of the library has a weakened symbolic importance; it is now the open-plan interior with its circulation patterns and dis-aggregated service points that embodies the symbolic value of the contemporary library ethos.

SPACES OF DEMOCRACY

Since the 1990s a number of city libraries have been built across the world whose design has consciously attempted to re-situate the public library at the centre of twenty-first century urban life and culture, with a strong orientation to the age of the Internet and globalised access to information. Indeed the past twenty years have been something of a golden age for library architecture: 'Not since the Carnegie era has there been so much interest in library buildings' (Black *et al.*, 2009: 2). Moreover, there has been in this period much more freedom to innovate in both programme and design, and this has led to greater architectural flair and experimentalism (even if accompanied by occasional lapses into self-regard and public grandstanding). In North America, Shannon Mattern writes:

> Over the past decade and a half, librarians, civic officials, architects, and library users have made myriad architectural packages for their public libraries. But with each

re-packaging, it has been not only the exterior representation of the institution that has changed; this repackaging has involved much more than fitting an old institution into a new box. With each new physical embodiment of the institution, each new architectural expression, some functions and identities and values of the public library have metamorphosed, too.

> (Mattern, 2007: viii)

One of the earliest and most radical of these new prototypes was that for the new Münster City Library in Germany, designed by Bolles-Wilson + Partner and opened in December 1993. The city authorities decided to commission a new library and museum in the 1980s intended to mark the anniversary of Münster's 1,200 years as a city. However there was insufficient space on the chosen site to have both and it was decided to focus on creating a new library which, it was felt, would not only meet the needs of the past and present, but of the future too. As Francisco Sanin has written:

The decision to go ahead with the library as the main monument to the city's anniversary celebration is highly significant. Not only does it relate to the origins of Münster as a seat of learning, but more than that, it also reflects a desire to engage the more dynamic and relevant aspects of life in the city.

(Sanin, 1994: 8)

This is almost certainly the narrative arc of the new library era: the growing wish to create a significant new civic building which not only functions as a library but also as an emblem of modern pluralist democracy, freedom of thought – as well as urban vitality. The Strategic Design Brief for the new Library of Birmingham states that: 'The City Council recognises the power of cultural activities to change lives and increase prosperity. The Library of Birmingham...will enable the city to provide a stronger, more co-ordinated cultural offer and lead people to new and richer cultural experiences.' More than that, in Birmingham it is central to the design brief that 'The roles of the library as a development agency and city meeting place will be foremost.'

But there have been other drivers of change, initially less alluring. In Tower Hamlets in the 1990s local politicians realised that that visitor numbers and book borrowings in the borough were in freefall, and something had to be done to reverse a pattern of rapid decline. A policy paper written in 2000 noted that, 'A staggering 72 per cent of the population never used the library services on offer and it was decided that a radically different approach to provision of library services in terms of marketing and presentation was needed' (Bryson *et al.*, 2003: 64). Hence not only a radical new building programme, but also a new branding concept of the library as an 'Idea Store' which, though not universally welcomed in the library world, has, nevertheless, completely re-energised the service in the borough, with four new libraries developed between 2003 and 2012, all recording high levels of public use and interest. In Glasgow, it was the challenge to a dull library service represented by the new glamorous book-selling chains such as Waterstone's which provided the necessary spur to action to upgrade the service and make it relevant to a new generation of consumer-savvy readers.

The Japanese library academic Yuko Yoshida visited Denmark in 2006, 2008 and 2010 while researching the political and social context of the library movement – with a view to providing lessons for Japan, where privatisation potentially threatens some of these historic values. His essay summarising this research highlights why new libraries in Europe continue to be built in what the author terms 'the revival of the civic library movement':

Public libraries are unique cultural institutes in local communities in that they are places that promote public discussions through a large range of media and *a self-learning place for people who want to solve their intellectual problems on their own.*

It is in this area that we find a means of survival and the significance of the existence of public libraries. It is hard to find places in local communities where people could meet and freely discuss issues in a neutral setting, despite their importance. *The physical presence of libraries has increased under this condition.*

(Yoshida, 2009: 16; italics in original)

This notion of the library as a central meeting-place in the town or city – of people, of ideas, and of diverse cultures and affiliations – is today becoming as important as the historic ideal of the library as a collection of books for the purpose of individual study and private reflection. 'Now knowledge is virtually everywhere,' argues Brian Edwards:

it has broken free of the constraint of buildings. Today, if you were to destroy all the world's libraries, it is unlikely that more than 20 per cent of human knowledge would be lost ... If a library is a repository of knowledge, this is now just one of its functions. The library's prime function is now making that knowledge available and encouraging exchange and reflection upon it.

(Edwards, 2009: xi)

This implies big changes in the basic library plan and programme, particularly in the allocation of space. Here, again, Jens Thorhauge, Director-General of the Danish National Library Authority, wrote in 2006:

The main challenge is to abandon the 'book depository hall' as [the main] organisational principle for the physical library, and replace it with an interior design principle that allows for the library being a multi-functional house with room for the classical free space for reading and working – while at the same time making room for many more scheduled activities than today – exhibitions, events, computer classes and many other learning initiatives, and meetings. And finally, [it is] a place that still signals that help is available to find the right information, and that produces a forceful cultural promotion both of the new books and of subjects of topical interest.

(Larsen, 2006: 10)

In architectural terms libraries have moved from being buildings symbolising intellectual power and authority for a select few to

Figure 4.1 Idea Store reception desk, London Borough of Tower Hamlets

ones embodying ideals of accessible and democratic knowledge and self-development for the many. In its proceedings from a 2010 conference in Barcelona on *The Futures of the Public Library*, it was agreed that: 'The users are really the centre of the service. It is necessary to think of the space for the users and not for the collection: the library is for people not for books' (Barcelona, 2010).

This is a radically new conception indeed. Yet it contains an important truth for the twenty-first century, which is that the modern library now prioritises human self-development and social community as much as it conserves the traditional sanctity of the book collection. Indeed the Barcelona accord goes on to assert that, 'The library is a public space that acts as an *agora* and helps to construct the community' (Barcelona, 2010). In this regard it has exchanged one ancient ideal for another. It is worth noting that in 2010 the MLA published a policy paper – with a small funding programme attached – called *Opening Up Spaces* (2010a), encouraging libraries, in particular, to create spaces where adults could organise their own learning. They gave the example of the wholly self-organised 'University of the Third Age' as a classic example of this new direction in informal education. More and more, as we shall discover in the case studies, the spaces of the library are becoming more flexible, offering not only individual carrels or desk spaces for study, but also places for seminars, training classes, performances, exhibitions, lectures and other events. At Aberdeen University, they have designated

the new library there as 'not so much a stronghold but rather as a threshold'.

A municipal councillor in Newham described the purpose of the newly designed library in Stratford thus:

> I suppose one of the things that we've tried to do in Newham is to breathe some life back into libraries and make them be an important meeting place where people would exchange information as well as just traditionally take out books. I think we wanted them to be a place of cultural life so they wouldn't be just a place where you went and got a book or went and accessed the IT ... but they would also celebrate what it was that our people were bringing, what Newham people were contributing...
>
> (Bryson *et al.*, 2003: 85)

In this, libraries are anticipating much wider changes in the townscape arising from more consumer lifestyles, as traditional retailing disappears from the high street or main street (either to out-of-town retail parks or to home delivery for goods ordered online), and personal services take over many central urban areas. When asked what the British high street would look like in 2030, leading data and retail analyst Matthew Hopkinson suggested that:

> It's going to be full of services, and social aspects. It'll be full of hairdressers, tanning salons, cafés and restaurants.

There might be doctors and dentists there. And it will become very leisure-focused. If there's an area where people like the architecture, and they can socialise, and not just shop, that's what will happen. You'll get a place where people will go for a community.

(Hopkinson, 2011)

This multiplicity of functions, and social effects, is not new. Writing about Alvar Aalto's seminal library at Viipuri, constructed in 1935 and still functioning, Michael Spens noted that,

Libraries remain places where individuals first assess their independent opportunities for growth and career progress. They also function as contemplative places, in the way churches have done; and for those whose life is mostly used up, they become places for calm re-assessment and leisurely study. Increasingly they can become centres of value to the whole family: single people can also find intellectual security and even group therapy through participation on a regular basis. The Library has become the repository for social values.

(Spens, 1994: 91)

It is said that Aalto's library at Viipuri was a momentous architectural breakthrough, in that it de-centralised and de-sacralised traditional library design, with its new emphasis on distinct compartments, wings, sunken floors and galleries (Edwards, 2009: 12).

In the course of an interview with John Harrington, Head of Information Services at Cranfield University – who himself had been involved in the development of the new campus library designed by Sir Norman Foster + Partners – he was clear that one of the main purposes in commissioning a distinctive library building was to provide a high-status meeting place in an otherwise random collection of buildings and residential blocks. Otherwise, he worried, many students would stay in their study-bedrooms and attend lectures, without ever feeling that they belonged. For Dutch architect Wiel Arets, the Utrecht University Library he had designed 'is emphatically intended as a meeting place for the whole university' (Arets, 2005: 136).

THE OLD AND THE NEW

But how do library users regard these new architectural interpretations of the twenty-first century public library building? What evidence we have comes courtesy of the Mass Observation Archive (MOA) which, in 2005, was commissioned to seek a range of views on 'Public Library Buildings' by library academic Alistair

Black. These came from the MOA's long-standing sample of public volunteers, spread out across Britain, and were solicited by letter and open-ended in response – and therefore highly subjective. But they certainly catch a flavour of differing attitudes towards the old and the new:

A library needs to be, and look, accessible to attract people. Older buildings tend to be more off-putting and formal in nature.

(Older buildings are) far more impressive and have an atmosphere of knowledge and learning.

I have found old libraries rather intimidating in the past, with a rather musty smell. At our (modern) library I feel at home.

The modern library has robbed a section of society of a place to hide, to be warm and to nurse their delusions in comfort and to be in company yet alone. Modern libraries have nowhere you can hide and disappear into a book and newspapers; few fuggy little corners. Accessibility and friendliness are wonderful but the magic has gone and the mystery.

As Black (2011a) suggests, however tentatively, older correspondents tended to remember the libraries of their childhood with warmth and affection – and perhaps a large degree of nostalgia. In my own discussions with library staff, there is no doubt that young people are much more attracted to the new, the colourful and the bold. These are, to a degree, generational issues around expectations, though the increased visitor figures to some of the most modern libraries suggests that all age groups can be won over if it looks good, and works well.

LOOKING GOOD, INSIDE AND OUT

It is such thinking that prompted the Dutch architect J.M. Coenen – who has specialised in designing libraries, including the new central library in Amsterdam – to write of this new emphasis on the social nature of the new library space:

Public spaces have become interiors. And this applies equally to public buildings. Today it is the interior which shapes our lives, and indeed it is this interior which links the inside with the outside. The skin of a building is no longer falsified with deceptive, symbolic ornamentation as it was in the nineteenth century. We no longer have any simple symbolism that we could openly display to the outside world. Indeed, people have become ashamed of such symbolism. Awakening negative associations, it has become superfluous.

(Coenen, 2002: 5)

Many would not go so far as to entirely reject the important symbolic aspects of the public exteriors of buildings such as libraries – or for that matter, schools, police stations, railway stations, or other public buildings which need to announce their presence and functions without an over-reliance on previous acquaintance or pre-existing information. Bas Savenije, one of the client body which commissioned Dutch architect Wiel Arets to design the Utrecht University Library, remains convinced that external appearance has to suggest something of the inner world it represents: 'The building as it is now has something almost "sacred" about it. That's a better word for it than "classical". But it's the same idea: you can tell by looking at the building that it contains material of great value' (Arets, 2005: 134).

It may suit corporate business to rely on a modest brass name-plate on a high-rise office block to identify a company identity, but architectural style in referencing historical templates and associations can play a positive role in creating meaning and attachment in the townscape. 'Does it look like a library?' is a question still asked by both politicians and public. This is especially true when it comes to commissioning a new building, and people are first confronted with the initial design ideas or architectural sketches.

Yet in several recent libraries in the USA – in Chicago (designed by Hammond, Beeby and Babka, opened 1991) and Nashville (designed by Robert A.M. Stern, opened 2001) for example – one could argue that designers have gone too far, whether in the spirit of postmodernism or old-fashioned revivalism, in retaining the classical tradition of public library architecture, producing highly symmetrical monoliths, with porticoes, pediments, and monumental granite or marble facades, which may do the library cause very little good in the long term. This argument has been made by the Benton Foundation in America which has reported that 'this traditional view of libraries makes it difficult politically for libraries to remake their image and surge forward in a digital age' (Mattern, 2007: 57).

It has been one of the main attractions of Dutch urban understanding that what is public space is larger than the mere issue of ownership or formal role or function. As Maarten Kloos and colleagues demonstrated so vividly in their study of Amsterdam architecture and public life, *Public Interiors* (1993), for many Amsterdam citizens and visitors, there are a wide range of places, including certain bars, department store restaurants, museums, libraries, arcades, churches, hotel lobbies, theatre and concert hall foyers and even supermarkets, where people arrange to meet, and maybe have a coffee or sit down to talk, often oblivious of the formal purpose or commercial nature of the setting. Similar arguments have been advanced by Ray Oldenburg in America. Yet these uses are as valid in respect of the vitality of the town or city as the more deliberated functions of shopping, theatre-going, book-borrowing or catching a train.

Furthermore, a new public library can add status, a sense of keeping up with the times, and even a 'wow' factor to a town or city centre. This has certainly been the case according to one business leader in Norwich interviewed about the effect of the Millennium Library:

> I think having a flagship library that looks good and has all the facilities that everyone's talked about, slap-bang in the city centre only helps to create, reinforce the fact that Norwich, despite the fact, is a medieval city, isn't lost in medieval times – it is still a vibrant centre. So in a way I think it benefits my business, as perceptual for the whole area, as in the nitty-gritty of what it's actually supplying. The other side of that is that it's actually a cracking good library.

(Bryson *et al.*, 2003: 60)

Looking good is not just an aesthetic issue. As the Audit Commission noted in 2002, appearance was a significant factor in library use. Young people in particular were, and are, reluctant to use a building that looks as though it belongs to a past age and culture, especially when almost everything else in the High Street or town centre is constantly updating itself and appears to be directly linked into a more globalised world of information, entertainment and life-chances. This is why such striking new buildings in urban districts exhibiting higher than average levels of social deprivation, such as the libraries in Canada Water, Shepherd's Bush, and even in the northern part of Barcelona close to Plaça de Lessops, quickly become adopted and heavily used by local people, as symbols of status and public esteem.

PART 3
Planning and processes

Passers-by stop to look at site hoardings with plans for new Library of Birmingham, displayed by Mecanoo architect, Francine Houben

design

CHAPTER 5

Developing the brief and establishing a project management team

When planning a new library or the major refurbishment of an existing library, developing a comprehensive brief is vital. This process should include all the key library stake-holders, including budget-holders, librarians, library users, architects and designers, as well as representatives of appropriate civic bodies. A precautionary list of 'The Seven Deadly Sins of Library Architecture' is presented based on past experience on what can go wrong. The project itself needs a steering group which has sufficient time and resources to think through all the possibilities and potential problems well ahead of signing contracts and starting work. Members of such a steering group would certainly benefit by travelling to see a range of new libraries both in their own country and elsewhere. A schema is suggested which links four key issues which are inter-connected in developing the brief: people, places, partners and programmes. In a mixed economy, based increasingly on a variety of public–private partnerships, and with many towns and cities experiencing rapid social, cultural and demographic change, planning for flexibility is vital.

ESTABLISHING THE GROUND RULES

As with all public buildings designed to serve complex needs in a changing society, the library buildings of tomorrow need even greater foresight in preparing the brief than has been previously required. There are of course some basic requirements, notably providing the right amount of space for the population to be served. In 2001 the DCMS supported the figure of 23 square metres per 1,000 population for public libraries, though in 2007 professional opinion suggested this might need to rise to 30 square metres per 1,000 (in the USA and Canada this may be up to 56 square metres for joint-use libraries), and 5 reader spaces per 1,000 population, given the role that the 'new libraries'

were now playing as civic meeting places (Khan, 2009: 122). For colleges and universities, space is calculated per student and work-space. Thus the 1993 Follett Report recommended one study space for six full-time equivalent university students, with 4 square metres study space per reader. All these figures are broadly indicative, though each library, whether public or academic, will need to assess the nature of their own needs based on the specifics of the situation and the wider purposes of the library to be constructed. This is the argument of IFLA: 'The amount of floor-space required by a public library depends on the unique needs of the individual community as determined through a community needs assessment and the level of resources available' (McNicol, 2008: 53).

They need to be 'future-proofed' against a rapidly changing economic and cultural future. Yet even before starting, there is the advantage of past experience and hindsight, and a list of dangers to avoid based on hard-earned wisdom.

For the American library specialists Fed Schlipf and John Moorman, writing in the 1990s, the 'Seven Deadly Sins' of modern public library architecture were:

● Bad lighting

● Inflexibility

● Bad location

● Complex maintenance

● Insufficient work and storage space

● Bad security

● Signature architecture (Bryson *et al.*, 2003: 32).

These are mainly functional, nuts and bolts problems relating to the building plan and structure itself, though they obviously relate directly to the changing and varied services which modern libraries provide. However if these basics are ignored, problems are inevitably stored up for the future. Since then American library consultant Fred Schlipf has written an acerbic *tour d'horizon* on the dysfunctional design of so many library buildings, as well as the propensity of commissioning bodies and architects to carry on repeating the same mistakes. This is contained in his required essay on 'the dark side of library architecture: the persistence of dysfunctional designs' which should be read by anyone working in the field (Schlipf, 2011: 227). Not everything that Schlipf finds unacceptable is necessarily bad – if it were none of the libraries discussed in this book would see the light of day. For there is little that Schlipf can find to say positively about rooflights, atria, balconies, non-standard light fittings, non-standard staircases, courtyards and non-rectangularity. But he provides a salutary lesson in counting the trade-off costs of going architecturally off-piste.

Matters such as the socio-economic and age characteristics of the population to be served are equally important. It is thus *a combination of hard and soft factors* which matter, not just of form and function but of adaptability and a people-based approach to the design and provision of services. In current library jargon this means being first and foremost 'customer-focused', or, more simply, designing for effective use. If the building and its location themselves present obstacles to access then trouble is sure to follow.

Compare the list of deadly sins above, with the following factors highlighted by Christine Fyfe, University Librarian at Leicester University, when accounting for the successful refurbishment of the David Wilson Library there, undertaken by Associated Architects. They represent a natural counterpoint. The key elements of success as far as library staff and users were concerned were in:

● Maximising natural light

● Providing a welcoming and warm ambience with the gravitas of the library

● Creating vistas and visual interest – and intimacy (with nooks and crannies)

● Replicating the aesthetics and proportions of the existing building to create a seamless space

● Designing a place that is a pleasure to be in for long periods of time

● Providing clarity and coherence of layout leading to ease of use

● Delivering the most sustainable building possible within the budget

● Using zoning to accommodate a range of behaviours – from silent to social spaces

● Designing settings which encouraged positive behaviour (Rossiter, 2011).

In 1996 the library organisation SCONUL published a collection of fourteen separate architects' briefs for higher education libraries subsequently designed and built, which, though somewhat dated, is still of great interest (Revill, 1996). In most it is the 'vision' or set of final outcomes desired from the creation of a new library – usually prefacing the brief – which is most telling (and occasionally inspiring) rather than the spatial, structural and technical specifications. What, ultimately, is the educational benefit of the new building on its users and staff, and how does it galvanise the whole campus in its role as a centre of life and learning? The brief for a proposed new library at the University of Abertay Dundee, was mature enough to recognise that even visionary statements require trade-offs and compromises. For, as it observed, the wish to create a building which was 'Welcoming', 'Warm', 'Diverse', 'Cultured & Dignified', had also to fulfil obligations for security – to users, staff and stock – as well as designating clear boundaries between quiet and active spaces. Furthermore, it had to be exciting to be in, as well as architecturally profound. 'Externally striking' with a 'non-inhibiting interior': how easy is that?

DISABILITY DISCRIMINATION ACT 1995

It is a legal obligation to take into account the Disability Discrimination Act when drawing up the building brief, especially so given the very public nature of the building. There are also many kinds of new enabling technologies, for example Braille and Kurzweil machines, along with software for the visually impaired, and expert advice should be sought on the best way of incorporating these facilities into the mainstream of the building, along with the requirements necessary for physical access to all parts for those in wheelchairs.

Ayub Khan provides a comprehensive list of considerations to be taken into account when designing for good access, circulation and support amenities for those with disabilities, including:

- Access
  - Parking
  - Building approaches – curbs & signage
  - Entrances – ramps, steps and handrails
  - Doors – ease of opening
  - Lifts and stair lifts
  - Wide aisles and clear sight-lines
  - Good emergency exits
  - Alarms system for alerting deaf people
- Décor and materials
  - Floor surfaces which aid navigation
  - Floor surfaces which are slip-resistant
  - Windows – low enough for wheelchair users to see through
  - Good task lighting
  - Switches and controls that are easy to find and easy to use
  - Signage & notices – clear, bold lettering, use of non-linguistic symbols and Braille
  - Aural messages in lifts and emergency procedures
- Facilities
  - Toilets – including wheelchair accessible
  - Loop systems at counters
  - Textphone facilities
- Robustness and stability of furniture (including different sizes)
- Desks and study spaces suitable for wheelchair users
- Furniture and equipment height
- Accessible meeting rooms (Khan, 2009: 129–130).

INCLUSION BY DESIGN

Along with the above technical issues to be resolved in the interests of access for everybody, inclusive design is also about ambience and ethos. In CABE's short document on inclusive design libraries and centres for learning are highlighted as being places where, ideally, inclusion means:

- A building to be proud of
- A library where you can't hear a pin drop
- A library where you can linger and be warm
- A library where people far from home can connect up to their families
- A library where students are welcome – even on a Sunday morning when many need to study
- Affordable facilities
- Accessible shelves
- A diverse staff team that reflects the make-up of the community (CABE: 2008a).

SUSTAINABILITY

Given that public libraries are exemplars of the open society, along with the latest thinking about people and place, it follows that they ought also be models of best practice in adhering to the principles of environmental sustainability too. The Strategic Design Brief for the new Birmingham Central Library clearly states that:

> The new facility must be designed and built in accordance with sustainability best practice and in particular must comply with the city Council's Sustainability Strategy. It must achieve a Building Research Establishment Environmental Assessment Method (BREEAM) rating of 'excellent'. It should be highly energy efficient, carbon neutral and have a lower than average environmental impact throughout its lifecycle.

In many of the case-studies detailed in this book, BREEAM compliance to a high rating has been a central requirement of the design brief, and, rather than this inhibiting creativity on the part of the architect, has in many cases – as with the Brighton Jubilee Library – been a key driver for better design (and a useful weapon against late-stage cost-cutting.) This is a good example of what Brian Edwards notes as 'the increasing impact that environmental accreditation is having upon design.' Where once upon a time design was linked to the social idealism of the library ideal, today it is more likely to be linked to ecological design, with the library building itself a message-carrier of sustainability (Edwards, 2011: 213).

In a detailed essay on 'Sustainability as a driving force in contemporary library design', Edwards delineates the many ways in which environmental requirements and opportunities are re-configuring library design in radical ways. Paradoxically nowhere is this more true than in the rather old-fashioned 'expectation that daylight, controlled sunlight, and fresh air should be provided in all or most parts of the library' (Edwards, 2011: 193). The days of the standardised deep-plan, artificially lit, air-conditioned 'universal space' are gone. New buildings are no longer study or book collection factories but civic meeting places, designed to provide a sense of uplift and personal well-being. As such, environmental factors – light, air, colour, furnishings, physical comfort, acoustics, sight-lines and visual interest – become even more important, privileging interior design as much as architectural structure.

At Mecanoo's university library in Delft, the glazed facades along with the turf-clad roof play a significant part in the building's environmental control strategy. The former provides both thermal and acoustic insulation as well absorbing rainwater which later evaporates or is dispersed more naturally, and in winter warm ground water is channelled through a heat exchanger to raise the building's temperature while in the summer the opposite process occurs. The double-glazed facade contains a 140mm ventilated air cavity into which air is pumped and released on each floor.

LIFE-CYCLE COSTINGS

This matter of lifecycle economies and environmental impacts is crucial – or as Ayub Khan has aptly put it, balancing 'cost, quality and time' (Khan, 2009: 32). Public and commercial buildings are today rarely designed for posterity. In earlier times the major economic factor was the size of the capital outlay – worries about maintenance and running costs were left for future generations. Today, however, any new building budget is increasingly required to factor in subsequent operating costs and maintenance – together

with a realistic estimate of how long the building is expected to last, thus amortising these costs. These can still vary widely. The 'pop-up' library in Seven Kings, London was a cheap but effective fit-out of an existing shop, only designed to operate for up to five years, before re-considering what might be needed next. Similarly, the Willesden Green Library Lab is another 'pop-up' project, a 6 month programme in 2012 taking advantage of an empty shop to provide IT training, workshops and lectures, based on a collaboration between Brent Council and Architecture 00:/ with the support of the London Mayor's Outer London Fund. At the other extreme, the life expectancy of the new British Library is estimated as 250 years (Architectural Review, 1998: 50).

It is easy to build cheaply, and then find endless expense involved in maintenance, or frequent refurbishments needed to keep up with changing environmental requirements. Better by far to build into the initial capital outlay the costs for high quality, environmentally friendly materials and flexible design, which may produce a more efficient and lower-costing maintenance regime in the long term. As the 2003 CABE report on *Creating Excellent Buildings* noted:

> The costs of running and managing buildings over their whole life is proportionately much higher than the initial capital cost. Extra resources spent on design or construction to achieve high quality can pay for themselves many times over during the life of the building.

When Andrew Carnegie provided funding for the many libraries built in his name, he only provided the capital costs, and subsequently some municipalities found themselves with buildings they could at times barely afford to staff, stock, heat or light. Even today, having spent over $165 million on its new library in Seattle, the city authorities there have already had to impose revenue cuts which mean that the new library will be open fewer hours than the one it replaced.

This has clearly been one of the major attractions of PFI (Private Finance Initiative) schemes, in that repair and maintenance costs are built into the outlay equation for a defined period – usually thirty years – leaving the client with no doubt at all as to what they need to be paying in the foreseeable future to keep the building properly maintained. However, a UK Parliamentary Public Accounts Committee published a highly critical review of PFI schemes in September 2011, noting amongst other things that lost tax revenues due to off-shore arrangements by PFI investors had not been factored into the cost-benefit analysis of such schemes, that public sector partners had insufficient information about the returns made by PFI investors, nor any share in gains made if shares were sold at a later date, and that the full costs and benefits of PFI schemes were obscured to public view by claims of commercial confidentiality. While the schemes certainly delivered effective long-term maintenance, they often proved more expensive than other kinds of financing in the long term.

PLACES, PARTNERS, PEOPLE AND PROGRAMMES

In the following schema these more complex externalities are assembled under four headings: Places, Partners, People and Programmes. This model was originally developed by a Steering Group involving CABE, RIBA and the MLA to which I acted as adviser.

The virtuous library circle

In developing the brief for a new library building, or even a refurbishment, then it is crucial to find the right equilibrium between four inter-connected factors: the *people* for whom the library service is intended (along with the staff providing the service), the *programme* of services, events and activities required to fulfil that obligation, the *partners* with whom the library authority might wish to undertake a joint development or venture, and the *place* of the library itself (along with the spaces it offers to meet its designated programme most efficiently and effectively).

This process is iterative and reflexive, and is thus best represented as a continuous circle which can be represented schematically as shown in Figure 5.1.

In the next two chapters it is proposed to follow the order of places, partners, people and programmes – given the nature of most development briefs. In reality the design brief can begin to be developed at any point in this circle. For example, the 'pop-up' library at Seven Kings in London came into being as a result of successful campaigning by community groups for a library in their neighbourhood to replace one which had closed more than a decade previously. Once the decision was made to create a new library – however temporary in this case – the use of a redundant shop premises in a busy shopping street was in reality the only option. All design considerations flowed from that specific decision. Similarly it was clear from the start that the target audience for this library would be families with young children, as the local authority and community groups had made increasing educational resources for young children a priority in the area.

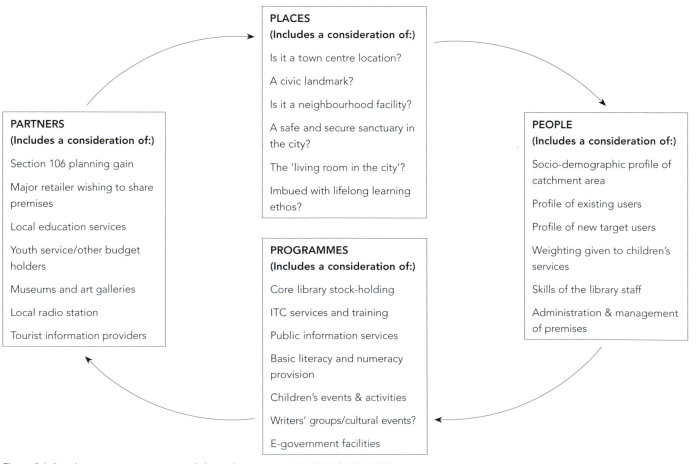

PLACES
(Includes a consideration of:)

Is it a town centre location?

A civic landmark?

Is it a neighbourhood facility?

A safe and secure sanctuary in the city?

The 'living room in the city'?

Imbued with lifelong learning ethos?

PARTNERS
(Includes a consideration of:)

Section 106 planning gain

Major retailer wishing to share premises

Local education services

Youth service/other budget holders

Museums and art galleries

Local radio station

Tourist information providers

PEOPLE
(Includes a consideration of:)

Socio-demographic profile of catchment area

Profile of existing users

Profile of new target users

Weighting given to children's services

Skills of the library staff

Administration & management of premises

PROGRAMMES
(Includes a consideration of:)

Core library stock-holding

ITC services and training

Public information services

Basic literacy and numeracy provision

Children's events & activities

Writers' groups/cultural events?

E-government facilities

Figure 5.1 People, programmes, partners and places: the virtuous circle (CABE & RIBA, 2004)

Seven Kings Library – the pop-up library

The concept of the 'pop-up' building emerged in the wake of high street retail closures in the recession of 2008. Empty shops were let on peppercorn rents to local individuals, voluntary groups and small businesses as galleries, charity stores, cafés and open-access workshops. This was considered much preferable than leaving them empty and boarded up.

In Seven Kings, London, a former discount store was re-opened as a community library – a pop-up library if you will – by the London Borough of Redbridge in 2010. There had not been a library in the district for many years after a spate of library closures in the 1990s, yet there was growing demand for one in the area following local campaigning. The Seven Kings library cost just £150,000 for the refurbishment and fit-out of a single shop interior, on the basis of a five-year life expectancy. The whole shopfront is fully glazed to give the public an instant view of what's on offer inside. Apart from the wall shelving, all the other bookshelves are on wheeled trolleys which can be moved to provide space for meetings of readers, local writers, and others. There are four computer terminals. The stock selection is focused on child and family interests, and the library proved an instant success, with more than 200 visits a day.

Figure 5.2 Pop-up library: Seven Kings Library, London Borough of Redbridge, converted from a vacant discount store

Figure 5.3 Interior of Seven Kings Library, London Borough of Redbridge, converted from a vacant discount store

Thus some opportunities to create new libraries, or refurbish existing libraries, come from planning or development opportunities, often retail-led, while others are responses to local demand, or the need to replace a building that is no longer suitable for what is required. Where you step into the cycle of developing the brief doesn't matter, as long as you follow through the four key elements: places, partners, people and programmes.

PROJECT STEERING GROUP

Once the decision is made to create a new library, or major refurbishment, it is crucial to establish a project steering group to draw up the overall design brief. Too often in the past this task has been simply handed over to an architectural practice to fulfil

– either selected by competition or chosen from an agreed list of approved architects drawn up by the local authority – and library professionals or library users have had little or no further say. Alas this still happens, for I was told in one recent building project that once the contract had been awarded no librarian was allowed to visit the site until the job was complete – upon which they found a whole series of elementary mistakes which could have been rectified or avoided had library staff been consulted throughout. At another new library in another town, I was told by the manager that, 'We didn't have any say in the architecture of the building, nor were we asked anything about the interior design.'

Such a project steering group ought ideally to be assembled by the main client – usually the local authority – together with key library staff, representatives of local community interests in the neighbourhood in which the new library is to be located, architectural consultants, people with business planning experience, and building management experience. Other members of the steering group should be up to date with the latest legislation regarding disability access and a degree of expertise in the principles of 'sustainable design'.

Though fewer and fewer local authorities have their own architects' departments today, the most successful projects seem to emanate from towns and cities where there is an established and forward-looking regeneration or development team. In Newcastle upon Tyne a consultant was engaged to help the development team articulate a vision for the new PFI library, both as a new 'brand' but also to develop a new ethos for the building and the services it was intended to provide. Head librarian, Tony Durcan, later wrote that, 'He helped us articulate what was needed. Communicating our vision for the library was crucial to helping the design team create a building of this quality. Working closely together we were specific about what we needed, then the designers came back with practical and often beautiful ways to achieve it.' The team also had assistance with writing briefs from CABE, working towards the rubric of 'a building that will delight and inspire'. The new library at Clapham One in south London grew out of a 'fantastic brief' put together by Lambeth Council's regeneration department, according to architect Christophe Egret.

When Cranfield College received the funding for a new library, a Library Building Committee was established, consisting of library, academic and estates staff. This

> met once a month to monitor the progress of the project. In addition to this, the project team, together with three or four representatives of the client, would also formally review progress on a monthly basis. A member of our estates staff attended project cost control meetings and there were many *ad hoc* meetings between library staff and the architects. Considerable and continuing emphasis was placed on the need to keep within budget. Many of the early designs were well over budget, but interestingly, as we got the designs back within budget, we frequently achieved a better solution – elegance through economy.
>
> (Blagden, 1994: 20)

In Birmingham consultants were engaged to draw up a 'Strategic Design Brief', a preliminary exercise in setting the fundamental aspirations for what a new library might achieve, and it was this that competing architectural practices were invited to discuss with the client before moving on to more detailed design stages. This strategic document set the tone of what followed with its opening statement that, 'Our mission, simply stated, is to deliver the best public library in the world.' Furthermore, the new

library 'must combine stunning visual impact with broad appeal, functional excellence and efficiency'.

When refurbishing the David Wilson Library at Leicester University, the following factors were given high priority in developing the brief:

- Architects shadowing library staff to develop an understanding of how the building functioned
- Allowing proper time to develop the brief
- Giving the management of acoustics significant priority
- Use of raised flooring with services running underneath
- A retail-style 'street' running through the centre of the building
- Consistent flooring used throughout to ensure visual coherence
- Bespoke furniture to ensure design coherence and best use of space
- Looking at life-cycle costs rather than solely capital outlay (Rossiter, 2011).

WORKING WITH ARCHITECTS

How do people know what they want until they have seen it? And then, what if it looks wonderful but doesn't work? As Stewart Brand has famously written: 'All buildings are predictions. All predictions are wrong' (Brand, 1997: 178). A new public building is always something of a political risk, and a showcase building most certainly a hostage to fortune. The temptation to stick to the tried and true – even if the library programme everywhere is in a state of constant change and development – is usually countered by an understandable wish to create a building that draws gasps of admiration, and even becomes a landmark or flagship for the town or city.

In talking to senior library staff in UK towns and cities where new libraries have been commissioned over the past decade, it is clear that there is no single formula for finding the right architect or – a quite separate matter – developing the best design. Certainly some degree of competition is essential to the process, in order to avoid charges of favouritism, corruption, or insider dealing, and in Finland, for example, architectural competitions have played a part in all of the major projects there since the Second World War (Mehtonen, 2011: 168). In North America, Shannon Mattern claims that 'Nearly every major urban public library design project from 1991 to date has made use of an architectural competition to select its design team' (Mattern, 2007: 9). She then goes on to adumbrate not only some of the drawbacks of this process but also, even worse, the failures of some of the buildings developed through this 'winner takes all' approach.

What is wrong with competitions? Competitions requiring concept drawings and designs can easily pre-empt the role of the client (and especially library staff and users) in having any real say in the basic programme of the building. They also tend to favour dramatic exteriors and bold contours, rather than workable interiors with a large degree of flexibility. Indeed some of the most famous architects or architectural practices working in America still feel obliged to impose their signature style on a building, irrespective of local context and local need:

> Because the same architects and firms – Safdie, Cesar Pelli, Hardy Holzman Pfeiffer, and Michael Graves, for example – appear repeatedly on libraries' short lists, the similarities between their proposals for diverse cities becomes obvious. As a consequence, it becomes clear that the designs they present to the client as inherently contextual, and the design elements rationalized by references to site and local character, are really just revisited signature elements that lend themselves to customized justifications in different contexts.
>
> (Mattern, 2007: 58)

On the other hand, as Mattern points out, an equal number of highly regarded North American architectural practices have refused to enter such competitions, on the grounds that they regard the design brief as quintessentially a collaborative, iterative, reflexive process. Some practices – often the same ones – also point out that the fees available for entering the competition by no means cover the cost of serious contextual development and thinking, and once again favour the architectural practice or design team which goes for visual excitement over functionality – let alone long-term sustainability. Even worse, low development fees can too easily result in established architectural practices presenting a template made for an earlier project – but now dusted off, re-badged and presented as new.

The more complex the building, the less likely is competition to produce the most satisfactory end result. When Denver's mayor announced a competition to build a new library at the beginning of the 1990s, the Denver chapter of the American Institute of Architects opposed the competition, arguing that the 'highly complex nature of the building would require significant client input into the decision process' (Mattern, 2007:13). The eminent architect Denise Scott Brown also wrote at the time to express her disapproval of this and other competitions with regard to major public projects: 'Our own experience in over thirty competitions has taught us that they are not a vehicle for handling the sensitive programming and urbanistic issues that require testing, development and fine tuning in order to provide a

building worth a city's investment' (Mattern, 2007: 14). Her firm declined to participate in the Denver competition, and Cesar Pelli and Associates later withdrew, claiming 'the process was moving too fast for careful consideration of the complexity of the project.'

Different funding arrangements can circumvent the competition process, sometimes to good effect. This happened at Canada Water in London's docklands, where the commissioning client was a private company, British Land, not subject to European rules for choosing architects. They chose CZWG, with whom they enjoyed an established relationship, even though the practice had not designed a library before, which would have ruled them out of the competition following other criteria. The result was a stunning success. Local authorities may choose to go with a 'design-and-build' process, in which the designer and construction company are part of the same team. This has the advantage of cutting costs and being more reliable in terms of ironing out design problems ahead of construction. It can, however, lead to blander buildings, as well as buildings in which the architect loses all independence, being part of the contractor team rather than being on the client's side.

The selection process also depends upon who is paying ultimately, and therefore who the 'client' or end-user actually is. In the UK, whether in PFI schemes or in Section 106 planning gain agreements, the financial package often involves a commercial developer or private finance company, already in a close working relationship with a design team or master-planning team, in which the new library is just one element of a larger scheme, such as in Brighton and Huntingdon. In such cases the architect or design team is already in place, and the project then becomes one of ensuring that the design adheres as much as possible to a brief developed by the local authority on the basis of its specific vision and needs. For it is usually the local authority – although in the case of the Bournemouth library a special trust was established to manage the library scheme – which will subsequently own, lease, or in other ways manage the building over a specified time, during which it has to work effectively as a public building that staff and users enjoy, and which fulfils all the needs of a modern library, not just as a visual grace-note to a larger scheme.

In the worst case scenarios – and this has most certainly happened in the USA according to Mattern, and to my own knowledge in the UK too – library professionals have been completely overlooked in developing the design or working with the architect. Politicians and/or urban development professionals or private sector developers, have done deals with architects over the heads of their own library staff and library public, either because they wanted to commission a 'star' architect for status reasons, or because they simply deferred to professional design expertise irrespective of local knowledge and experience. 'These kinds of details were not shared with us,' a librarian said, when asked about problems in the newly opened Denver Library (Mattern, 2007: 20). During visits to two new UK libraries built in the past five years, as mentioned earlier, it was clearly evident that library staff had not been consulted at all upon the design. In both cases there were substantial – and now permanent – problems of poor adjacencies, access and visibility, along with the use of inappropriate materials, which might have been easily resolved if library professionals had been invited to discuss briefs and plans.

Such problems are avoidable, though they often stem from confusion as to who the principal 'client' is. For example, in a joint public/private partnership set up to master-plan or develop a run-down urban quarter in which a library is going to be a key element, who is the principal client? Is it:

● the partnership providing the funding package?

● the local authority which has historically provided and managed libraries and has designated the library element?

● the senior library management team who have the professional expertise required to develop the programme and brief?

● the tax-paying public whose monies are contributing to the library of which many will be the principal end users?

'Identifying the client' is a great game to play, but when it goes wrong the results can be expensive and long-lasting. Surely in the end it is the community of library staff, library users and would-be users whose interests represent the core of the 'client' persona.

Increasingly clients are selecting architects by a mixture of long-listing, short-listing, discussion and negotiation, rather than straightforward competition for a finished design. In the case of the commissioning of the new library at Cranfield University, a shortlist of six practices was compiled based on the following selection criteria:

● Quality of existing buildings – both interiors and exteriors

● Functionality – did these buildings work?

● Library experience preferable

● Commitment – how much did they want the job?

● Size of practice

● Cost control and management experience

● Personalities – who will actually be doing the job as opposed to the presentation?

● Client empathy – could they be sympathetic and constructive to work with?

Each company on the shortlist was asked to nominate three of their buildings which could be visited, and many were. At the end of the process Sir Norman Foster + Partners were chosen, by widespread agreement, largely because of the quality of their buildings, and the effectiveness of their presentation.

In the case of the Utrecht University Library, there was a European call for tenders to which 42 practices responded, and of which twelve were long-listed. This long list was then reduced to five practices, all of whom were visited, 'and asked to present their vision to us. So we didn't ask for a design sketch but rather for a story' (Arets, 2005: 134). The winning architect, Wiel Arets, was chosen on the basis that his presentation consisted of passing round a postcard of Piet Mondrian's famous late painting, *Broadway Boogie Woogie*, with its free flow of spaces and forms, and then some on the spot sketches and discussion about how one embodied freedom in form. After several concept sketches and lengthier exchanges of ideas, according to project manager Bas Savenije, 'there was an immediate interchange and that's what we fell for' (Arets, 2005: 134).

LEARNING FROM OTHERS

When thinking about a new library it makes sense to see what people are doing in other parts of the world. Without this wider perspective, people often are limited in their imagination to what they already know, and consultation simply becomes a form of asking how a new building might do the old things better rather than marking out entirely new territory. 'Few authorities appeared to have undertaken a rigorous approach to planning their new libraries,' Jared Bryson and his colleagues noted in 2003. 'Many have relied on previously successful local models and only a handful appeared to have considered national and international standards.' American library planning consultant Robert Rohlf is quoted as saying that in large libraries, 'the majority of the professional staff have never worked in any other library, so their options for change are "more" or "bigger", not "different"' (Mattern, 2007: 15).

Development of design possibilities by accretion can work, but from time to time a particular building type needs an entirely new configuration – or, if you like, a paradigm shift. This is particularly the case where, as we shall discover in the case studies, a new city centre library is intended not only to provide new library facilities but is also intended to contribute to re-shaping the identity of a new district or development area, and set a strong civic mark on the terrain, as has happened in Bournemouth, Brighton, Cardiff, Dagenham, Newcastle upon Tyne, Norwich and in other towns and cities.

Encouraging politicians and planners, library staff and users to travel to see what is exciting and innovative elsewhere is a good way of raising the stakes. In the Norwich case, visits were made to major English, European and American public libraries. In preparation of the design brief for the Newcastle city library, a small contingent of the bid team 'did a quick hop across to Malmo, in Sweden, taking in Copenhagen's Black Diamond library in Denmark at the same time'. They and others also visited a number of new libraries in London, including the new British Library and the Idea Store in Whitechapel. The Cardiff team were bowled over by Jo Coenen's Amsterdam library when they visited it, and the influence shows at every level – and succeeds. Birmingham library officers visited new libraries in Amsterdam, Helsinki and Seattle, as well as attending several conferences devoted to matters of new library design. When planning a new library in Salt Lake City, the existing library board

> was given books and articles to read, and speakers were invited to give the board a basic knowledge of architectural styles, contemporary architects, and architectural criticism. They visited the new public libraries of the western United States, with each board member evaluating designs based on some general and some personally defined criteria.
>
> (Mattern, 2007: 86)

The facilities and services which public libraries provide are changing to meet new cultural needs and interests, at an ever-increasing pace of cultural and technological transformation, particularly in response to the development of new media in digital form, whether music, film, e-books, talking books, computer software, online access to the Internet, and so on. Even within the last two decades records, videos, CDs and audio-tapes have come and gone, as the whole cultural sphere becomes increasingly de-materialised as part of the new 'weightless economy'. This process of adaptation is not new: library buildings in Britain in the 1930s often incorporated a small art gallery, theatre or even a film theatre. They also loaned out framed prints and jigsaw puzzles. Today, libraries may well incorporate computer training suites, advice centres, careers services, cafés, toy libraries and homework centres. They are rapidly becoming 'plug-in' hubs for people who want access to cultural products – books, music, films, spoken word, and information – but want to download it rather than carry the physical items home.

Thus each library programme is different depending on the community it serves. This increasing 'differentiation of library type' which we are seeing as a result of co-location projects and customised facilities means that there is no longer a single model

Figure 5.4 Amsterdam Public Library designed by Jo Coenen & Co Architecten, opened in 2008, and much visited by librarians from around the world (Photos: Mike Llewellyn)

to be adhered to – hence the importance of visiting a range of new libraries elsewhere to assess the extent to which customisation can work to provide something different and new in library design depending on the people and place it is intended to serve. In America this process of increasing differentiation is also happening:

> There are new libraries in cities as diverse as New York, Minneapolis, San Antonio, and Nashville, and no two of these buildings resemble one another, at least in terms of their exterior shape and skins. There are indeed some programmatic elements and interior design elements that have become common to many newly constructed buildings, but the diversity of shapes and structures and styles of the modern-day public library evidences the search for localised, particularized solutions for some widely shared design problems.
>
> (Mattern, 2007: 63)

Figure 5.5 Interior of new public library and community centre in former mining community of Houghton Le Spring, near Sunderland

Figure 5.6 New art gallery in refurbished public library at Bishop Auckland by Ainsworth Spark Associates

March Library and Learning Centre, Cambridgeshire

Opened in August, 2000 in the small market town of March, in Cambridgeshire, this inexpensive, ostensibly simple design is a wonderful building to visit and use. Designed by Bernard Stillwell Architects, it is 1,000 square metres of single floor space, with significant glass walling and clerestory, giving high levels of natural light, and uncluttered sight lines across the main library open plan floor. The timber-framed building seems both traditional in its easy-to-understand basic construction, yet it offers all the light and space usually associated with steel, concrete and glass forms. Interior design was by Leonore Charlton, a library design consultant.

Unusually, this public library also shares the building with the town's Registrar of Births, Marriages and Deaths, and is licensed for marriage services, which are frequent. Both wedding suite and public library share the same entrance doors and lobby. The marriage room doubles as a 50 seat meeting room, and there are also individual interview rooms, 21 computer terminals, and a programme of formal and informal courses leading to Level 3 qualifications. The capital cost of the building was £1.25 million, an extremely modest outlay for a building which has won national esteem and won a Civic Trust Award in 2003. It is set in a small landscaped park, set back from the main high street.

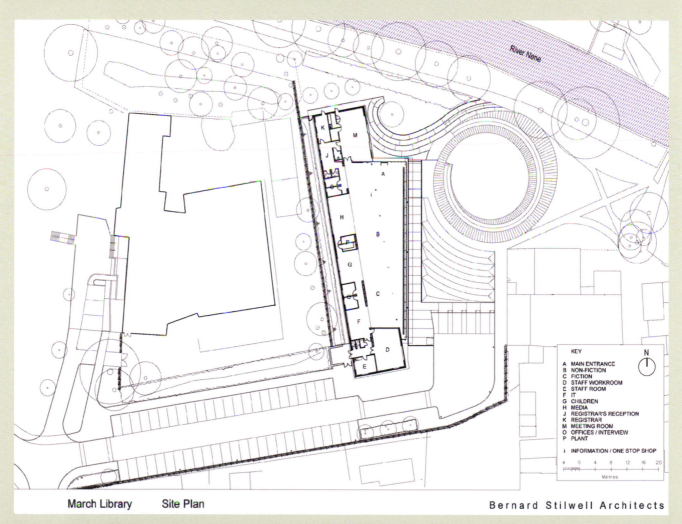

March Library   Site Plan   Bernard Stilwell Architects

Figure 5.7 Site plan of March Library, Cambridgeshire, designed by Bernard Stillwell Architects

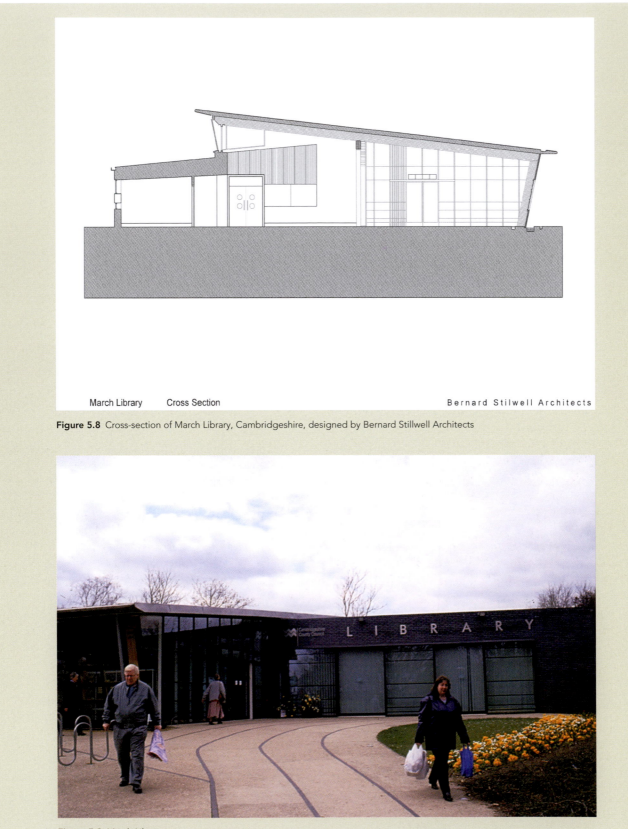

March Library   Cross Section   Bernard Stilwell Architects

Figure 5.8 Cross-section of March Library, Cambridgeshire, designed by Bernard Stillwell Architects

Figure 5.9 March Library

Figure 5.10 March Library interior

Furthermore, today's library services may be offered in buildings alongside other public services, sometimes in unusual and intriguing combinations. A number of libraries in former mining communities in Durham and Sunderland also operate as 'electronic village halls'. In Bishop Auckland, the library shares a rehabilitated town hall with a beautiful art gallery and theatre. In Houghton Le Spring close to Sunderland, the design of the new library centre also incorporates a children's nursery, a youth centre and local police facilities. The library in March, Cambridgeshire, designed by Bernard Stillwell Associates, and winner of a 2003 Civic Trust Award, houses the local Registrar of Births, Marriages and Deaths, as well as a marriage suite. Changes in services and functions obviously mean changes in design and plan. Traditional library design has to be adapted or superseded, sometimes by radically new configurations of services and spaces.

A particularly imaginative assembly of library and cultural facilities can be found in Apeldoorn in The Netherlands, designed by Herman Hertzberger. Known as CODA (Cultuur Onder Dak Apeldoorn) it brings together two museums, a theatre auditorium and a public library in an elegant meeting place for the town. A variety of very different sizes and volumes of spaces are typically connected by bridges, galleries and ramps so that people can move easily from one facility to the next while observing a range of different activities going on around them. The sloping curved roof of the auditorium falls to ground level and can be used as a children's play area, as well as an outdoor performance space.

LIMITS OF CONSULTATION

Some forms of consultation are more credible and strategic than others. During the long building programme for the Library of Birmingham, the site hoardings were very effectively used to show plans, drawings, computer generated graphics, and timetable for the development, and these attracted a lot of interest. Keeping the public informed is important. It is likely that existing library users have a greater investment in the success of a new library than non-users – though this latter group might be attracted by services and facilities not currently available. Any form of provision, whether commercial or public, is more sustainable in the long term if it succeeds in keeping the existing clientele satisfied – and building on that base – rather than aiming for an entirely new audience. We know that families with young children, as well as older people, are amongst the most loyal and committed of library users, and therefore basic things like the provision of toilets, baby-changing facilities, comfortable seats, as well as an opportunity to buy refreshments, are all important. In the consultation exercise for the new library in Huntingdon, according to designer Leonore Charlton, the main requirements the public emphasised were 'a café, toilets and car parking'.

However, in an interesting example of how consultation can sometimes produce failed predictive information, the consultation for the Newcastle library found that many users of the local history library asked for public lockers to be installed there. On paper this made sense, as many of those studying local or family history often came for long periods, and wanted somewhere to put hats, coats, bags, etc. Yet though provided they have been rarely used, and take up valuable space that could have been used for other purposes.

In the USA Shannon Mattern reports that public involvement in library design has had mixed results:

> When done well – that is, when the public's comments are taken seriously and applied to the design and when discussion is kept at an abstract level rather than fixating on details – public processes can rally a community around a design project and promote a tremendous sense of civic pride. When done poorly – that is, when the public is asked to financially support a library but is then completely shut out of the process, or when a public is led to believe that every voice will hear itself echoed in the library building (a promise impossible to keep) – a public process elicits resentment and may damage the library's place in public culture.
>
> (Mattern, 2007: 29)

Thus in designing the brief, no single interest group or partisan point of view should be allowed to prevail. Librarians know many things which architects don't – but the reverse is equally true. In some of the best new libraries in the UK, librarians have told me how they have been fascinated and greatly impressed by the design solutions which architects have proposed to what were thought to have been intractable problems. In turn architects have often been surprised to realise just how diverse the modern library 'offer' is, and the range of people and needs that today's public libraries serve.

The public interest in these matters is best described as a matter of trust. Library users rely on library professionals and architects – though they may no longer defer to them – to work together to provide a building which delights and is a pleasure to use. But then again, library users know from experience many things that designers need to know too. In truth one suspects that not many architects are avid users of public libraries, and therefore they should listen to, and observe, those who are. A multi-perspectival view is required today.

Figure 5.11 Corner entrance to Apeldoorn Cultural Centre in The Netherlands, designed by Herman Hertzberger

Figure 5.12 Facade of existing Apeldoorn Library

Figure 5.13 Café and gallery at Apeldoorn Cultural Centre and Library

CHAPTER 6
Places and partners

In the previous chapter, the four elements of 'places, partners, programmes and people' were identified as being central to the design brief. As with any public facility, locational issues are crucial to the success of any new-build development. Most of the newer libraries occupy key city-centre sites as part of their role in urban renewal. A number have benefited directly or indirectly from planning gain agreements, land swaps, funding from major developers and other financial arrangements made with private sector bodies and development agencies, which have helped provide them with strategic city-centre sites where they operate as part of the retail/cultural mix. Furthermore, the new open plan spaces of the modern library often continue the life of the street and the public domain. Younger people, especially, are drawn to modern design and bold interiors, and are becoming more committed library users. Many newer libraries, both large and small, also incorporate space and facilities for other activities, whether drop-in clinics, complementary medicine services, art galleries, recording studios, performance spaces, local radio stations and a variety of other services wishing to 'co-locate' in the new facility.

It is time to consider a number of key generic elements of any design brief for a public library, starting with the matter of location.

PLACES
Location

There is no doubt that the once extensive network of central, district and branch libraries is retreating in the UK. In recent years the number of library buildings in continuing use has diminished. Local authorities claim that they no longer have the money to sustain a large number of small branch libraries, and have either closed those which are less busy, or handed them over to community management in some form or other. In this

they are able to argue that they are following government advice which is that: 'Local authorities should regularly review the footprint of the library service to determine whether they have the right buildings in the right place' (Hodge, 2010: 9).

While library design issues share much the same priorities in the UK as in North America, with regard to the need to occupy a central or 'downtown' location, the one major difference is car parking. To my knowledge provision for car parking has barely featured in any UK design brief, though it was mentioned in Huntingdon. However, it figures strongly in American proposals – including provision for snowmobiles in some states – as it no doubt does in parts of Scandinavia. Indeed, as Shannon Mattern has emphasised, a number of new libraries in America have been designed so as to show their best face to the passing motorist, and have even put their main entrance opening out into the parking lot rather than on to the pedestrian street. Queens Borough Public Library in New York designed by the Polshek Partnership has been one of the great success stories in American public libraries in recent times, its bold street corner flagship building now a major meeting place in the downtown area. Its prow-shaped glass facade was designed 'as a counterpart to the vault-like and seemingly impenetrable character of public libraries of the past,' according to former library director, Gary Strong (Mattern, 2007: 39). Capturing and consolidating a corner-site so successfully has been echoed at Bournemouth, and at Calne in Wiltshire.

Despite retrenchment many new libraries have been built during this same period. They have either replaced existing buildings in strategic centres where demand remains high, or are integrated into new developments intended to bring cultural life to a new part of the town or city, as is the case with Dagenham and Canada Water as well as the beautiful Jaume Fuster Library in Barcelona. Thus location issues are central to the strategic thinking behind new library provision, either with the intention of maximising use because this is where people are now mostly to be found, or because there are funding programmes or partnerships to be had which can help underwrite the costs of the new building.

Not surprisingly, the location of many new library buildings has been largely determined by changing patterns and densities of retail activity during the daytime. A national survey in the UK found that 'exactly half of all new libraries were associated with retail developments' (Bryson et al., 2003: 68). Lest it be thought that libraries were beholden to retailers to bring their services to the most desired locations, retailers themselves are often even more enthusiastic to have this 'anchor business' integrated into their malls and shopping streets, both to consolidate the retail 'mix', as well as to bring a degree of civic status to any new development.

One of the earliest and most successful examples of this was the creation of a new central library for Hounslow in the new shopping centre, opened in the early 1990s. This had been agreed as part of the planning gain, though a number of retailers at the time were sceptical about having a public service in a setting geared to shopping. In fact the library quickly proved to be one of the busiest tenants in the development, and brought hundreds of people every day to the centre, who also used the surrounding commercial facilities. The new library at Shepherd's Bush in west London is part of the enormous Westfield shopping mall, and its new location, only a hundred metres or so from its former building, has tripled visitor figures compared with those of the library it replaced, now adapted for other uses. This £2 million library was built and fitted out entirely at the expense of the developer under a Section 106 planning agreement, which is used to procure public benefits from private development. It was designed by FaulknerBrowns architects.

Shepherd's Bush Library, London Borough of Hammersmith and Fulham

Opened in September 2009, the library is part of a Section 106 planning gain agreement from the large-scale new Westfield Shopping Mall – which the library bookends at its western extremity – with a Jamie Oliver restaurant perched on its roof. The £2million pound building – part designed by FaulknerBrowns – was built and fitted out at zero cost to the taxpayer as a result of this deal, and replaces the old Passmore Edwards library located only a street away. Where the previous library rarely attracted more than 500 visits a day, the new library is achieving daily visitor numbers of between 1,300 and 2,000, which is astonishing for a library still very small in terms of floor space and book-stock (though 10,000 new books were added to the existing stock). It appears to be a predominantly young group of library users, many attracted by free WiFi facilities, bringing their own laptops, and the upstairs mezzanine study area is always packed and the atmosphere remarkably quiet and purposive.

The exterior design is bland, but is part of the overall mall design code, though the library occupies a ground-level corner site which is much to its advantage. The entrance is made up of two sets of automatically opening double-doors. There is a minimal reception desk/library counter, as self-service is mostly used, and library staff concentrate on circulating and keeping the stock and shelves in order and answering visitor queries. The immediate entrance area provides little immediate orientation and is disappointing, whereas the children's area, the mezzanine study floor, and the rear ground-floor lounge area all have a very strong design presence and conviviality. The most serious design flaw is that the public toilets have been located in the (mostly unsupervised) children's library, contrary to child-protection principles, allowing unrestricted public access by adults to dedicated children's facilities.

There are several small meeting rooms and interview rooms for hire, though those upstairs – including the staff area – are mostly small and windowless, as are the administration rooms. The library is too small to provide a café area, but the adjacent mall is full of eating places. Vending machines were installed at the beginning but were subsequently taken out as they failed to generate sufficient income to warrant their hire.

The library operates in one of the most intense, colourful and busiest urban environments in London, where there is also a degree of anti-social behaviour, as might be anticipated. A higher than average proportion of local people live transitory, isolated or economically marginal lives, and the library also has to serve these visitors too – which it does. Though library staff had little say in the design as far as one can gather, the building is extremely successful and attractive in its major areas, though poor in some details. Yet in terms of visitor numbers, for a library of this size it is phenomenally busy and well used.

Figure 6.1 Shepherd's Bush Library occupies a corner site, much to its advantage

The Cardiff library was part-funded by developers who were keen to add a strong cultural element to the extension of retailing in this formerly rundown part of the city. The combination of shopping and library-use is well established, and is particularly so for young people. A survey of young people's spending power undertaken by academics at the University of Sheffield some years ago revealed that combining a Saturday trip to go shopping with a visit to the library was a popular choice amongst those questioned.

In the case of the new library at Stratford in east London, a priority was given to attracting young people into the library, as this age group was forming a significant section of the population. As the then Head of Library and Information Services noted, 'It's an acknowledgement of Newham having the youngest population in London. It's one of the fastest growing populations and has the highest birth rate in London now. So all these considerations were taken into account in the design of the library' (Bryson et al., 2003: 42). This focus was not without problems, given that the large library foyer on the ground floor was laid out as a 'Teenzone' with armchairs, sofas and a large television screen showing music videos, which older library users disliked. As some librarians admitted later, when interviewed, 'While they got the teenagers in, they alienated a lot of the older people which make up a big group.' One result was that while other libraries locally continued to get lots of older users visiting and spending a long time in their libraries, this pattern almost disappeared from the new Stratford library.

To a lesser extent reduced use by the elderly was also reported at the Norwich Millennium Library, partly evidenced by a lower than expected take-up of large print material, with some older people admitting they prefer to use the smaller, quieter branch libraries. However, this was certainly not the case when I visited the Jaume Fuster Library in Barcelona, the ground floor reading room of which was packed with older people reading quietly and enjoyably. This library is, admittedly, a branch library serving a neighbourhood location.

Modern libraries have a much closer relationship to modern retailing than would have been expected – or even approved of – in the past. But this is a two-way process. The rise of the Waterstone's chain of bookshops in the 1980s was attributed to their high levels of design and bibliographical expertise; they also encouraged the culture of browsing, providing armchairs in which customers could relax and peruse the book stock, even while drinking a coffee. At the time Waterstone's management said they had tried to appear more like libraries than fast-turnover bookshops. The compliment has been returned, as libraries have been more active in the promotion of reading, in highlighting new books, and changing displays of different kinds of thematic books, music and film. Glasgow's library managers told me that the key factor for embarking on a large programme of library refurbishments was as a direct response to the arrival of Waterstone's Bookshop in the city, which had created a media frenzy.

Thus there is a continuing symbiosis between the modern library and the modern bookshop. In both cases staff are trained to be more outward-going, increasingly required to abide by a dress code which gives them an air of both service and authority, and are there to advise visitors and browsers on the stock just as much as they are there to stand behind an issue desk or till. Both bookshops and libraries cultivate something of a club-like ambience by providing comfortable armchairs and settees, as well as providing somewhere to buy coffee. The library in Newcastle is actively involved in promoting and selling books about local and regional history and culture, often produced by small amenity groups or publishing initiatives which otherwise would not have access to such premier retail space. Today the inter-relationship between the public library and the world of contemporary city centre retailing and commercial cyber-cafés is firmly established, though the library's civic remit will always make it somewhere special and unique for many people.

The living room in the city

An equally important aspect of the 'central place' aspect of the newer city-centre libraries is that the ground floor of many of them provides a floor space which continues the urban space of the city outside. In Rotterdam the ground floor of the large 1970s building (now after some controversy formally attributed to architects Bakema & Weeber) extends the life of the famous street market outside. It provides exhibition space, toilets, information bureaux and events, while acting as a viewing floor for the open-deck tiers of library floors visible above. In Newcastle this connection to the streets around was deliberate, according to the project architects:

> The development of the library site offered the potential to transform the urban landscape around the building and reinforce the physical and visual linkages between the Blue Carpet (an adjacent open square) and the Laing Art Gallery on one side, and Princess Square on the other. *At the core of the concept was a synthesis of the architectural and townscape design so that external spaces and movement patterns could flow into and through the building*. This required the creation of a distinct personality for each space.
>
> (Phethean, 2009: 71. My italics).

Furthermore, as Tony Durcan, the librarian principally responsible for overseeing the Newcastle scheme, has elaborated: 'When

I'm waxing lyrical I say a good library is one of the best quality public squares with a roof on top where you can sit and be warm, you can work, or you can look at newspapers or you can just feel secure' (Phethean, 2009: 32). This could be a verbatim description of the penthouse café at Whitechapel's Idea Store. The concept of the public library as 'the living room in the city', originally a Scandinavian concept, is now being emulated across the world.

I first heard of the 'living room in the city' when visiting a new library in Ornsköldsvik in the north of Sweden in the late 1990s. My visit occurred in the midst of winter, with temperatures well below freezing, and thick snow lay everywhere. People visiting the library often came for the day, using lockers to change from heavy outdoor wear and snow-boots, into casual clothes and footwear, sometimes even slippers. In many of the libraries featured in the book *Nordic Public Libraries* (Larsen, 2006), there is a glazed conservatory-style entrance lobby, tiled, operating as something like a domestic porch or lobby, where people change shoes, divest themselves of wet clothing, and put umbrellas or pushchairs. At Ornsköldsvik library users often brought sandwiches and flasks of coffee, though catering facilities were provided. They not only came to borrow books or to browse the collections, but also to meet friends, listen to lunchtime concerts, and to attend talks or lectures. Outside the temperature was bitterly cold; inside the library it was room temperature, warm and welcoming. It was, in short, the town salon, or living room. In time this has become something of a prototype for the new library.

In the new Birmingham library it is envisaged that:

> The foyer will be a vital element of the new development. It will be large, capable of hosting events, containing 'tasters' and trails to entice people to explore further within the library, and mounting an exciting programme of performances relevant to the collections of the library – examples might include poetry in performance, promenade theatre, children's entertainment, street artists, author readings, musical events and community information programmes. The foyer must be designed to serve a number of purposes and different audiences, throughout the day and evening.

A new high profile location creates an opportunity to make a bold statement about the importance of the library in contemporary life and culture, and this has not been missed in many of the newer city centre UK libraries featured in the case studies. One of the library staff working in the new Stratford library in east London, designed by Miller Bourne Partnership (with FaulknerBrowns responsible for interior design), said that 'The simple fact that the building is where it is, is its biggest promotional statement.' In Stockholm three new subway libraries located at busy metro stations have proved popular, and the initiative was awarded a prize by the city's Chamber of Commerce for making the city a better place to live. The new library at Canada Water designed by Piers Gough's practice, CZWG, sits literally on top of a combined overground and underground railway station. A strategic and high profile location not only

Figure 6.2 Uppsala Library Reading Room

brings new people into the library, it also adds a substantial drawing power to the shops and services which surround it. In North America this 'living room in the city' is more customarily called an 'urban room', and is specifically called so in Moshe Safdie's Salt Lake City Library, where it is a distinct space leading to the library and can be used out of hours. In this it is like the large public atrium at Norwich.

With this new premium on providing space to congregate, however briefly, or to sit down and browse a collection of books, more than usual space is needed. IFLA guidelines suggest circulation space of 15 per cent–20 per cent for public areas and 20 per cent–25 per cent for staff areas, but this may not be enough for the former, if the library is to function successfully as a meeting-place. The new wing at Enfield Library, an elegant Miesian glass box designed by Shepheard Epstein Hunter, looks light and airy from the outside but the foyer is cluttered, and the ground floor is filled with an over-abundance of display stands, tables and badly placed shelving failing to create any sense of arrival or coherent resting space whatsoever.

One design principle which can work against this idea of the library space – or part of it at least – as an urban living room, is an equally powerful tendency to design the interior spaces around an atrium – criticism of which by Rem Koolhaas has already been noted. While this can produce stunning and highly transparent interiors, in which users can at a glance see all the floors and the escalators and lifts to access them, it renders the idea of sanctuary space problematic. Certainly the ground floor becomes a public arena rather than a public lounge or quiet place.

World of interiors

'It smells of beige, if that's possible,' said one respondent to the MOA survey of people's views of the libraries they use. 'Everything inside is beige or chocolate, plastic brown. It was supposed to be exciting but it isn't.' One library manager told me some years ago that he thought many library staff 'lacked visual imagination'. Pre-occupied with books, texts, maps, archives and cataloguing systems, they appeared at times indifferent to the quality of their surroundings – even though we know that when questioned many library staff in fact attach a great deal of importance to their working conditions, even if this is not the same thing. As Brian Edwards has shrewdly pointed out, 'Architects perceive libraries as space, librarians as service' (Edwards, 2009: 70). Today the public most certainly are interested in design, legibility and accessibility. While older people recall the dark brown wood and high shelving of the libraries of their childhood, along with a sense of the mystique of the library staff and their arcane world of card indexes, pastel cardboard library cards and rubber stamping machines, for today's library users the building

has to exude an air of brightness and efficiency – as well as connectedness to global networks.

In the MOA study cited earlier, though many respondents idealised the Victorian, Arts and Crafts, or other mannered architectural styles of pre-war library provision, younger respondents enthused about the steel and glass libraries of the present day. However, there seemed to be a shared dislike of post-war brutalist styles, not only for their outward appearance, but for their interior colour palette too.

> (Our 1960s library) looks like nothing so much as the headquarters of the Secret Police in some dingy corner of Eastern Europe. It is an ugly block of grey concrete made even greyer by the water that runs off its flat roof; all sharp angles and blank plate glass windows...

> (My library) is fifties-built brick. Stalin era, one storey edifice with grilled and barred windows, fortified doors, vandal proof benches outside and a small litter strewn car park...
>
> (Black, 2011b: 34)

Figure 6.3 Cardiff Central Library designed by BDP: connecting views

Figure 6.4 Aberdeen University Library: the view from above of the café-foyer area

In fairness, the problem with so much now-derided public architecture of the post-war era, was lack of maintenance and repair, rather than a failure of architectural imagination. Refurbished libraries of this period, such as Sheffield University's Western Bank Library opened in 1961, designed by Gollins Melvin Ward (wholly refurbished by Avanti Architects in 2009), or Sir Basil Spence's 1964 Swiss Cottage Central Library (refurbished by John McAslan & Partners in 2003) or the 1970 Ewell Library in Surrey designed by A.G. Sheppard Fidler and Associates, have all emerged from under wraps looking startlingly fresh and exciting. Perhaps the most welcome development in building budgets in the last decade or more has been the time and thought given to life-cycle costing rather than capital outlay – realising that spending more on quality materials at the outset along with a fully worked out maintenance schedule, over time ends up costing less than economising on costs at the beginning but having to constantly spend large sums of money on repairs, and even premature abandonment or demolition.

Colour plays an increasingly important role in differentiating different parts of the library, through what is now called a 'colour mnemonic': each floor may be colour-coded differently to emphasise its distinct sphere of operation, whether this be children's section, fiction, non-fiction, and so on. However, some designers have reservations about too much fixed differentiation – either by colour, floor surface or other design cue – as this reduces opportunities for the future re-configuration of the spaces.

Opinion is mixed with regard to the use of colour. The new Canada Water library has multi-coloured carpet tiles throughout, except for the ground floor which has hardwood flooring. The rest of the building is mainly handsome light-wood shelving, with white walls, not dissimilar to the British Library, the Jaume Fuster Library in Barcelona and dozens of Scandinavian libraries. The over-exuberant use of colour at Barking Library is somewhat dizzying and almost aggressive.

Letting the light in

A long-standing feature of library architecture has involved trying to create as much natural light in the main reading areas as is possible, whether by the round clerestory in Asplund's Stockholm City Library dome, in Aalto's revolutionary roof-lights at Viipuri, through to the astonishing conical rooflight which illuminates the heart of Mecanoo's university library at Delft. It is no accident that Henning Larsen's extension to Malmo's historic city library is called *Ljusets Kalender* ('The Calendar of Light'), described by Peter Davey (1998) as a great hall where a 'continuous skylight circles the whole space, so that the volume continuously changes with the time of the day, weather and the seasons.' In the case studies provided in this book, designs to encourage the larger areas of the library to be lit naturally can be seen in the circular clerestory at Ewell in Surrey, in the large ceiling lantern at Cambourne, the central light well at Huntingdon library, the clerestory panels at March, the three-sided glazed atrium at Newcastle upon Tyne, the north-facing glazed side-panels which run the full height of Sheffield University's Information Commons, as well as Rem Koolhaas' glass and steel mesh skin which covers the whole exterior of Seattle Central Public Library. Good lighting is essential to the act of reading, whether it is achieved by natural lighting, general lighting or task-lighting on desks – or a combination of these.

New building materials and curtain-walling techniques have allowed more of the modern library's walls to be almost wholly glazed, and more and more study and informal reading spaces are being pushed out of the centre of the library space to the well-lit edges. In the case of Delft University Library, the conical light well is encircled on each floor with study desks taking advantage of the light flooding in from above. This renewed emphasis on natural light is not only desirable as a form of energy conservation, but it enables library users to spend more time in the building, and to regard it as a meeting place as well as a place in which to burrow away in order to study – though these latter spaces are also still available between the stacks.

The modern library now looks outwards to the world, metaphorically and literally: certainly compared to earlier models of library design emphasising the closed, interior world of study and contemplation. Views of adjacent parks, street scenes, rivers and harbours (the latter a feature of Copenhagen's Black Diamond as well as Canada Water in London's docklands) are available from the reading areas and study desks of these libraries.

The library at Linköping in Sweden, designed by Arkitektkontor, is essentially a large triple-height glazed wooden shed, triangular in plan, with a slightly tilted flat roof supported by internal cylindrical concrete columns. Inside there is a mezzanine floor containing an art gallery, lecture theatre and staff accommodation. A series of roof lanterns bring light into the centre of the deep-plan book hall. There are of course dangers to providing too much glazing, especially in south-facing facades such as those at Linköping (and in the UK at Brighton and Cranfield for example). At Linköping a wide roof overhang, combined with automated blinds, is the principal means of combating over-heating, along with a limestone surround to the floor below, in which pipes are inserted to provide cooling or heating at the edges as required. The Brighton glass facade is shielded by louvres which deflect the sun in the summer months but allow the low winter sunlight to enter, along with automatically opening vents which circulate air (supported by five wind towers). The Cranfield interior is protected from direct sunlight by a large roof overhang – though on a particularly bright winter's day a low sun can reach some areas and dazzle users.

Large glazed exterior walls also allow library buildings to glow after dark – illuminating the interior like a stage set – and this offers an invitation to passers by to enter and join in the activities on view. Indeed, the view at night is now as much a feature of the architectural photography of the modern library as is the daytime image. The photograph of the Médiathèque Jean-Pierre Melvillle & Bibliothèque Marguerite Duran in Paris clearly demonstrates the enlivening effect of this urban transparency. The library is not only a beacon architecturally and symbolically, it can literally become one in the night-time townscape, especially when much else around the building is closed.

PARTNERS

Public libraries have often been incorporated into buildings serving other functions, whether they be art galleries, theatres, health clinics or apartment blocks. This is usually so that costs can be shared with other providers. In modern parlance this is termed co-location, and the range of partners or facilities conjoined in recent times includes swimming pools, health centres, youth services, police offices, radio stations, as well as major retail chains and brand-name coffee shop franchises. In the new settlement of Cambourne in Cambridgeshire, the library shares a building, as well as an entrance and common reception area, with a health centre, as it does at Clapham One, the latest new library in London, designed by Studio Egret West, which opened in 2012. At Clapham, Dagenham, Dalston and Boscombe near Bournemouth, the new library was achieved in partnership with an adjacent or integrated housing development.

Figure 6.5 Mediathèque Jean-Pierre Melville in Paris, with strong visual connections between library and street

In their 2002 survey, completed by 70 UK libraries, researchers at the University of Sheffield found some 44 different organisations sharing premises or enjoying partnership arrangements for the provision of services, including arts organisations, housing associations, community groups, health boards, regeneration companies, adult learning services, after-school clubs, universities, early learning centres, Citizens' Advice Bureaux, careers services, schools, tourist information, amongst others. In the case studies described in this book, new libraries have worked in close co-operation with commercial coffee-shop franchises, local radio stations, registry offices and repertory theatres. In Bournemouth a number of external agencies have a presence in the Central Library, including Connexions (information and guidance for 13–19 year olds), Connect2Learning, Care Direct (monthly drop-in centre for over-60s), Businesslink Wessex and European Information Centre, Dorset Record Office. The library at Hook houses a recording studio on the first floor.

The Winchester Discovery Centre is a new concept of the public library, since it now provides library services in an integrated building which also houses two exhibition galleries (one large, one small), a fully equipped 150-seat Performance Hall (which can be used for dance classes or conferences), a self-contained assembly room with catering and bar (which also houses the fiction stock during the day-time) and a variety of other amenities which brings a very wide range of additional users to the building.

Likewise, the University of Worcester's new city centre campus in Worcester, 'The Hive', designed by architects Fielden Clegg Bradley Studios and completed in the summer of 2012, brings together in one landmark building:

● A fully integrated public and university library

● Worcestershire Record Office

Figure 6.6 Library & Health Centre at Cambourne in Cambridge, designed by West Hart Partnership (Practice)

Figure 6.7 Interior of Library & Health Centre at Cambourne in Cambridge, showing common foyer, waiting area and reading room

- Worcestershire Historic Environment and Archaeology Service
- Worcestershire Hub Customer Service Centre.

Its design is intended to achieve a BREEAM environmental assessment of 'Excellent', embodying as it does a range of environmental features such as bio-mass heating, river water cooling, rainwater harvesting, use of recycled materials and a core structure of concrete providing the thermal mass to assist both heating and cooling.

Such partnerships not only bring in additional funding – particularly revenue funding vital to long term maintenance and repair – but also bring in new library users whose activities can underwrite the provision of expensive hardware such as computers, scanners and photocopiers. However dual-use libraries can bring additional headaches along with the welcome joint-funding. These have been ably summarised by Ayub Khan, who notes some of the following disadvantages:

- A site that is not central and thus a drawback for one partner
- Misunderstanding of the roles of the joint partners
- Mixed perceptions of the library's clientele by other partners
- Governance problems
- Problems of public access at different times to different parts of the building (Khan, 2009: 81).

Researcher Sarah McNicol, who has studied the place of libraries in co-location developments, amusingly describes them as being of three kinds: the lodger, the flat-mate and the marriage partner (McNicol: 2008). In the former case the library is largely stand-alone and neither takes advantage of its partner's services, nor suffers any deleterious effects by sharing the same site or building. If it enjoys flat-mate status then there is some synergy between what the services are offering (e.g. health centre or sixth-form college). If it is a proper marriage then the library is actively co-producing services and achieving economies of scale, such as might be found in a joint public and university library.

The majority of new libraries involve either some kind of public-private sector funding or planning concordance, or are co-located with other rent-paying, cost-sharing amenities, whether this be a performance space (Birmingham, Winchester, Seattle), an art gallery (Bishop Auckland, Winchester), or a restaurant/café in many cases. Not all co-located projects work. In smaller libraries it is very difficult to run a café at an operating profit, and the key strategic decision here is to what degree the library service is prepared to subsidise a facility that may not add significant value to the overall enterprise, particularly if there are plenty of other cafés nearby.

Mattern describes a series of failed café and restaurant facilities in new American libraries, and this story is echoed in the UK. In the otherwise highly successful and admired library in Bournemouth, the large ground floor space allocated to a café-franchise witnessed a succession of caterers come and go, though a successful franchise is now operating there. At the new Barking library, the ground-floor atrium café proved commercially successful, but, alas, noise and odours permeated the upper library and reading areas, and it has now been closed off. In a refurbished library in Lewisham some years ago, the lobby café proved initially successful but over time lost its popularity. It ended up providing a rather depopulated space, sometimes dominated by noisy teenagers, and therefore become a 'negative' space, potentially deterring some people from entering.

Figure 6.8 Boscombe Library, Bournemouth, a development by Hawkins Brown, including apartments

Figure 6.9 Gallery and art workshop at Winchester Discovery Centre

CHAPTER 7

Programmes and people: the changing library programme

Though libraries are now taking increasingly different stylistic forms, the core programme has remained much the same. Today's designs do, however, have to emphasise flexibility, given the rapidly changing material forms and modes of consumption which contemporary culture is developing. Hence the rise of the open-plan, non-segmented library floor plan. Given the rise of many new media formats available in libraries it has to be decided whether to keep books and digital media separate, or integrate them along with study spaces and reading areas. Circulation patterns were once almost wholly determined by book-shelving layouts; today the mixture of spaces and the sequencing of them is an important element in way-finding – which also needs clear signage. Opening hours are longer, and people are likely to stay longer if they are studying – hence the need for coffee shops and toilets, along with spaces for events.

The core function of a library is to provide access to books and information in a variety of media, in an ordered and managed environment. In the case of the public library this provision is available to everybody, and free at the point of delivery. Charging fees for the loan of CDs, videos and DVDs was a late development, opening the door to continuing debates about which cultural materials might elicit a lending charge. This then led to on-going discussions about cultural relativism and the role of libraries in providing free domestic entertainment. Anxieties about the new mixed economy of library provision have now subsided, with most people now less worried about a range of charges for add-on or specialised services.

Libraries have often offered associated services and facilities which consolidate and support this basic book-lending function. The Victorian libraries consisted principally of three main areas:

the lending library, the reference library and the reading room. Separate children's libraries or children's sections came later, but soon joined the core plan. Other provision designed to supplement the building might have included lecture theatres, meeting rooms, art galleries, exhibition space. In a few places cinemas or screening rooms were added. Over time the reading room lost its distinctive place in the library schema and casual reading was integrated into the main lending library area, though often in an area with formally arranged tables and chairs. Public toilets were often provided, with access usually controlled in some form, via a key issued at the library desk. Many libraries abandoned the idea of providing public toilets, because of problems with cleaning and/or vandalism, but the new libraries, with their understanding of how users are staying in the library for longer periods of time, once again feel obliged to provide toilets, especially if they are also providing a coffee shop.

ANDREW CARNEGIE LIBRARY
& READING ROOMS
WEST DERBY, LIVERPOOL

Figure 7.1 Floor plan of West Derby Carnegie Library, 1905, re-drawn by Ian Worpole. Clear allocation of spaces to functions, including separate reading rooms for 'Boys' and 'Ladies'

Though libraries in many towns and cities are stylistically different, the programme has remained fairly common. Today's designs do, however, have to emphasise flexibility, given the rapidly changing material forms and modes of consumption which contemporary culture is developing. Hence the rise of the open-plan, non-segmented library floor plan. Even so, each individual library project will be different, responding to a different set of client needs, projections, site conditions, townscape and historical context. Thus the design will need to be wholly interwoven with the programme in an iterative, self-correcting process. As architect Denise Scott Brown acutely observed in a letter regarding the competition to design a new library in Denver in 1990:

> It should not be thought that the creation of a building is a linear process: programming, design, documentation, construction. Design informs program as much as program informs design. Eliminate that interaction and the question may never catch up with the answer.
>
> (Mattern, 2007: 18)

There are still some enduring patterns in the library programme which form the basis for the ground rules of design and scale, largely demographic and related to the catchment area and population to be served.

SO WHAT DO PEOPLE USE LIBRARIES FOR?

According to the most recently collected statistics on library use in England alone (DCMS: 2010), the following percentages are given for the most common activities pursued by library users:

● Borrowing a book (81 per cent)

● Research (30 per cent)

● Children's activities (20 per cent)

● Borrowing music, films or computer games (19 per cent)

● Using a computer (16 per cent)

- Accessing information on jobs, health, etc. (15 per cent)

- Taking advantage of a quiet place to study (13 per cent)

- Other (9 per cent).

What the priorities are in the programme may well differ between those of the staff providing them and what library users want. Nowhere was this more graphically expressed than in research cited by Bryson *et al.* (2003) when library staff and library users were asked to score the strengths and weaknesses of the library service. The two main weaknesses identified by the public – by a very significant margin – were opening hours and the range and quality of the stock. For librarians these ranked as low priorities. For library staff the key weaknesses were too little space and building faults. Not surprisingly it is library staff who especially focus on building matters – because it is where they spend most of their working time, a lot of which might be compromised or constrained by inappropriate space or building efficiency.

As the 2010 MLA national survey of library use concluded, 'Books are still the main reason why most people use public libraries – and are seen as the core offer of the library service by users and non-users alike' (MLA, 2010b). While the modern library may not be designed specifically around the armature of the library shelving – as it was in the book-lined dome or series of tiered galleries – and while modern shelving may be much more flexible in its design and mobility, nevertheless the attractive presentation and massing of the book-stock remains a key feature of the library presence. Some people find the ground floor lending library in the otherwise much-admired Brighton Jubilee Library disappointing – especially when compared with the same library's fine upper floor and side galleries. This is because it feels somewhat shed-like, or even a place of temporary storage. Nor does the quality of the shelving and other aspects of the fitting out on the ground floor rise to the quality of the building itself.

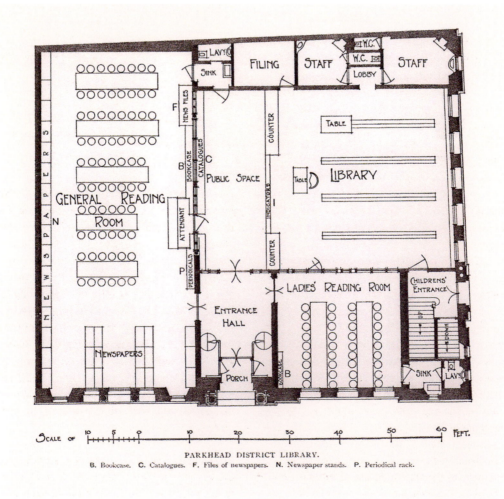

PARKHEAD DISTRICT LIBRARY.
B. Bookcase. C. Catalogues. F. Files of newspapers. N. Newspaper stands. P. Periodical rack.

Figure 7.2 Floor plan of Parkhead District Library, Glasgow (Courtesy of Gerald Blaikie, Scotcities). The children's library has its own entrance into a separate basement, as at Viipuri. Separate Ladies' Reading Room

A PLACE FOR TECHNOLOGY

One area where there is broad agreement as to what the library of the future needs is a significant increase in the amount of study space: both individual spaces, as well as those designed for group learning. Over three-quarters of new libraries surveyed by Bryson *et al.* (2003) offered separate study space and increasing amounts of it. 'To meet the library's growing role as provider of lifelong learning, greater space is being devoted to group work and training areas,' they reported. The fact is that the exponential rise in the student population – as a proportion of the adult community – has resulted in a demand for study space that many of the newer universities have failed to provide. In the early 1990s, many public libraries reported that students were 'squeezing out' other library users in the competition for desk space and seating. At present it appears that the demand for attractive study space in pleasant surroundings (as well as the added bonus of free Wi-Fi and power sockets) is unlimited, especially in urban areas with large student populations, as is evident at the new library at Shepherd's Bush.

In nearly all the libraries visited during this study, computer terminals used to access the Internet were filtered centrally for inappropriate material. All local authorities have now developed 'Acceptable Use' policies. Either the children's library card and the adult ID library card used to log-in automatically de-bars users from accessing many sites, including social networking sites for younger people. It was a surprise to read, therefore, that in America there is an ongoing battle over the rights of library users to access pornography on public computers, and librarians have filed complaints against their own employers for creating a workplace situation which they find hostile and offensive (Mattern, 2007: 171).

In many of the newer libraries, computer access and use is integrated into the spatial layout of the book stock, rather than separated. As the Head of Library and Information Services in Norwich observed:

> You've got to have the two. And I think that what is nice is that the two are integrated. We go into a lot of libraries where the IT is all in one space together, and the books are all in another space, so you're almost recreating what we used to have in a lending and a reference section. Ideally the two need to be integrated.

Despite these developments, the principal service of providing a wide range of books to browse through, to use as reference material, or to borrow, is still the core business of the public library, whether old or new, and provides its essential visual appeal. 'The visibility of books is a primary concern in many

Figure 7.3 Photographs of local scenes enliven ends of stand-alone shelving units at Huntingdon Library

recent (library) design projects in the USA,' according to Shannon Mattern (Mattern, 2007: 103). When people come through the door of a public library they need to come into a place whose tone and ethos is set by the presence of books, no matter what other media are available elsewhere in the building. This is why I find the ground floor of Richard Meier's Central Library in The Hague problematic – it is basically an empty lobby with café, chairs, information desk, in too large a space with little visual or intellectual stimulation. In contrast, although the ground floor of Hans Scharoun's State Library in Berlin is similarly given over to exhibition space, catalogue cabinets, library counters and public foyer space, there are profoundly powerful and direct visual connections to the open plan reading room immediately above and all around, via the atrium space and the wide, elegant ceremonial staircases.

The danger of creating a void at ground-floor level was noted at the 2011 Helsinki conference on new library design where it was said that it 'is also good to remember the danger of creating a non-space. If the space is not enough of something, it can become nothing.' By contrast with the ground floor of the

Figure 7.4 The Hague Library, designed by Richard Meier, opened 1995

Hague library, when you enter Whitechapel's Idea Store, through a labyrinth of street market stalls and bustling streets, the attractive book-filled spaces immediately establish a different tone and tempo. Likewise, although the fore-shortened ground-floor of Canada Water library is largely book-free, the astonishing staircase leads visitors almost immediately upwards to the main, expansive, library floors, leaving behind the everyday life of the street and reception area below.

Book stacks not only signal the presence of knowledge, culture and memory, but their configuration and mass are also vital in many other ways. As Ayub Khan has enumerated, the layout of book stacks:

● Helps define routes through the library

● Acts as acoustic barriers (very important in children's sections)

● Can be configured to create distinct reading areas at perimeter of floorspace

● Helps provide thermal mass (Khan, 2009: 113).

For the more technical aspects of stack sizes distribution and aisle clearances, Khan's book is excellent. Interestingly the quiet, busy, self-absorbed tone once set by books in the library has been to a degree consolidated by the very high numbers of people now using libraries for study, research, and Internet browsing. Dagenham's upstairs computer suite is designated a Quiet Area, but here and in most other libraries the proliferation of computer terminals or spaces for people to use their own laptops has given the public library a restored ethos as a place where people quietly get on with their own learning and development.

NEW MEDIA FORMATS

Nevertheless, the rate of change in media formats is now capable of undoing a library's allocation of space in a very short space of time. The neat, easily shelved, orthogonal printed book dominated the way libraries, library cataloguing and storage systems were designed, managed and presented within the public library until very recently – with the familiar exception of maps, newspapers and original documents usually held in the reference section. Children's books, often large format, offered some challenges to conventional shelving, mostly solved with free-standing book boxes in which different sizes could be accommodated in one container. Nevertheless, the quality and configuration of the shelving established a key design feature of the historic public library. It was often very high, blocking sight-lines across the space or spaces of the library, becoming somewhat claustrophobic, though some people liked this sense of the library as a labyrinth or bibliographical maze.

This core programme changed in some of the larger libraries with the rise of the music library after the Second World War, and was solved by creating a new section – and in Brighton, for example, a separate building – for long-playing records and music scores. In time different music formats emerged, including spoken word recordings, in the form of cassette tapes, CDs, videos, DVDs and other formats, each of which required different forms of shelving and presentation.

As the newer libraries worked hard to encourage users to spend more time in them – as opposed to coming and going with 'quick loans' – it became necessary to provide listening stations and even viewing stations by which people could sample or enjoy in entirety some of the music and films now provided in a variety of formats. 'The need for media-specific access spaces seems to necessitate format-defined departments,' according to Shannon Mattern writing about libraries in America. Hence the living room or lounge in some libraries where people can sit in armchairs and listen on earphones to a symphony or poetry reading on tape or CD. I first saw this in the 1970s in Stockholm's Kulturhuset library and then thought it overly luxurious. Today this level of comfort and amenity is now taken for granted. More people are coming to the library to 'consume' or use media *in situ*, rather than borrowing materials for home use. This is why the new Aarhus library is to be called Urban Mediaspace Aarhus, or why the new Library of Birmingham will have the atmosphere, it is hoped, of a club for members, rather than a 'one-stop shop' to which people come and go as quickly as possible.

Many libraries converted their original music libraries or departments into audio-visual libraries, though some – uneasy at the growing separation of formats and cultural assumptions – attempted to integrate some formats, by, for example, interweaving talking books (on cassette or CD) with traditional books in the same alphabetical grouping. In Seattle for a brief period they tried mixing books and other formats alongside each other, but the public response was distinctly negative. This continuing headache about providing for a proliferating range of new media formats may now be coming to an end.

It is likely that in the near future many of these issues will resolve themselves, as more forms of cultural product are digitised. Already much music is now accessed digitally by downloading material from the Internet, and this is becoming increasingly the case with film material too. A growing proportion of library users who are sitting at desks or in armchairs are using their own laptops to read, listen to or watch library materials – as well as take advantage of free Wi-Fi provided by the library to browse the Internet. The space once occupied by racks of CDs, videos and DVDs (let alone vinyl records) is rapidly diminishing. Today libraries are making licensing deals with providers of digital material for their members to access such materials for free via their library membership card. The reading room of the past, or the space allocated to viewing or listening, becomes the 'mixing chamber' symbolised in the Seattle library, where people congregate to sit and quietly study, browse, watch or listen, almost entirely in their own worlds.

WAY-FINDING, SIGNAGE AND NAVIGATION

A number of architects interviewed mentioned the poor quality of signage and use of visual reference points in many existing libraries. At their worst, windows are filled with outdated notices and events flyers, and basic way-finding practices are ignored, requiring users to negotiate endless corners and dead ends which offer no support in clear and easy navigation of the library's various spaces. Many of the newer libraries have commissioned graphic designers to produce an overall signage system which is bold, clear and easy to understand, and which complements a floor-plan and layout which intuitively leads users from one key area to the next. (Lest it be thought that this suggests that architects are without fault in this regard, one library authority had to completely replace the signage insisted upon by the architect – which in the event was largely illegible to users, comprising as it did of small silver lettering on metal panels that in most lighting conditions proved impossible to read).

This problem occurs everywhere, for as Shannon Mattern (2007: 80–81) has written of the new American libraries, 'Most libraries I visited have had to redesign their signage once or more within a year of the new building's opening, simply because it is difficult to predict the public's navigational patterns or to know what directional cues visitors will need before the building is put to use.' Nevertheless some basic principles of clear sight-lines across the main space of the library uninterrupted by high shelving, allied with bold lettering indicating different sections, can allow users to see at a glance where to go and what they may find there. In this the new Dagenham Library is a model of clear way-finding and simple, efficient graphic design, as are the neatly signed white pillars in the Jaume Fuster Library in Barcelona.

Figure 7.5 Good use of columns for clear sign-posting at Jaume Fuster Library in Barcelona

Some traditional way-finding icons are disappearing too. The once dominant library counter at the entrance, to which users had to return for help or advice wherever they were in the library, is being replaced by smaller satellite enquiry points distributed equally throughout the building. This also allows greater supervision of the library's many spaces, and intranet services and mobile phones allow easy communication between service points as and when needed. The design of signage, especially in a building over-supplied with typefaces and lettering serving many different purposes, is a professional job today. The age of hand-written notices allied to a labyrinth of high bookshelves, poorly labelled – and in which one could get lost – is no longer acceptable to many library users, especially the young who have grown up with highly professional forms of design and product display.

Way-finding should also be as much instinctual as sign-posted: one space should appear to lead naturally to the next, related space. This raises the issue of adjacencies in libraries: what spaces, facilities and activities fit best next to each other, and which should be kept as separate as possible too. Khan summarises these as:

- Positive adjacency – spaces are directly related
- Neutral adjacency – spaces share no common relationship
- Negative adjacency – spaces should be separated (Khan, 2009: 120).

OPENING HOURS

At first it may seem that opening hours may have little design implications, but not so. Time and space are always in some kind of dynamic relationship. Several of the newer libraries such as Norwich, though open on Sundays, nevertheless restrict access to the ground floor lending library, keeping other areas or zones closed. At the library in March, Cambridgeshire, where the library shared facilities with the local registry office, there were times when access to the registry office was needed when the library itself was closed, and this access had to be designed separately. In Peckham where the lift system takes you to the fourth floor library, access to the intermediate floors is denied by the lift system's over-ride. The new library in Time, Norway, opens its ground floor facilities at 7am for self-service loans and returns, access to study areas and for breakfast in the library café, retaining a minimal library staff presence during these hours.

All public buildings which are shared with other services or commercial partners have to be designed for separate access at different times of the day or week. Where facilities such as toilets, lifts, kitchen facilities or disabled access of other kinds are involved, these are major design considerations. Where academic libraries are concerned, some of these issues are resolved by having access restricted electronically through membership cards, so that, for example, Cranfield University Library is open until midnight most evenings, without library staff in attendance, though there are paid student monitors. The Information Commons at Sheffield University is open 24/7, but similarly with access only open to registered members via electronic gates. Thus the public library poses issues of access and regulation, not usually shared by academic libraries, though in some Danish villages, according to the country's Director-General of Library Services, public access is now available, even when the library is unstaffed, by use of people's individual medical cards which are electronically tagged. He wrote in 2011 that, 'The public library that I frequently use in a small village is open from 6.a.m. to midnight every day, and last time I used it was a Saturday evening, where there were five other users during the 20 minutes I was there.'

LIFE WITHOUT COFFEE?

There is no denying the fact that today's public take a very dim view of any public amenity that does not provide a relatively attractive coffee bar or tea-room. In the 2010 MLA report (2010b), the top five changes that the public said would encourage them to use libraries more put 'Coffee shop on site' as the first priority both for current users as well as for lapsed users too. In an important sense a coffee shop converts any facility also into a meeting place, and a destination in its own right.

Many existing libraries simply lack the space to provide this facility, though a number do offer self-service coffee machines and drinks dispensers. The danger when designing new facilities is that the tail ends up wagging the dog, as suggested by the notorious advertisement for the V&A Museum in the 1990s: 'A very nice coffee bar with an interesting museum attached'. Even so, the penthouse café at Whitechapel's Idea Store is not only a popular meeting place serving good food, but is also integrated firmly into the library milieu, as it shares a whole floor with the art gallery, art library, lounge area and newsroom (a large screen television tuned to a channel running news stories with the sound switched off, displaying surtitles), which people can watch while sitting in armchairs and drinking a coffee. Likewise the top floor café area at Swiss Cottage Library is self-contained and sealed off from the more public library areas, and works well as an intimate and attractive meeting place.

TOILETS

Maintaining public toilets in a public building such as a library is often a headache – particularly so if the library becomes known for having the only free public toilets in the immediate area, which then become used (and occasionally abused) by everybody. Few of the newer libraries or major refurbishments such as Bournemouth, Brighton, Cardiff or Winchester report problems. Indeed, at Canada Water the ground floor café and toilets serve those using the bus and underground station as much as they serve library users, all under the careful watch of security personnel. At Shepherd's Bush library, the adult toilets have been inappropriately located as leading off the children's library, and are only accessible by knowing a security code – which means that library staff have to accompany the user to toilets to provide access, an unsatisfactory arrangement. In Norwich the toilets are provided as part of the larger public atrium which is shared by other businesses and managed independently.

When designing the Seattle Public Library, it was already known that there had been a problem with a number of the city's

homeless population using the previous library's toilets as their own personal space. As a result the 'men's restrooms' in the new library have 'been painted a hideous green' to discourage long-term use by patrons or the homeless: hardly a viable solution in the long term, surely?

THE MODERN LIBRARY IS ALSO A PERFORMANCE SPACE

The last two decades have seen an enormous rise in public readings by authors, along with book promotion tours, children's story-telling sessions, and a proliferation of local writing and poetry groups, all wanting to use the library network as a collection of local and popular venues. Most libraries now feel it important to offer live events and meeting space for book-related activities, and this means either designing auditoria, or ensuring that in a prominent part of the library shelving can be easily moved to create a space for chairs, with a PA system easily put in place. The refurbished Winchester Discovery Centre not only now has a dedicated 150-seat performance hall, but the new single-storey, double-height extension wing to the east – containing the café, box office, gift shop and fiction section – can also be quickly adapted to create a performance space with its own entrance, bar and catering. The Whitechapel Idea Store has a fourth floor penthouse café/gallery/newsroom area. This is where large format art books are to be found, many on display, where there is a programmed exhibition space, and where 150 people can be accommodated for events and readings. All this makes a very successful cultural space. Each year there is a ten-day reading festival at the library.

As has been mentioned, the number of library-based reading groups trebled to 10,000 in England between 2004 and 2008, and are now a feature of many local library services. Reading groups require space in the library and possibly an extension in opening hours for those groups which meet in the evening. Many are accommodated by shifting mobile shelves aside in the lending library to create space. Reading groups and talks by authors now seem to be an integral part of what libraries do – which is not just to lend books but organise social gatherings in which they can be discussed.

MEETING ROOMS

Most new libraries provide a range of meeting rooms, often as potential sources of income generation. Such rooms can be let out in the day for seminars, conferences, interviews, and, when free, can provide additional study space. At the Idea Store in Whitechapel many meeting rooms are booked well ahead, and by each door is a panel saying who has booked the room and from what time and until when. If the room is not booked then it is freely open to public use for quiet study. Such provision also enables the library to act as a small conference centre, or as a venue for seminars and meetings, adding to the mix of users.

The Idea Store also provides a home for the public face of the major Crossrail project – a large new rail development connecting east and west London. This comprises a small exhibition, leaflets, but also showcases job opportunities. Something similar can be found in the Workzone at Shepherd's Bush Library, where the job opportunities in the adjacent retail and development area are promoted to library users.

BACK OF HOUSE FUNCTIONS

A lot of work is done behind the scenes to keep a library functioning effectively. Books are being delivered from other branches or from library suppliers on a constant basis, which requires good access for van deliveries at the rear or to the side, and adequate space in which to receive, store and process these books for public use. As more and more library users browse for books and reserve them online – many of which will come from other branches or even from national collections or regional consortia – there is a high level of traffic in the physical movement and delivery of books. Furthermore, books, CDs, DVDs have to be frequently checked for damage, and this requires space and support equipment.

Library staff also need their own rest-rooms and places for tea-breaks and lunch-breaks, with basic kitchen equipment and comfortable chairs. This is especially important in libraries serving neighbourhoods poorly served by cafés, shops or places to sit outside during coffee breaks and lunch-hours.

The American library consultant Jeanette Woodward has drawn attention to the fact that libraries, as with many other public buildings, are opened and closed each day by staff who often access the building themselves by a separate entrance – and this side or rear entrance is sometimes poorly protected and vulnerable. Staff entrances should be well-lit, and offer secure sight-lines and access to the public street system, and able to be used in complete safety whatever time of day or night.

There also needs to be good vehicular access to the service areas of the building, as well as parking space for disabled library users.

THE OUTDOOR LIBRARY

The winner of the 2010 European Prize for Urban Public Space was the highly unusual Open Air Library in Magdeburg, Germany, designed by Karo with Architektur + Netzwork. This town in former East Germany has been suffering from under-development and high levels of social deprivation. From the outset creating this library was a community-led process, with an empty shop adjoining the site used as a base for workshops with local people discussing and developing the core idea. Some 20,000 books were collected along with a thousand beer crates, the latter used to create a 1:1 model of the final building. Though the books are stored inside, much of the library space consists of green space surrounded by benches, together with a stage on which local schools can put on performances, bands put on concerts, and poetry readings can be given. The library is supported by a café and is managed by residents as a community facility and meeting place.

This project is exceptionally unusual, though the idea of a library possessing its own gardens and courtyards is not. Many Victorian libraries were designed with a formal garden in front of them, as in Bromley and Middlesbrough for example. Of course it is not possible to allow books to be taken outside without being formally issued, but the idea that a library might have an open-air space adjacent to it for outdoor reading is still viable. The new Canada Water Library will have a designed public space connecting it to the waterfront, while the library in March, Cambridgeshire, has a designed landscape created around it to bring a sense of detachment and tranquillity to its 'back of the High Street' site. In Winchester the new extension to the refurbished Discovery Centre has an attractive café terrace on to the busy street.

Figure 7.6 Open Air Library in Magdeburg, Germany, designed by Karo with Architektur + Netzwork

Figure 7.7 Terrace garden and entrance to new extension of Winchester Discovery Centre

CHAPTER 8

A vital space for children and young people

Children's use of libraries remains high, and the newer libraries are becoming increasingly popular as meeting and study places for young people and students. It is a matter of some debate as to whether the children's library should be seen as a place apart, self-contained and with its own safeguarding and child protection protocols, or more integrated with the adult library. It is also a matter of contention as to whether it should have its own design code – often colourful and imbued with fairytale imagery – or whether it should share the same design palette as the rest of the library, avoiding charges of infantilisation.

In a short essay published in the *New York Times* on 27 March 1994, and cited by the Mid-Hudson Library System on their website, American novelist E.L. Doctorow wrote that, 'The three most important documents a free society gives are a birth certificate, a passport, and a library card.' For many children the library card was and is their first official badge of recognition – and in a way, citizenship. At around the age of seven I was delighted finally to have my own cards – two for fiction, two for non-fiction. It is still the case that the public library remains a familiar and important place in children's lives. In libraries throughout the UK it is refreshing to see so many children and young people completely at home in their local library, where they are treated with a respect that is frequently denied them in the streets and shopping centres outside.

Compared with the gradual decline of adult borrowing figures, the statistics for children's borrowing have held steady, and even increased in recent years in the UK. Moreover, children's actual use of the library as a space or destination has also increased, whether they are borrowing books or not. It has already been noted that children who were taken to libraries as a child have significantly higher attendance rates at libraries in later life than those who did not. It remains in the interests of all those concerned with the cultural horizons of future generations, therefore, to carry on investing in library services (DCMS, 2010). Architect Christophe Egret, who designed the new Clapham Library in south London, told me that the first principle of contemporary

library design is that 'children must love it'. Once they become familiar with such spaces, they are more likely to remain library users throughout their lives.

Librarian Ayub Khan confirms this: 'Spaces for children can no longer be "add-on" but must be integral to the library experience. Family-friendly public libraries are a growing requirement' (Khan, 2009:11). School visits are still a common feature of the library service in many areas, and the ability to cater for up to thirty children at a time, with space to sit and listen to stories, or to engage in private study or group work, is now essential in library planning briefs.

Though specific provision for children – both in terms of dedicated space as well as book stock – was not part of the earliest public libraries, it soon became so. In 1924 a detailed study of children's library provision was undertaken and published, complete with evocative photographs, delineating the care and attention newly given to creating uplifting environments for children in this new area of the then widening public domain. Here is a description of one such library:

> The room is large, being 70 by 25 feet, and will accommodate from 200 to 250 young folk. There are folding tables, enabling the quick and easy clearing of the room for lectures, and small chairs. The chairs and tables are two inches lower than those of adult size. One end wall has been

treated with white-wash paint for lantern purposes, and although oak panelling and lincrusta are considered by the librarian of Croydon to be ideal decoration for a children's room, Spanish red paint as dado, two green lines above, and beyond that cream paint with a blush of pink has been found to be a very effective substitute.

(Rees, 1924: 38)

The early children's libraries or reading halls made an attempt to provide a more domestic atmosphere than that found in the adult libraries. This was largely achieved by providing armchairs as well as wooden chairs, along with flowers in vases on the shelves or tables, and a selection of framed pictures hanging on the walls. These often depicted national myths, historical events, famous people, romantic landscape scenes or reproductions of paintings such as John William Waterhouse's *The Lady of Shalott* or John Millais' *The Boyhood of Raleigh*. There were elements here of creating an image of the ideal home, even a national home, as imagined by worthy designers and idealistic local politicians.

What with story-telling sessions, reading groups, homework centres, and access to new technology, the best children's library services are now busier than ever. What is increasingly obvious to librarians and visitors is how many of the newer libraries now feel like young people's places, a remarkable transformation from the time when the public libraries had too often become associated with an older generation.

CHILDREN'S LIBRARIES – A PLACE APART?

Nevertheless the space and place of the children's library within the larger design remains problematic. Total separation of the children's library can mean that children feel isolated from the larger community. On the other hand, total integration creates problems of children having easy access to inappropriate material, or, of more concern today, failing to protect children from the attention of adults who may not have their best interests at heart. Their excitable presence can also disturb adult library users, particularly those at study. In Aalto's library at Viipuri, the children's library was located in the basement, with its own door, and approached through a separate play area and garden. This was then seen as a very positive statement. In Coenen's new Central Library in Amsterdam, the children's library is also located in the basement – not to everybody's approval it is claimed.

Very occasionally a municipality will commission a separate children's library, such as the one in Paris, in the 15th arrondissement, designed by Franck Hammoutene. Although this is a striking building architecturally, a black concrete, steel and glass monolith hugging the ground, and would serve well as a security outpost, it appears to the passer-by intimidating and off-limits. It is designed to be principally lit by a large roof-light, but this fails to create any real sense of belonging to the public domain, though for some children it might just offer the appeal of a secret cave. No exterior lettering on the facade announces that it is a library, nor does anything about the design suggest it might be. Having only visited it once I am unable to say whether over time it proved successful in meeting the intentions of its municipal client.

Traditional ways of creating a border zone between adult and children's areas within a shared space have often been achieved either by raising the children's area on a platform, bordered by shelves or toy structures, or by creating a sunken area, with child-scale seating, bright carpets and other means of distinguishing it as a distinct sphere with its own rules of entry.

Building a playful barrier of shelving designed as castle walls – with a drawbridge in the case of one Bournemouth library – has proved another effective way of making a distinct area of the library dedicated to children's provision obvious to all other users. The employment of large soft toys, along with fairy-tale murals, floor coverings – and even floors painted as scenery – all aid this process of visual differentiation. In Sidcup Library high quality wooden shelving has been used to create a clearly designated compound without too much exaggerated visual and tactile emphasis.

Not all library staff, let alone interior designers, are happy with the perceived 'infantilisation' of the children's library space: too many over-sized stuffed animals and jungle imagery can over-determine the nature of the space and exclude other age ranges in what Alistair Black has termed the 'theme park children's library'. What is colourful and exciting to a three-year old can have a deterrent effect on an eight-year old. Richard Cowley of BDP, who was responsible for the interior of Cardiff Library, was insistent on using the 'same kit of parts' for the children's library, though on a slightly smaller scale – resisting any pressure to produce something that didn't integrate into the overall aesthetic of the building. Though this may not please everybody, the decision is likely to produce a stronger sense of loyalty amongst older children, integrated as the design is with the building overall.

In the USA, a children's library manager who researched the design of children's libraries discovered that 'very little had been written about the design of children's libraries'. She and colleagues then arranged a study tour of visits to the children's sections of other public libraries, mainly to return with a series of negatives:

Through their visits to other libraries, they learned how *not* to design a children's section. They learned to avoid such clichés as bright primary colours, a school-like atmosphere, and child-sized versions of adult furnishings.

(Mattern, 2007: 30)

When CABE was asked to comment on the proposed design of the new Liverpool Library extension and refurbishment – now underway at a cost of £50 million – they were also critical on this issue of potential 'infantilisation':

The children's library is another area of the proposal that we think could benefit from further thought. Whilst we understand the desire to create a welcoming, playful environment...we think that a calmer aesthetic, less reliant on bright colour and organic forms, could be more successful. We think it would be a mistake to underestimate the ability of children, especially those in the older age range, to enjoy high quality public spaces.

(CABE, 2010)

Such decisions of course need to be based on the location and demography of the area the library is serving, and the degree to which the children's library is focused and programmed as an activity area as much as a reading space. Some American libraries also incorporate craft areas, with sinks and taps, washable floors and tables, and space to display artwork and paintings. Though this is rare in the UK, the new C.L.R. James Library in Hackney, London, opened in January 2012, incorporates a 'wet room' where children can play with water and painting materials. It also has a small tiered seating area for story-telling. The most impressive children's library I have seen was at Barcelona's Jaume Fuster Library, where the library occupies its own wing of the building and is furnished to the same high standard and design palette as the rest of the library. It is a place in its own right, not simply an adjunct.

In Alsop & Störmer's Peckham Library, the children's section occupies a separate double-height room to the north of the suite, with stunning views through parti-coloured glazed walling to the London Eye and Westminster to the north. The whole children's area sits in its own glass box, resolving the issue of separation

Figure 8.1 Childrens's Zone clearly dermarcated at The Hub, Kinson, Bournemouth, designed and installed by Radford HMV Group Ltd

and belonging very effectively. A staircase in the children's library leads upwards and across a truncated bridge into one of three pods located in the main lending library, providing a space-ship style space floating above the adults. In Brighton the children's library occupies a large side-gallery to the main ground floor lending library, with port-holes connecting the two.

More and more libraries also now distinguish a teen area, another staging post between children and adult sections, where the growing literature especially designed for teenage readers (including graphic novels) is to be found. Such areas also incorporate study desks and computer terminals (though these computers are likely to be filtered, as they are in the Winchester Discovery Centre, for age-appropriate uses), and here style is again an important factor. In the children's 'Internet Zone' at Ward End Library in Birmingham, some very stylish Philippe Starck chairs add a glamorous note to the interior space and milieu.

From the USA comes a very well documented and positive lesson in involving teenagers in library design and provision. A Teen Library Council was established by Phoenix Public Library to help create a distinct library area for this age group, and out of an initial meeting of over 150 teenagers, some 20 or 30 met regularly to plan the new provision. The new library section was not to be 'themed' the young people insisted, but simply carried a range of modern media, occupying a variety of individual, group and public spaces, with regular film showings and events to attract young people after school, as well as for a large number of organised school visits from an ever wider catchment area, such was the popularity of 'Teen Central'. As Mattern reports:

> Phoenix has managed to simultaneously inspire some of its teenagers to become architects; to provide a wholesome, constructive alternative to the mall and the streets; to empower a marginalised community; to activate a public sphere around a design project; and to provide its city with a space that is the quintessence of publicness.
>
> (Mattern, 2007: 32)

These are large claims, but they surely point to a positive outcome resulting from the involvement of users and potential users in design. Having segmented and created boundaries of varying degrees of permeability around the children's library, there are also design issues associated with how this space itself is divided. As Nolan Lushington has written:

> Spatial density and the degree of openness present something of a design problem. The need to monitor children can conflict with the child's need for privacy.

Research into design options has produced somewhat contradictory and ambiguous results. Studies have shown that spatial density tends to increase aggression among pre-school children. At the same time, open areas tend to result in running and cross-room talking. Research has also shown that activity areas with partitions tend to increase co-operative behaviour. The answer may be low dividers between activity areas with higher dividers and increasing privacy for older children. Furnishings and dividers should always be low enough so that children can see and be seen by staff.

(Lushington, 2008: 101)

Child protection issues are now rightly seen as central to design philosophy as are matters of disability access, which is why the location of the adult toilets within the children's library at Shepherd's Bush was such a basic misjudgement.

PROVIDING BUGGY SPACE AND LOCKERS

Very young children will usually be brought to the library in pushchairs or 'buggies'. A library story-telling session can attract up to 30 young children and their parents or carers, which also means finding space for as many pushchairs, secure and out of the rain. That has to be planned for. At the other end of the spectrum, the reference section of many libraries – including specialist collections – require users to store away coats and bags in lockers in the interests of security and the avoidance of theft, which can be a problem in children's libraries too. The wider the range of library users and the longer their stay in the library, the more these secondary forms of provision and support services are needed.

Figure 8.2 Stylish Philippe Starck chairs in Internet Zone, Ward End Library, Birmingham, designed by John Hunt Associates (Photo: Kevin Duffy)

PART 4
Selected case

studies

CHAPTER 9
Public library case studies

Jaume Fuster Library

Opened: November 2005
Client: Barcelona City Council
Architect: Josep Llinàs Carmona/Joan Vera
Project description: New public library
Library size: 4,800 square metres
Cost: Euro12m

This new library in a busy urban quarter near Park Güell occupies the corner of a major road intersection, though its wide paved frontage on two sides sets it back from the traffic, additionally protected by planting – enough so that the library services its own outdoor café at some distance from the library entrance, a café which is a popular meeting place in its own right.

The building is diamond-shaped inside, faceted on the outside with a series of angular roof canopies and elevations, with the main entrance set back under a large canopy which provides shade to the entrance and vestibule. This dynamism is continued inside with a large internal lobby where people sit and gossip, a bright reading room to one side, a café to the other side, a gallery to the rear, a reception desk, stairs up to the main library floors, and a corridor leading to a very large children's library (the *Àrea infantil*) established in its own wing – a very satisfactory arrangement, perhaps one of the best spatially independent children's libraries to be found, and one which employs the same design palette as the rest of the interior.

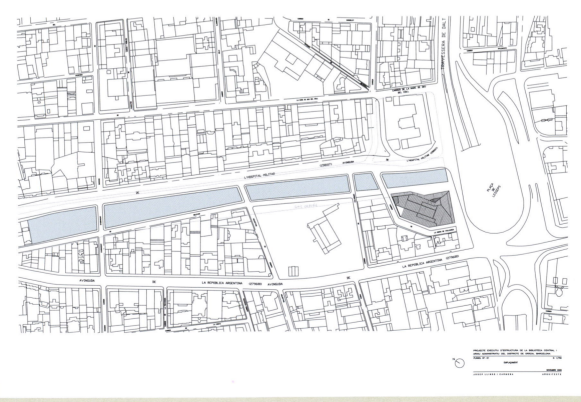

Figure 9.1 Site plan, Jaume Fuster Library, Barcelona, Courtesy of Josep Llinàs

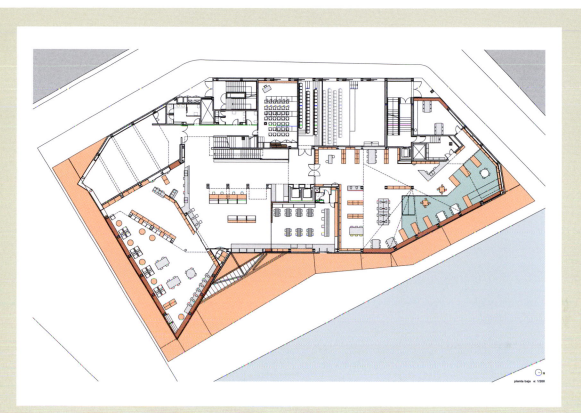

Figure 9.2 Ground floor plan, Jaume Fuster Library, Barcelona, courtesy of Josep Llinàs. The self-contained children's library is to the right. The cafe is bottom left, and the art gallery top left.

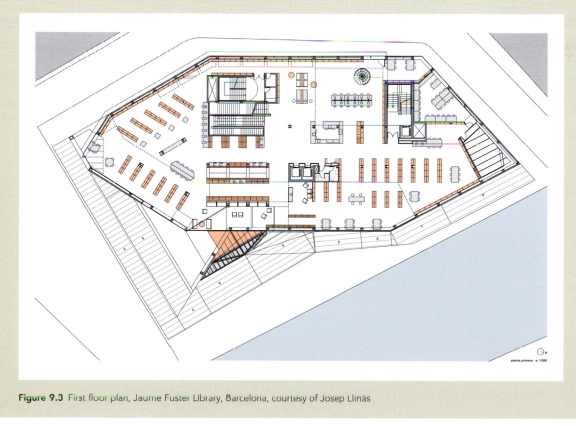

Figure 9.3 First floor plan, Jaume Fuster Library, Barcelona, courtesy of Josep Llinàs

The flooring throughout is terazzo tiling, with light-wood shelving and furniture, and white walls everywhere, giving rather a Scandinavian feel to the interior. There are sight-lines between and across floors in all directions, across light-wells and bridges, with bold, elegant lettering announcing the different bibliographical sections painted in black on the white support columns. A white concrete spiral staircase adds a dynamic feature to the first floor study area, leading up to more gallery study space.

The public library tradition is less well established in Spain, though this is now being remedied, and this particular library has won international attention and rightly so. When I visited it in December 2011, it was very busy with very many older residents using the reading rooms and lounge areas, while the café traded to both the street outside and to library users inside.

Figure 9.4 Street corner view of Jaume Fuster Library, Barcelona, commanding a major intersection

Figure 9.5 Canopied, set-back entrance to Jaume Foster Library, drawing visitors in

Bournemouth Library

Opened: April 2002
Client: Bournemouth Borough Council via PFI Management
Company: Information Resources (Bournemouth) Ltd
Architect: Building Design Partnership
Project description: public library and ground floor retail
Library size: 3850 square metres library space
Cost: £9.5 million
Stock: 111,432 book and audio visual stock
Visitor numbers: 1,100 per day

The new Bournemouth Library was officially opened on 28 June 2002, designed by BDP (Building Design Partnership). It occupies the site of a former surface car-park, close to the city centre, reinstating the line of two streets which meet at an area known as The Triangle. Thus the building resolves some historic townscape elements as well as providing a new facility, providing a satisfactory 'end stop' to the former ragged edge of the historic town centre.

It is consequently triangular in shape, with an entrance at the building's prow, and therefore fits neatly under the rubric of the public library as a 'street-corner university'. It won the Prime Minister's Better Public Buildings Award in 2003 as well as a Civic Trust commendation. Because it was an early 'pathfinder' project under the Private Finance Initiative (PFI), the development benefited from additional government funding. This contract runs for 30 years, with Kier Project Investment holding 50 per cent equity in the overall management company, Information Resources (Bournemouth) Limited. As with Norwich, all building services are provided by a dedicated team on site, charged with all repairs and cleaning, with strict penalties. This arrangement, library staff claim, has proved very effective, and taken a major headache away, given that librarians should have others things to worry about than dirty toilets, chipped paintwork and smeared windows. Eight years after it opened the interior looks pristine. The building provides 3,850 square metres of very high quality library space in the town.

The first thing the visitor notices is that the library occupies the first and second floors of a three-storey building. The ground floor was allocated as commercial letting space for

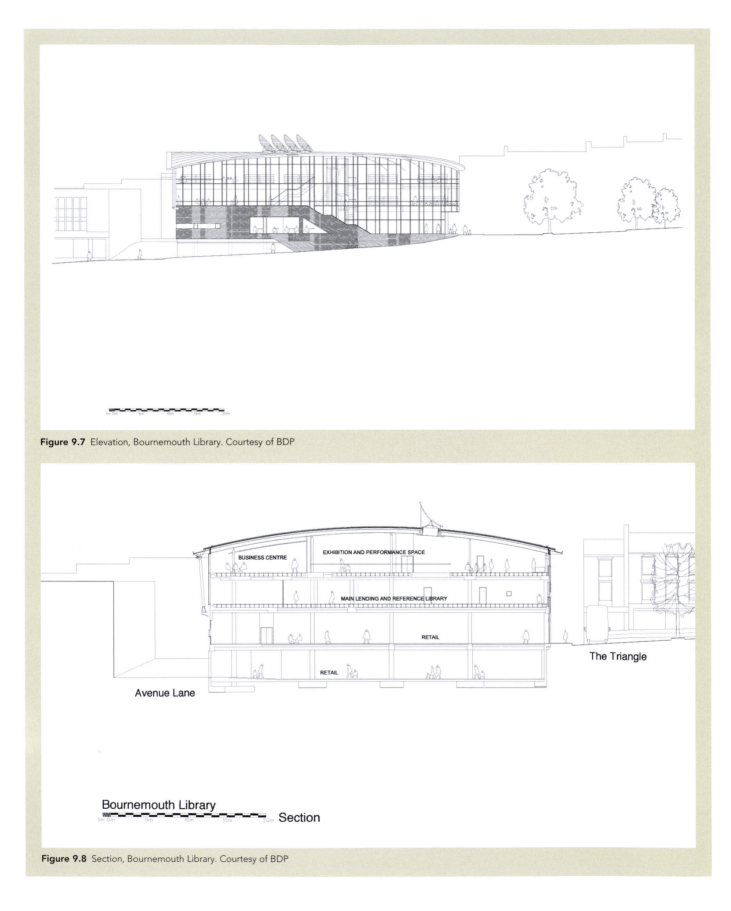

Figure 9.7 Elevation, Bournemouth Library. Courtesy of BDP

Figure 9.8 Section, Bournemouth Library. Courtesy of BDP

retail and a café. While the entrance stairs and lifts are generous and well designed, this does present something of an initial barrier to people's expectations. However, once arriving at the first floor, the space is exceptionally attractive and engaging, beautiful even, with clear sight-lines across a range of spaces and places, with an immediate air of being 'above' and separate from the surrounding streets in a quite special kind of way. This sense of a floating space station is continued on the third floor where the reference library, local history library, music library and events island are equally calm and well-ordered, with abundant views down into the main lending library on the floor below.

In her review for *Architectural Journal*, writer and critic Katherine Shonfield rightly enthused not only about the building's verve and panache but praised BDP's 'expertise' which she found 'effortlessly apparent in the acoustics'. 'It is a place,' she wrote, 'where people can have a conversation comfortably, or concentrate without hearing any untoward pin drop.' The building spaces get quieter the further 'up and out' you go from the staircase and lift services. There is a very fine line of study desks along the window area, as well as other study spaces scattered about the two floors, a number of which have personal desk lamps which can be operated manually by the reader. This sense of control over lighting can be very rewarding, and can help personalise space in a public environment.

The library now gets over 1,100 visits a day, and the study desks are always occupied, possibly as a result of a large student population living in this part of Bournemouth. A large and very beautiful painting, *Adoration of the Sea*, by Nicholas Charles Williams, looks down upon library staff and users, providing additional colour and flair to what is already a stunning interior. A number of external agencies have had a presence in the library, including Connexions (information and

Figure 9.9 Interior view of main first floor atrium at Bournemouth Library

guidance for 13–19 year olds), Connect2Learning, Care Direct (monthly drop-in centre for over-60s), Businesslink Wessex and European Information Centre, Dorset Record Office. Some of these have been superseded or joined by new partners including Next Steps (careers advice) and Skills & Learning (adult learning courses).

As with a number of other new library buildings, the interior is much more dynamic and exciting than the exterior, which struggles to proclaim or express the building's inner vitality and seriousness (though it is a different matter at night when the building glows). There is a large flank wall of red brick facing the Triangle that seems dead above the first floor retail area which now houses a Tesco Express. The ground floor site

designed to be a café serving library users and passers-by proved difficult to manage, and several companies attempted and failed to make it work commercially, detracting from the liveliness of the building at entrance level. However, the café space is now under a new franchise and open until 11pm, attracting a wide usage, especially from students and young people.

The very solid and handsome staircase with bright painted steel support columns at 70 degree angles, immediately attracts the eye and draws the visitor up to the first floor and the engaging world to be found there. A pioneering new town library rightly regarded as a great success.

Figure 9.10 Brightly painted angular support columns add dynamism to interior of Bournemouth Library

Jubilee Library, Brighton

Opened: March 2005
Client: Brighton & Hove City Council
Architect: Bennetts Associates & Lomax Cassidy Edwards (now LCE Architects)
Project description: public library
Library size: 3900 square metres
Cost: £14.5 million
Stock: 175,000 books, 13,000 AV items plus 45,000 items in Rare Books & Special Collections
Visitor numbers: Up to 1 million per year

The new Jubilee Library in Brighton has won plaudits all round for a building that became the focal point and driving force of a master-plan to develop a former area of run-down streets and demolition sites. Opened on World Book Day, 3 March 2005, it was funded as a PFI project with cross-subsidies from the development of shops, cafés and restaurants immediately around it. Both the project and the design were a long time in the making – a public discussion about a new library in Brighton and where to site it had been going on for many years – but in the end a team was put together which consisted of local firm Lomax Cassidy Edwards (now LCE Architects), Bennetts Associates, with the local authority's own 'Major Projects Team' acting as the client body. The PFI contract allows for the building to be maintained for the next 25 years, and capital costs amounted to £14 million.

Central to the design brief was the Council's demand that the building achieved the highest BREEAM category of 'Excellent' – which it did. Furthermore, this requirement to fulfil the stringent environmental demands of BREEAM supported the architects against cost-cutting pressures, allowing the designing of the splendid glass facade, providing wind towers, and in other ways creating a building that was more than a square box which PFI pressures might have resulted in. This was an interesting example of environmental considerations

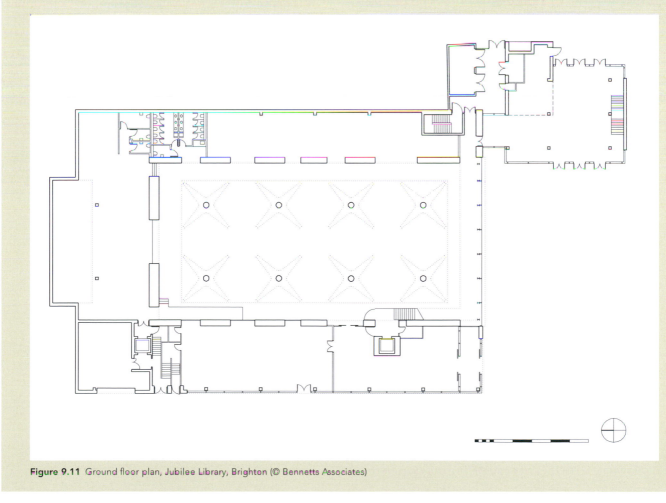

Figure 9.11 Ground floor plan, Jubilee Library, Brighton (© Bennetts Associates)

raising the level of design creativity and excellence, and worth highlighting.

The building dominates the new square in front of it, and this square is now a popular meeting place, especially for young people. The library facade is magnificent from the outside, the glazed walls reflecting the seaside sky and the activities in the square. The main entrance consists of two sets of sliding glass doors, creating an environmentally protecting lobby, leading into and through a substantial gift shop. The rationale for this unusual decision is that the flank wall of the library on the street continues the 'shop window' appeal of the rest of the street, and library users now take this in their stride, though some might argue that it also mutes the effect of arrival into the building: in effect it is an ante-chamber to the library proper. Furthermore, while the gift shop delays the sense of arrival, it also acts – inadequately one has to say – as an exhibition space, as well as preventing heat loss from the library proper.

Once inside the spaces are as dramatic as the facade suggests – the first floor non-fiction library especially so. Connected by glass-sided bridges to the outer frame, and resting on a series of substantial white columns which rise from ground floor to ceiling, it seems to float in the air of its own accord, 'as if it were a magic carpet of knowledge,' said the Head Librarian, Sally McMahon, at the time of its opening – and on this occasion without exaggeration. This particular effect is stunning. The side galleries on both floors, including a large children's library at the rear of the ground floor and a rare books library on the floor above, also work well, providing both separation and intimacy on the edge of the more public library floors (there's an element of the trading floor at ground floor level). A small franchised café operates at the front of the ground floor, giving views into the square and the street-life beyond. An electronic set of screens provides up to the minute bus timetables in the area.

In total the library offers 3,900 square metres of space. There are public toilets on all floors, as well as a conference centre, a training room and staff facilities. What doesn't feel so fully resolved, however, is the main ground floor lending library which appears somewhat cavernous, largely because of the almost random configuration of mass production shelving (and poor signage) which diminishes the overall effect, and over which the architects had no control. The need for a professional interior design approach is badly wanting here. In recompense, all the shelving is on wheels, and can be moved easily, thus clearing a very large ground floor space for events, such as the annual 'White Night' festival, when over 4,000 people visit the library on a Saturday evening.

Visual contact between the ground floor and the floor above is weaker than one would find in a more conventional atrium design (though not the other way round), and the high walls of the main concourse can appear bland – until one learns that these large areas of light-coloured wooden panelling are responsible for the pitch-perfect acoustics of this very large space, which is no small achievement. The acoustics are exceptionally good wherever you are, as is air quality and ventilation, all of which make the building a thoroughly comfortable setting for reading and studying even for long periods.

The building is highly energy-efficient 'within the limits of PFI,' according to architect Nick Lomax. 'It's been designed to take advantage of natural energy provided by its south-coast setting. The sun's energy is gathered through the glass south wall in winter, though in summer fan-assisted cooling is required to keep the temperature down. Heat is stored in walls and a specially constructed hollow floor, then released slowly into the building.' The exposed concrete columns and first floor table absorb heat by day and release it at night, maintaining an even ambient temperature. The plant needed to heat and cool the library is a fraction of that required in a

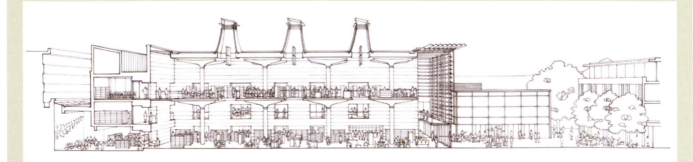

Figure 9.12 Section perspective, Jubilee Library, Brighton (© John Bradbury)

Figure 9.13 View of ground floor of Brighton Library

Figure 9.14 Corner view of 'floating' first floor reference library, connected by walkways and bridges

conventional air-conditioned building. Three, five-metre tall wind towers draw off excessive heat in the summer. In the winter heat recovery units capture heat from lighting, PCs and people, and recycle it back through the system. Lavatories are flushed with rainwater collected in a tank below ground. What the architects have no control over of course are the energy requirements of the library's users. Larger than expected numbers of visitors, extended opening hours, and increasing numbers of users plugging in their own laptops, mobile phones and ICT equipment (as well as on at least one occasion an electric kettle) have all contributed to higher than anticipated electricity use.

The library is open seven days a week and hosts around 500 events every year. With over 1 million visits each year – more than three times the visitor figures for the former central library – it is one of the busiest public libraries in the country. There is no doubt that the Jubilee Library has done wonders for what was formerly a back-street location, and has turned the area inside out. The public square created in front of it is already a major meeting place in the city, and library membership has soared. The project has won the Prime Minister's Better Public Buildings Award 2005, Civic Trust Award 2007, and was one of six finalists for the 2005 RIBA Stirling Prize.

Canada Water Library, Southwark

Opened: 2011
Client: London Borough of Southwark
Architect: CZWG Architects
Project description: public library
Library size: 2,678 square metres
Cost: £14.1
Stock: 55,000 items; 40,000 shelf spaces
Visitor numbers: 1400 per day

The new library at Canada Water designed by Piers Gough's practice, CZWG, sits literally on top of a combined overground and underground railway station, and has its own station entrance and exit, making it ideal as a place to pop into before or after school or work – which many people do. The arresting shape gives the appearance of an inverted pyramid or ziggurat, or even an ark out of water, which is highly suitable for a dock-side location. The design and programme of the library was based on widespread public consultation which elicited over 5,000 responses. Local young people were taken to visit Peckham Library and Whitechapel's Idea Store to give them an idea of different models of library provision, other than what they already knew.

Because the commissioning client, British Land, was a private company it was not subject to European rules for choosing architects, and the developer chose CZWG for their imaginative approach to the project as planning permission architects, even though the practice had not designed a library before. This lack of 'experience' would have ruled them out of many competitions, providing a cautionary lesson as to how

over-protective procurement policies can sometimes undermine their own best intentions.

It was always clear that this particular site required a building with a 'Wow' factor, as it is at the heart of a key docklands regeneration area, which is otherwise rather piecemeal in its assembly of housing, warehouses, retail sheds and other services. The new library is immediately adjacent to the hi-tech Canada Water bus station designed by Eva Jiricná, which adjoins Buro Happold's dramatic railway station, the latter of which serves both the Jubilee underground line and the London Overground. The dynamic inverted mass of the library is clad in anodised aluminium sheets which gleam in the sun and reflect the water in the nearby dock, making a strong 'point of arrival' statement to everybody using the transport terminus.

Because of the inverted volume, the ground floor is the smallest floor-plan in the building, and works as a busy café, reception area and enquiry point. The café is franchised out to a private company experienced in working at this scale, and it works well, serving a rather fine, sunlit, south-west facing corner. From the centre of the ground floor the drama begins, as the interior of the building is dominated by a large circular staircase which rises within a dramatic, almost slightly-larger-than human-scale, wooden-slatted drum, turning a full 360 degrees. Architect Piers Gough said that he 'was keen that people really would walk up from the noisy downstairs to the quieter, more relaxed place above.' In the event, this has proved to be the case, as from several visits it is clear that most people choose to use this ceremonial staircase, even though there is ample lift provision.

Arriving at the first floor the building opens out into a panoramic space containing the main fiction library, children's library, lounge areas, with views out on all sides. This is both an exciting space and a successfully functioning space, enlivened and given solidity by high-quality staggered book-shelving. Close to many of the windows are sofas and comfortable chairs for reading by natural light, with added lighting effects provided by the glistening water immediately outside.

On the top floor is a perimeter gallery containing the non-fiction stock, with long study desks overlooking the main atrium. Though these desks are enormously popular the book-stock is somewhat left stranded as all the shelving is against the wall almost as backdrop, and may be much less

used. Flooring uses multi-coloured carpet tiles throughout, except for the ground floor which is of hardwood.

The library is already proving enormously popular with high visitor and borrowing figures. Serving what was once an established working-class area, now transformed by the rise of nearby Canary Wharf employing tens of thousands of office staff, many from overseas, the library's clientele is incredibly mixed and the library really does function as an integrating feature in the social landscape. It is also heavily used by school-children from a neighbouring 2,000 student comprehensive. Full of praise for the design, Southwark's head of library services, Adrian Whittle, says that success is also due to having a brand new, wide-ranging book-stock, which accounts for a record number of book-issues for a library of this size. 'Good design with good book-stock is the secret of a successful library,' he says.

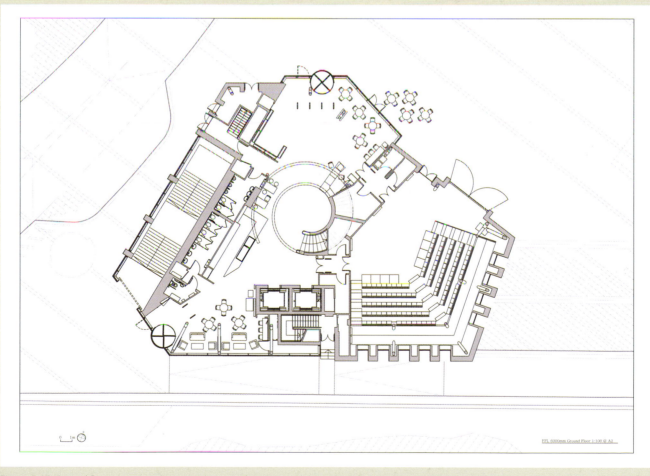

Figure 9.15 Ground floor plan, Canada Water Library. Performance auditorium to the left, courtesy of CZWG Architects

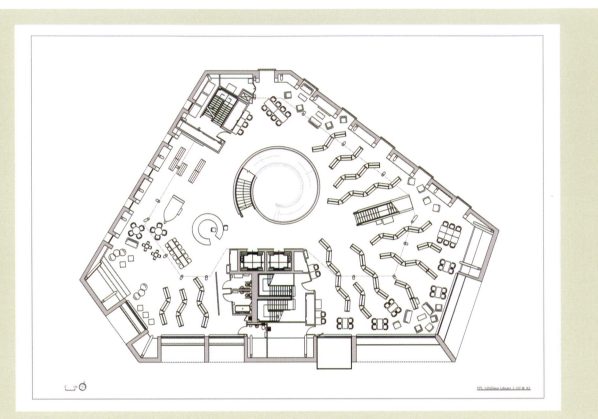

Figure 9.16 First floor library floor plan, Canada Water Library, courtesy of CZWG Architects

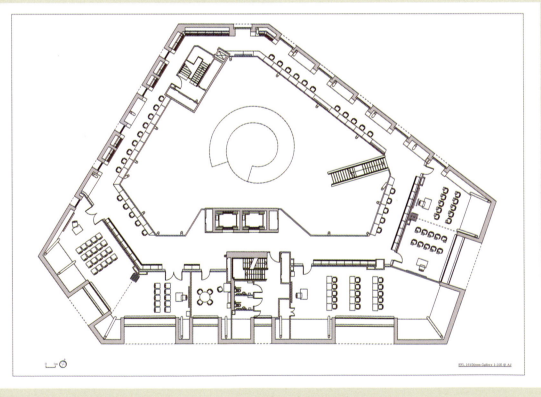

Figure 9.17 Second floor library plan, Canada Water Library, courtesy of CZWG Architects

Figure 9.18 View from upper tier of Canada Water Library to first floor lending library

Figure 9.19 The new Canada Water Library end-stops a public piazza linking bus, underground and overground rail services

Dagenham Library (London Borough of Barking & Dagenham)

Opened: October 2010

Client group: London Borough of Barking & Dagenham, Bouygues UK, Southern Housing Association

Architect: ArchitecturePLB

Project description: public library and 82 flats in combined development

Library size: 1,818 square metres in total, including Council One Stop Shop

Cost: £14.3M

Stock: 28,573 items (including 23,518 books)

Visitor numbers: 38,000 per month

This new library was opened on 13 October 2010 as part of the regeneration of a run-down shopping parade adjacent to Dagenham Heathway underground station, and serving the large Becontree housing estate. This area of suburban east London traditionally provided homes for workers in the nearby Ford car factory and other major industrial sites, and has been poorly served in the past by public and commercial amenities. The new library is unexpectedly generous in scale and has already been a great success, proof if any were needed that a new library can make a big difference to the self-confidence of a neighbourhood.

The new development occupies and emboldens a busy street corner site which it uses to full advantage, possessing a large massing of volume as a result of being a combined library and residential block. The library facade is striking in its angled monumental steel support columns, allowing the entrance to be recessed, and the use of large lettering announces the presence of the 'Dagenham Library' on the street with imagination and panache. From a distance the library seems to be comprised of a steel and glass box on stilts, projecting out from the surrounding apartment building. It possesses a strong architectural dynamism – unusual in the rest of the surrounding townscape, but it works very well, and is immediately visible from the railway station several hundred metres away.

The library is entered through automatic sliding glass doors set under the overhang but clearly demarcated. Most users arrive on foot, and the project architects were keen not to put the building on a plinth or in any way create a monumental entrance, and it feels very easy to cross the threshold and immediately become an active participant in what the library has to offer. 'People can get to the information themselves,' one of the project architects told me. 'That is the ethos of

Figure 9.20 Bold corner canopied entrance of new Dagenham Library by ArchitecturePLB, with apartments above and either side

this new kind of library building.' Inside the space is extremely generous, with a council information service, reading area with newspapers and magazines, computer suite, teen and children's library sections and service point on the ground floor. The interior design – by Evolution Architects – combines a mix of white, grey and mauve finishes, and the signage is excellent.

On entering the library it is possible to see at a glance the different sections displayed by their large, clear signs suspended from the ceiling. The large foyer area is supervised by a concierge/security manager who sits at a console facing the main doors, combining greeting and monitoring functions in a low-key and unobtrusive fashion – most effective. Glass

lifts at the rear, along with a grand staircase at one corner lead to the first floor gallery areas – the centre of the library is a double height atrium – where the main book stock is well displayed, and where there are study areas, meeting rooms, toilets, and the principal library service reception desk. Roof-lights and large areas of glazed facade at the front and side produce very good natural lighting.

There are 48 computers for public use and free Wi-Fi hotspots. This is almost certainly one of the best public library developments in recent years specifically designed as part of a long-term urban regeneration strategy. It exudes confidence and a belief in a better future.

Figure 9.21 Main staircase and atrium at Dagenham Library

Ewell, Surrey: library and cultural centre

Opened: 1970
Client: the Borough of Epsom and Ewell
Architect: A.G. Sheppard Fidler and Associates
Project description: public library and social centre
Library size: 4,000 square metres approximately
Cost: £369,000

An early attempt to re-imagine the public library architecturally, Ewell was opened in April 1970. This dramatic circular library and cultural centre was designed by architects A.G. Sheppard Fidler and Associates, and was likened at the time to a space ship which had landed in an ornamental garden. The main public areas are situated in a single domed structure 140 ft in diameter and 37 ft to the top of the central roof light. A mezzanine floor accommodates the museum, exhibition areas, workshop and archives. A beautifully detailed helical staircase takes visitors from the library upstairs to the museum. On the lower ground floor can be found the main assembly hall with seating for 300 people along with a stage. This is a double height space whose roof provides the floor of the mezzanine level.

This is a bold re-working of the traditional prototype of the library as a domed reading room. The principal dome is formed from 20 precast concrete half portals joining at a 30ft diameter compression ring which supports the central circular roof light. A clerestory window runs the complete diameter of the building.

The building has always been regarded as a great success and is very popular, providing a sense of occasion, space and a good mixture of cultural amenities. It replaces a former mansion house, Bourne Hall, and inhabits the historic gardens (including ornamental lake), which have now been somewhat islanded by a gyratory road system. Most people do seem to come and go by car, which is perhaps typical of this kind of well-established suburban part of south London. The building is surrounded by mature trees which soften the sharp contours of the main structure and provide that much hoped for harmony between dramatic white modernist buildings set in pastoral settings.

One problem with buildings with such large areas of glass wall sections, is that it seems inappropriate to put shelves or other items of stock furniture against them, obscuring the view. Yet this has to be done. Within the space the lighting is pleasant and the high roof and great circular roof light add a sense of drama to the space.

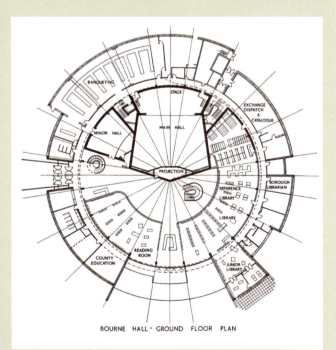

BOURNE HALL – GROUND FLOOR PLAN

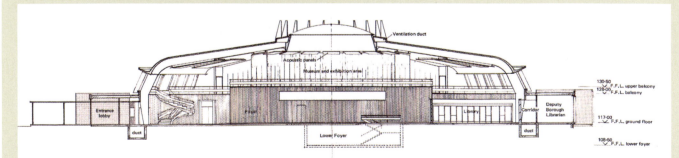

Figure 9.22 Floor plan and cross section of Bourne Hall Library, Ewell, opened 1970 (Images courtesy of Surrey Libraries and held in the Epsom and Ewell Local Family History Centre)

Figure 9.23 Art gallery interior, connected to circular edge of public library at Bourne Hall Library, Ewell, Surrey

Figure 9.24 'It looked as though a space ship had landed.' Bourne Hall Library designed by A.G. Sheppard Fidler and Associates

Glasgow: The Bridge Arts Centre and Library

Opened: 2006
Client: Glasgow City Council
Architect: Gareth Hoskins Architects
Project description: arts centre and public library
Library size: overall including college library and shared
    meeting space – 1620m²
Cost: £10 million
Stock: 25,602 books plus 2098 AV items
Visitor numbers: 13,000 per week

This new award-winning arts centre, incorporating a 250-seat performing arts theatre, dance studio, gallery, café and large public library, was squeezed into a sloping site between an existing swimming pool building and the new John Wheatley College. The new insertion acts almost literally as a 'bridge' between the two adjacent buildings, as well as a pedestrian route from one side of the Easterhouse Estate to another. As the photographs show, the library also functions as a public

thoroughfare, not only providing a lively and colourful covered space connecting two street networks, but also provides a busy atmosphere and natural surveillance to the boldly designed open-plan library, which deserves as much attention for its remarkable – and innovative – tiered staging as the earlier Peckham Library did. Both are bold experiments in the radical re-framing of the traditional library setting.

The pronounced incline of the wedge-shaped library provides a dynamic to the building which is immediate and arresting – but also complies with DDA requirements regarding the approved gradient of pathways for wheelchair use. The six library galleries, in ascending tiers, not only provide easy access to the bookstacks, but also create a series of separate public rooms and study areas which are well used. At the upper level of the library space there is a café and lounge area; at the lower level are to be found the continuously staffed library desk and reception area, which directly

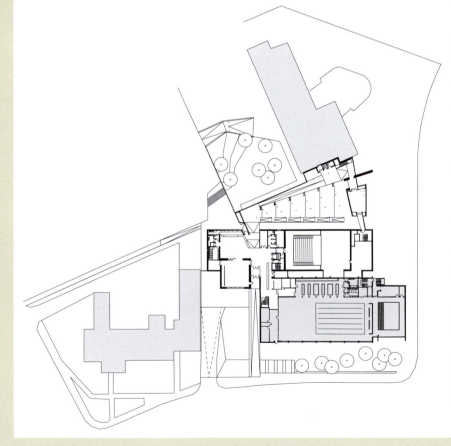

Figure 9.25 The Bridge Library at Easterhouse Arts Centre: floor plan and context, courtesy of Gareth Hoskins Architects

overlooks the children's library area and the second main entrance. Suspended above the children's library is a pod for seminars, meetings and story-telling sessions; adjacent to the children's library is an informal lounge area used as a drop-in centre by Macmillan Cancer Care. The high ceiling appears to float free of a series of slender white columns which pierce 'breathing-holes' or sky-lights into the canopy roof, providing additional light to that from the glazed panel walls. There are two main connecting walkways through the library, one on each edge of the library space proper, both in polished concrete, a material which evokes both indoor and outdoor suitability simultaneously.

At ground floor level the new 'Bridge' locks jigsaw-fashion into the adjacent buildings to provide an even greater sense of connection. To the east the library shares a computer suite and specialist arts library with the John Wheatley College; to the west the theatre takes up space in what was formerly the swimming pool boiler room to provide access corridors to back stage areas. The timber-boarded west flank wall acts as an exhibition gallery, curated by the in-house arts team, Platform. Thus the library sits at the heart of a highly programmed and successful arts centre, providing a different kind of space, but one which consolidates the cultural presence of the arts centre in the community.

Figure 9.26 The Bridge Library at Easterhouse Arts Centre: library section

Figure 9.27 The Bridge Library, Easterhouse, by Gareth Hoskins Architects. Internal walkway adjacent to main library space

The unusual sloping hall is a triumphant success, though it must have seemed a high-risk strategy on paper. It is intended to evoke the large inclined, top-lit, concourse of Glasgow Central Station, though the wedge shape has echoes of Lubetkin's Finsbury Health Centre – another dynamic insert – while the terraces echo football terraces, or possibly even a flight of canal locks. The library and its many distinct spaces and thoroughfares has been a great local success, both in terms of the high numbers of users, as well as amongst the staff who work there. There has been little vandalism or anti-social behaviour in this very public building, which serves a large housing area seven miles from Glasgow's city centre and which in recent decades has suffered high levels of unemployment and social deprivation. It has a higher than average amount of use by young people, especially on their way home from school, when they browse the computers and sit around tables to talk and look at books. Junior fiction and non-fiction issues rose by 91 per cent and 30 per cent in the first six months of operation.

Awards

RIBA Regional Award winner
RIBA National Award winner
Scottish Design Awards – Best Public Building winner
Scottish Design Awards – Grand Prix winner (best overall project)
British Construction Industry Awards – UK Regeneration Award winner
Glasgow Institute of Architects Award winner

Figure 9.28 The Bridge Library at Easterhouse Arts Centre at night. Photograph by Andrew Lee

Hook and Chessington Library

Opened: 2007
Client: Royal London Borough of Kingston Upon Thames
Architect: Dunlop Haywards & Quintessential Design
Project description: public library, skills training centre,
    meeting rooms & recording studio
Library size: 370 square metres.
Cost: £2.15 million
Stock: 31,000 items including books and AV materials

A model of a new community library, very much established as a community centre fronted by a good café/reception area, leading to a library, skills training centre and recording studio. Pressed tight to a main road, most people enter the library across a large car park, one of the weakest points of the design. (In these suburban libraries many users do come and go by car). It was jointly funded by the local authority and the Learning and Skills Training Council, and designed by London practice Dunlop Haywards, already contracted to supply architectural services to the local authority.

The library operates in a suburban area with few local amenities and is much valued; in such conditions the café, toilets and warm, welcoming space, are a real incentive to people to visit, and it is very much regarded as a 'family library', rather than a city-centre student or professional Wi-Fi networking hub. Most of the computers are to be found in the training suite on the first floor. Apparently many visitors comment favourably on the bright comfortable furniture and light-wood fittings, which brings a higher quality of interior design to the neighbourhood than had been expected. The reception area is used for craft fairs and quiz nights.

A doubling of new stock, compared with the previous library close by which was closed after being badly damaged by fire, has resulted in a doubling of library visitors. There is a very good space for children, overlooked by the library desk, although it also contains a fire escape door leading directly on to a main road, which is a very poor piece of design.

The building won a Public Library Buildings Award in 2007, under the rubric, 'The Heart of the Community'.

Figure 9.29 Street frontage of Hook and Chessington Library, Royal London Borough of Kingston upon Thames, by Dunlop Haywards & Quintessential Design

Figure 9.30 Hook Library and Community Centre: library, café, meeting rooms, computer training and recording studio

Figure 9.31 Main library desk at Hook Library overlooking computer suite

Huntingdon Library and Archives

Opened: 2009
Client: Cambridgeshire County Council
Architect: Crampin Pring McCartney Gant
Project description: public library
Library size: 1,750 square metres
Cost: £4.6 million
Visitor numbers: 1,000 per day

Designed by Crampin Pring McCartney Gant and opened in 2009, this new library and archive is part of a larger development in the central neighbourhood of this market town with a population of 32,000. It is built on the site of the old library, which was demolished. The design was a collaboration between senior library management and the architects, with the particular involvement of Library Design Consultant Leonore Charlton, who has specialised in library interiors for many years, working in Cambridgeshire and other counties.

The building occupies 1,750 square metres, incorporates the Huntingdonshire Archives, a specialist Cromwell Collection linked to the nearby Cromwell Museum, two meeting rooms, IT Learning Centre, café and toilets. Lighting and temperature is automatically adjusted for different parts of the building, though in the case of the Huntingdonshire Archives, the study area and store are especially designed to maintain the correct ambient conditions as well as to guard against fire or water ingress – which is additionally expensive compared to standard library building requirements. Total cost was £4.6 million, which included £400k fit-out costs.

The exterior consists largely of Cambridge brickwork, with a distinctive curve at one corner, and a cedar-clad first floor overhang or jetty to the north which partly accommodates the archive. The ground floor lending library is one large, high-ceilinged open-plan area with excellent signage and clear

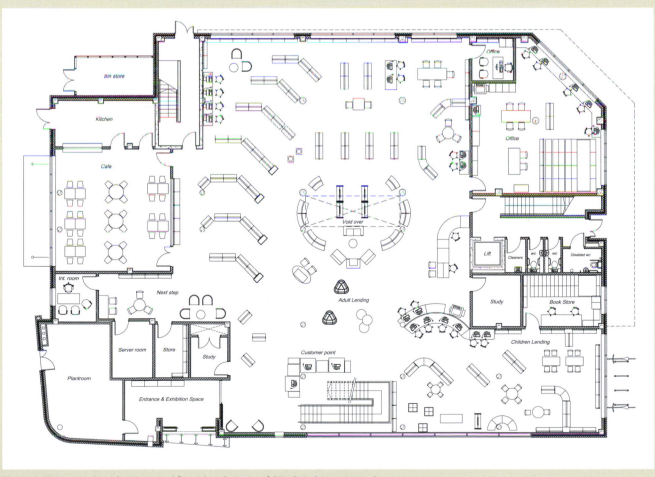

Figure 9.32 Huntingdon Library: ground floor plan. Courtesy of CPMG Architects Limited

sight-lines across the whole space, so that the different library sections and services can be taken in a single view on entry into the building. The high ceiling is supported by polished concrete columns, and a light well illuminates the central floor area. The building is entered by automatic sliding doors which open into a small lobby, where pushchairs or mobility scooters can be stored, with a further sliding door leading into the main library space. Though sliding doors are more expensive than automatic doors that open inwards or outwards, designer Leonore Charlton thinks they are much more efficient and easier for customers to use.

At the entrance an attractive chrome and plate glass staircase leads to the first floor archives, IT learning centre, meeting rooms and study areas. The walls are enlivened by high quality photographic panels which depict local historic houses, gardens and other scenes from the town's heritage, which add a sense of identity to the interior; equally, end panels of some bookshelf stands are also decorated with photographic panels, to good effect. The library café is very popular, serving cooked meals as well as providing snacks and refreshments, and is managed by Cambridgeshire Catering Service. The library is visited by up to 1,000 users on a busy day.

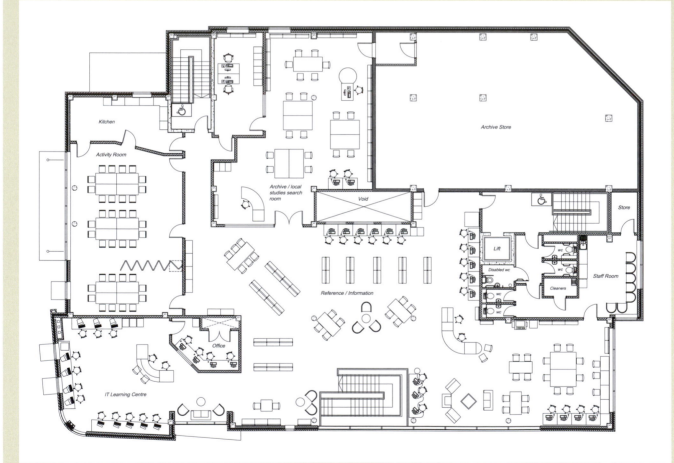

Figure 9.33 Huntingdon Library: first floor plan. Courtesy of CPMG Architects Limited

Figure 9.34 Pronounced corner of new Huntingdon Library and Archive, designed by Crampin Pring McCartney Gant and opened in 2009

Figure 9.35 Ground floor interior of Huntingdon Library and Archive

Newcastle City Library

Opened: June 2009
Client: Newcastle City Council
Architect: Ryder Architecture
Project description: public library
Library size: 8,300 square metres
Cost: £25 million
Visitor numbers: 3,800 per day

In March 2002 the Department of Culture, Media & Sport (DCMS) put out a call for PFI proposals, including new library buildings. By this time Newcastle Council had decided that it wanted to replace its existing central library which, though designed by Sir Basil Spence, and opened in 1967, had failed to stand the test of time. According to the Deputy Leader of the Council, Councillor David Faulkner, 'the old library was almost unloved from the time it went up. It was a product of that concrete building spree. Dan Smith and the Brasilia of the North' (Phethean, 2009: 21). The PFI process did not involve an architectural competition, but it did invite bids from consortia to cost and provide designs for a state of the art public library designed to meet a number of defined 'Outcome specifications'. A design panel was established including elected councillors, senior library staff as well as private sector advisers, along with the Regional Development Agency, the Civic Trust and CABE. The consortium chosen after much consultation and deliberation was led by a Japanese company, Kajima, in conjunction with the architectural practice of Ryder Architecture and the Royal Bank of Scotland. This consortium, once selected, was charged with the design, construction and maintenance of a new Newcastle City library for 25 years, creating a dedicated operational company for this purpose. Total cost of the project was around £40 million, with capital outlay of circa £24 million and lifecycle costs of £15 million. When the building opened on 7 June 2009, queues stretched all the way round the building, down to Northumberland Street.

A lot of work went into consulting with library users, non-users, library staff and others as to what should be the principal features of the new library, and apart from the obvious wish for brighter, cleaner, more attractive settings, the key idea which emerged was the notion of a place that *encouraged multiple and independent uses of the library* as and when people wanted to visit. Thus, for example, the traditional idea that library users are first and foremost confronted by a desk when they enter had to go. This notion of a hierarchy of spaces controlled and directed by library staff no longer seemed suitable or apposite for twenty-first century users. Instead the building was divided into five service areas

– information, local studies, music and fiction, children and young people, meeting rooms and café – all of equal status and all served by a number of information points where staff could handle enquiries as and when needed. The café is franchised out and has been a great success, contributing much-needed revenue to the library service.

Library services are provided over six floors. Several specialist collections were made more publicly accessible. So, for example, there is 'The Book Gallery', where interesting or unusual books from the stack are set out for display (and handling) on a series of bespoke shelves made from walnut. The library also houses 'The Newcastle Collection' which is mounted in a series of illuminated glass boxes, an idea inspired by the King's Library at the British Library. An interesting example of how consultation can sometimes produce failed predictive information, is that many users of the local history library clamoured for public lockers to be installed there, though once in place they are now rarely used, and take up valuable space that could have been used for other purposes.

Changing the status and fluidity of the spaces had to be accompanied by changing the working practices of the staff. Library staff were no longer desk-staff but floor-staff, 'working the room' so to speak, meeting and greeting and trained to handle a variety of book and information enquiries on the spot. This itself was precipitated by the decision to encourage 100 per cent self-service by library users, and library staff were pleased to see how quickly the public adapted to this.

The children's library occupies much of the third floor, easily accessible by lifts, close to the young people's library. There are no adult toilets on this floor, and the area is supervised by staff all the time, all trained in child protection issues, given public concern on this issue. The building is Wi-Fi throughout, and users know that the IT manager in the building is able to monitor what is on people's screens when they are online, and thus able to screen for pornography or other inappropriate uses.

The new library was built on the site of the old one, once this had been demolished. Indeed it shares exactly the same footprint and uses the former library's foundations, though this one resolves the almost impossible access problems of the former building, according to architect Ian Kennedy of Ryder Architecture, which 'was designed around a grand scheme for Newcastle city centre, with first floor access from raised walkways in the air and cars beneath. Many of these bridges and walkways are still in evidence round the city, but the

total scheme never materialised, so you were left with these idiosyncratic entrances floating in mid-air, almost inaccessible' (Phethean, 2009: 22).

Figure 9.36 Level 1 Floor plan, Newcastle City Library, courtesy of Ryder Architecture

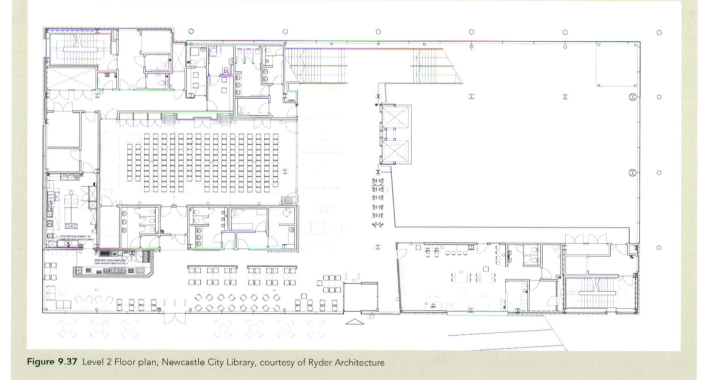

Figure 9.37 Level 2 Floor plan, Newcastle City Library, courtesy of Ryder Architecture

Though on the perimeter of the central area of the city, it is adjacent to the Laing Art Gallery; however, a busy ring road separates the two. It occupies a corner site with two entrances of equal status and equal use. One leads into the large and very attractive café area, the other straight into the main ground floor atrium.

The development of the library site offered the potential to transform the urban landscape around the building and reinforce the physical and visual linkages between the Blue Carpet (an adjacent open square) and the Laing Art Gallery on one side, and Princess Square on the other. *At the core of the concept was a synthesis of the architectural and townscape design so that external spaces and movement patterns could flow into and through*

the building. This required the creation of a distinct personality for each space.

(Phethean, 2009: 71)

Once you have entered the main atrium it is possible to take in most of the library and its distinct areas at a single glance, and way-finding is aided by a cleverly designed colour-coding scheme. Although the building is, in essence, a rectangular box, a glass extension overhangs the main street, so that people can see the library from a distance, as, for example, when they come out of the Metro Station at the Earl Grey's Monument. On the top floor of this glazed extension is a viewing deck furnished with pink leather Arne Jacobsen Swan and Egg chairs, sponsored by Ryder Architecture who helped design the building. This is like a penthouse sun-trap and is very popular. The library now receives about 3,800 visitors each day.

Figure 9.38 Ground floor of Newcastle Library by Ryder Architecture

Figure 9.39 Enquiry desks and quick access computer stalls on ground floor of Newcastle Library

Figure 9.40 Corner glazed tower of Newcastle Library

Norfolk and Norwich Millennium Library

Opening date: 2001
Client: Norfolk County Council (with major partnership funding from Millennium Commission & Norwich City Council)
Architect: Michael Hopkins & Partners
Project description: public library within large retail, public information and exhibition atrium called The Norwich Forum.
Library size: 4,621 square metres
Cost: £63.5 million
Stock: 325,000 items
Visitor numbers: 1.5 million per year.

Designed by architects, Michael Hopkins and Partners, this civic complex opened in 2001, within the larger Norwich Forum. The Norfolk and Norwich Millennium Library is just one element of the building, though the centre-piece and principal element. The development cost £63 million and includes shops, cafés and restaurants, the headquarters of the regional BBC, a Learning City (IT skills centre) and a Learning Shop (further education advice), all housed and accessed from within a great atrium entrance hall, which is also used for meetings, concerts and art exhibitions. The cost of the development was largely raised from Millennium Lottery funds. The new library within the Norwich Forum replaces the old Norwich Library destroyed by fire in 1994. In 2010 the library was attracting 1.5 million visits a year and has become the busiest library in the UK.

Why is this different from a traditional library in its design and service? For a start 90 per cent of books and other materials issued are issued through self-service machines, leaving staff to deal in person with queries and reader advice. Most of these materials contain RFID recognition inserts, which means not only that self-service simply requires the borrower to pass them under a scanning device, but also means that the library staff can track the whereabouts of all materials, and interrogate the system for frequency and patterns of borrowing, leading to a more intelligent understanding of the stock. There is no reference library as such; nearly all the material is on open access

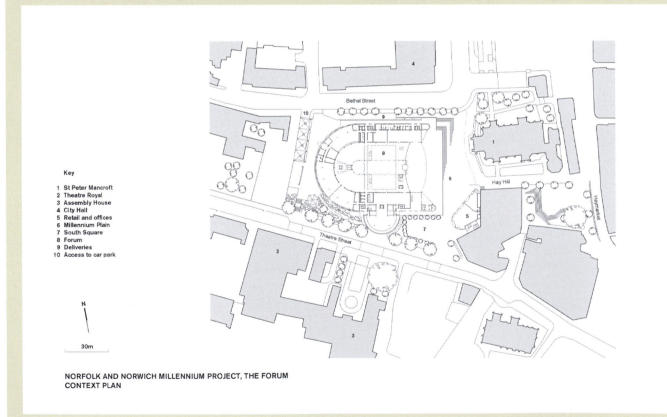

Key

1 St Peter Mancroft
2 Theatre Royal
3 Assembly House
4 City Hall
5 Retail and offices
6 Millennium Plain
7 South Square
8 Forum
9 Deliveries
10 Access to car park

NORFOLK AND NORWICH MILLENNIUM PROJECT, THE FORUM CONTEXT PLAN

Figure 9.41 Norfolk and Norwich Millennium Project: The Forum Context Plan. Courtesy of Michael Hopkins & Partners

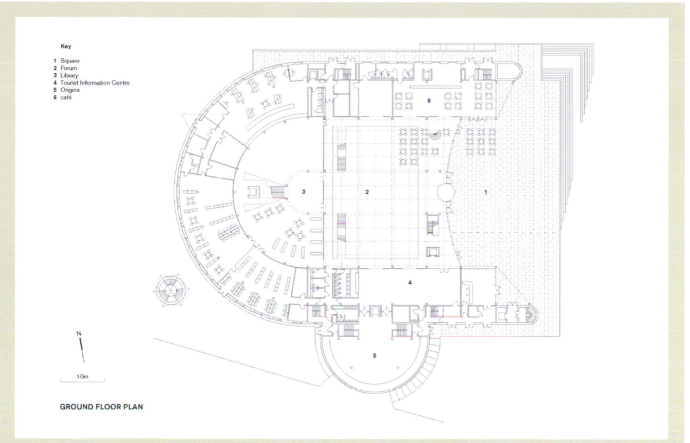

Key

1 Square
2 Forum
3 Library
4 Tourist Information Centre
5 Origins
6 café

N

10m

GROUND FLOOR PLAN

Figure 9.42 Norfolk and Norwich Millennium Project: Ground Floor Plan. Courtesy of Michael Hopkins & Partners

shelves and there are study tables and desks strategically placed throughout the library, providing some 220 study spaces. It has been a deliberate – and successful – policy not to separate the book stock from the ICT terminals. According to a senior staff member at Norwich:

> You've got to have the two. And, I think that what's nice is that the two are integrated. We go into a lot of libraries where the IT is all in one space together, and the books are all in another space, so you're almost recreating what we used to have in the lending and reference sections. Ideally the two need to be integrated.
>
> (cited in Bryson *et al.*, 2003: 31)

The library holds more than 120,000 books on open access, approximately the same number as the old library once held. There is free Internet access available at 115 computer terminals, the system being filtered for inappropriate material by a series of keywords. The library employs 75 staff, some part-time. The ground floor of the library, which contains fiction, the children's library, CDs and DVDs, is open seven days a week, and Sunday is promoted as 'Family Day'. The first

floor library, which contains much of the non-fiction and local history materials, is open six days a week. Many library users can be directly contacted by email newsletters alerting them to new books in stock, visits by authors, invitations to join reading groups, thus connecting the library service to people in their own homes – including reminders of overdue books to be returned.

The overall shape of the building combines two main structural elements – an urban civic library embedded in a large covered public concourse or mall. One of the project architects has well described this reference back to older building types as follows:

> You can analyse our building and say quite simply we've got a semi-circular library that you could say is half a classical reading room, literally chopped in half – around the outside of which we've got a relatively traditional construction with relatively modest window-sized openings with bay windows, with study booths, we've then got a panopticon-type radial plan which comes into a central space. And then the other half of that

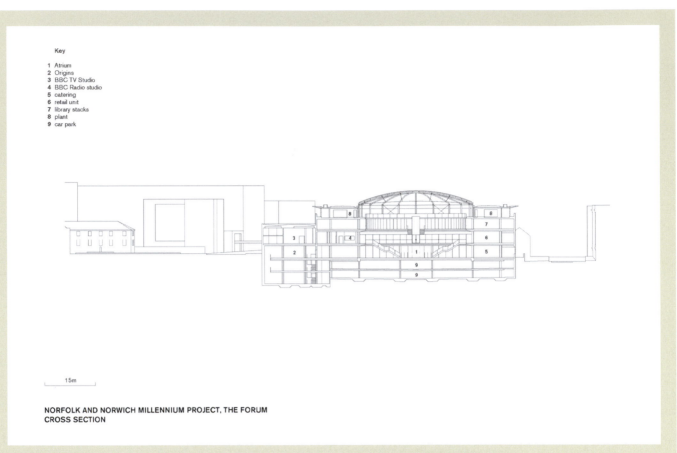

Key

1 Atrium
2 Origins
3 BBC TV Studio
4 BBC Radio studio
5 catering
6 retail unit
7 library stacks
8 plant
9 car park

15m

NORFOLK AND NORWICH MILLENNIUM PROJECT, THE FORUM
CROSS SECTION

Figure 9.43 Norfolk and Norwich Millennium Project: The Forum Cross Section. Courtesy of Michael Hopkins & Partners

we've got, instead of having your complete circle of the library we've got the equivalent of a Victorian railway station, really with a large open concourse with people milling through it. So in a way the Victorians had the prototypes and we've merged various ideas that have been around...The building makes an outside space and then that connects through a big glass wall to an inside space...so that it links directly into the streetscape...

We had a three-storey building and we had it at the back of a hub of this U-shaped space. And we decided to have this semi-circular form, and that had interesting aspects in terms of context on the outside of the building, but had an interesting aspect in terms of the inside of the building, in that it had very much a central space which could allow a more noisy activity, and then you could filter through that space towards the outside of the building and go towards quieter study areas. So there was a very clear idea on the plan how a circular arrangement might work architecturally.

(Bryson *et al.*, 2003: 30)

The library not only draws on certain architectural traditions, it also responds to the particular history of the city of Norwich and its culture. There is an especially fine collection of art books, partly a response to the presence of a well-known Art School in the city, but also because of a long tradition of a distinctive painting school known as the 'Norwich School' of landscape water-colourists and painters. Furthermore a room has been provided to hold the Second Air Division Memorial Library, which honours the American forces personnel based in East Anglia during the Second World War who lost their lives in the conflict. This attracts many visitors, including many American relatives of those memorialised, as well as historians and those interested in American history and culture.

Where others may have eschewed monumentality in the public face of new library architecture, the Norwich Millennium Library makes this a talking point and as one of its architects has said, 'it is a sort of public gesture to put the architecture out in the open realm.' The design has also brought a new element to Norwich life, as the then Head of Library Services noted:

On a lovely summer day the steps are just full of people, and it looks like a scene in Paris. There are these public spaces, but in Norwich there has never been that sort of public space. I think it takes time for people to realise the potential of a space like that.

(cited in Bryson *et al.*, 2003: 33)

The integration of inside and outside is highlighted by the comment of one of the Norfolk Business Focus Group when asked about how the new library feels:

First of all what really pleased me is that I've traditionally seen libraries as something you sit in, you focus inward in personal spaces – but this is a completely different sort of atmosphere! First of all it's very welcoming, you hardly feel like you've walked into a building. You've walked into an environment – which I really do like. You've got this immediate feeling like being a part of something. You can use the opportunity to learn, have fun and relax. You can look outside and see the most wonderful views, obviously which I think helps the whole creative process.

(Bryson *et al.*, 2003: 49–50)

Because the Millennium Library is part of the larger Norwich Forum, which is managed as an independent Trust, it benefits from a dedicated in-house Building Services team with 10 staff on site 24 hours a day, 7 days a week and 365 days a year. Thus all repairs, maintenance and cleaning are handled continuously, as and when needed.

In almost all respects the Millennium Library in Norwich succeeds brilliantly. The one outstanding difficulty to be resolved is temperature control within the building, both within the atrium and the library itself. Large glazed atria are subject to problems with ambient temperature, and the relatively deep interior of the library sections makes natural ventilation difficult. There is also a recognised need for secure storage space for buggies, so popular is the library amongst parents and carers with young children. This is a design issue which most Scandinavian libraries solved decades ago, providing ample space for buggies, self-service clothes lockers and places for outdoor shoes and wellington boots, all anticipated because of the weather.

Figure 9.44 Glazed facade of Norwich forum, from library, looking across to main market square and city roofline

Figure 9.45 Norwich Library purposely mixes reference and lending stock, causal reading and study areas

Figure 9.46 Main public area of Norwich Forum leading to Norwich Millennium Library

Idea Store Whitechapel

Opened: 2005
Client: London Borough of Tower Hamlets
Architect: Adjaye Associates
Project description: public library with dance studio, meeting rooms and further education programme
Library size: 3,500 square metres
Cost: £16 million
Stock: 100,000 items
Visitor numbers: 2,000 visitors per day

The principal motive for the re-branding of public libraries in the London Borough of Tower Hamlets as 'Idea Stores' was that visitor numbers and book borrowings in the borough were in freefall, and something had to be done to reverse a pattern of rapid decline. A policy paper written in 2000 noted that, 'A staggering 72 per cent of the population never used the library services on offer and it was decided that a radically different approach to provision of library services

in terms of marketing and presentation was needed' (Ezard, 2003). Working with design company Bisset Adams, Tower Hamlets staff set out a plan for a series of new libraries and major refurbishments at a reduced number of sites, starting in Bow, followed by Chrisp Street and then Whitechapel. Both the latter two were new-build projects designed by Adjaye/ Associates.

Idea Store Whitechapel opened in 2005 on the major thoroughfare of Whitechapel Road, on a site provided at reduced cost by Sainsbury's supermarket as part of a planning deal. This is one of London's busiest street markets on one of the city's busiest roads (A11), in an area rich with history. It provides 3,500 square metres of space over five floors, and was built at a cost of £16 million, with Adjaye Associates designing both the building and its interior. It won a RIBA London Award in 2006, and today is the busiest public library in inner London. In 2009 architects and designers, mackenzie

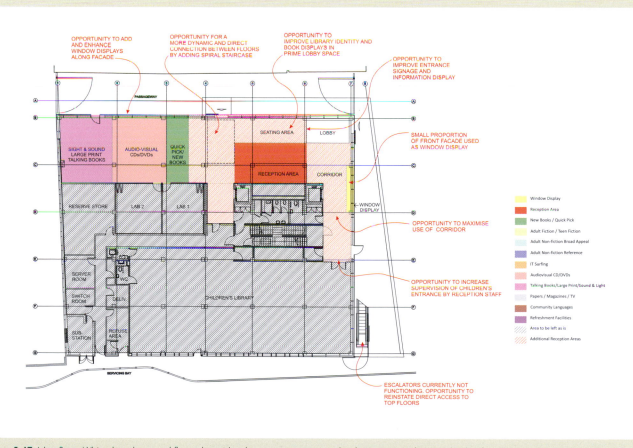

Figure 9.47 Idea Store Whitechapel: ground floor plan with subsequent suggestions by designers, mackenzie wheeler, for adaptations and enhancements after several years of intensive use

wheeler, were brought in to refine some of the interior design issues which had emerged after five years of intensive use.

Certainly the building struck a bold – if controversial note – in an otherwise historic streetscape. The most talked-about feature was a public escalator which 'hoovered up' passers by and visitors from the pavement to the first and second floors, within a tall narrow space behind the glass facade. This was in addition to two ground floor entrances, one at each end of the otherwise plain rectangular block. Unfortunately, high maintenance costs for this bespoke escalator, allied with security issues attached to 'opportunistic' access, have caused the escalator to be closed and boarded off to the public for some time, although, with a new layout completed in 2012, there are plans to re-open the escalator and make it an integral part of the building. Furthermore, one of the two ground floor entrances has been closed – there were problems with cross-currents of cold air – so that there is now a single entrance to the building, which seems to create no problems at all.

The interior quality is very high, with beautiful red rubber studded floor surfaces on all floors, bespoke wooden shelving in attractive curved and straight configurations, many comfortable armchairs and sofas in addition to over 120 study places. Access to all floors is mostly by lift, though there are staircases too, if rather narrow. A new spiral staircase linking the ground and the first floor was recently installed, and there are now plans to reinstate the original open staircase connecting the second, third and fourth floors.

Lifts, staircases, toilets are all located in a central core, which means that the basic floor-plate at each level of the building is in the shape of a square doughnut, or four connecting galleries – not entirely satisfactory. There is a brightly lit top floor café serving proper meals as well as snacks, teas and coffees, which is a popular meeting place. Adjacent to the café is a news lounge, where library users can sit in armchairs and watch news television (without sound but with sub-titles) at selected times of the day. This top floor also contains an exhibition space for art work, as well as for public events and talks, and the collection of art books is kept here, attractively displayed. This space also has a very good feel.

The third floor is currently given over to learning materials and a number of learning laboratories, where an extensive programme of adult education classes are held. One of the implications for calling these libraries 'Idea Stores' is that they are very much an integration of library and further education services – very pro-active, and able to access both revenue and project funding for many different kinds of educational courses. When these learning laboratories are not in use they double up as additional study space for library users.

On the first floor is the principal computer suite, heavily used, along with non-fiction collections, a dedicated dance studio with sprung floor, and a complementary therapy suite with showers and related facilities. All these spaces are programmed directly by Idea Store staff. The ground floor is largely taken up with fiction and a large, separate children's library, with its own glass entry doors and continual supervision. At present Idea Store Whitechapel attracts 14,000 visits per week.

Overall the building has a very colourful feel to it. It is heavily used by people studying or attending classes – many vocational or offering 'life-skills'. The 'penthouse' café and gallery are very popular spaces, and possess an admirable degree of quiet conviviality and studiousness. The interior design, furnishings and materials are all high quality and integrate the building. The drawbacks are the breaking up of the floor-plate by the central lift shafts and staircases, and the over-ambitiousness of the street escalator entrances. At first sight, the front curtilage of the building at street level is almost extinguished by the encroaching street market, but in practice it integrates the library completely into the life of this vibrant and dynamic neighbourhood – as it has always done at the Rotterdam Central Library which, too, is entirely surrounded by market stalls. An important success story in the continuing development of new models of public library provision.

Figure 9.48 Whitchapel Idea Store

Figure 9.49 Curving book display units and bright rubberised floors at Idea Store Whitechapel

Winchester Discovery Centre

Opened: November 2007
Client: Hampshire County Council
Architect: Hampshire County Council Architects
Project description: refurbishment of 1830s Corn Exchange –
   and new-build extension – for public library, art gallery,
   exhibition hall and performance hall.
Cost: £7m
Stock: 130,000
Visitor numbers: 500,000 per year

The wholly refurbished and extended Winchester Discovery Centre was opened on 21 February 2008. This new concept of a library is based in the Grade I Corn Exchange and Market House designed by architect Owen Brown Carter in 1838, where the city's public library had operated from 1936. Controversy surrounded the re-opening, notably around the re-branding of the town library as the Winchester Discovery Centre. The controversy was anticipated and possibly intended, as it signalled a remarkable change in the services provided in this new public amenity.

Although a very attractive and clearly recognisable library sits at the heart of the original building – lit by very large glazed roofing panels above – the visitor will also find an equally well-lit art gallery, an arts and crafts exhibition area, a 180 seat Performance Hall (with retractable seating), interior and terrace café areas, gift shop, meeting rooms, toilets, and a booking office for the many events held there. The building, which holds over 130,000 books and other stock items, now attracts half a million visitors a year and is generally agreed to be a great success, not only as a result of a beautiful re-fit and extension by the long-admired Hampshire County Council Architects' Department, but also by a very dynamic management team whose backgrounds embrace commercial

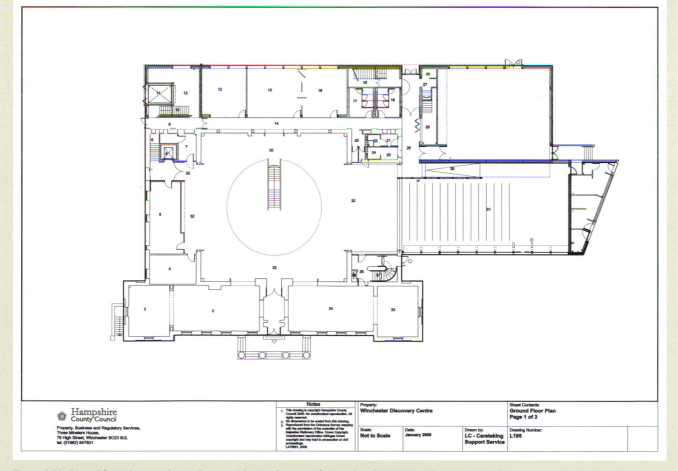

Figure 9.50 Ground floor plan, Winchester Discovery Centre. Courtesy of Hampshire County Council

book-selling, events management and a dedicated interest in literature and the arts.

Those fearing that the re-branding might result in an overly corporate look, or embody a cheap and cheerful retailing ethos, will be disappointed. Both interior and exterior exude seriousness, a delight in light and colour, and civic professionalism. The interplay between the arts – in the form of the vast tapestry mural by Alice Kettle in the café/ fiction gallery, the arts and crafts display area, the temporary exhibition walls, as well as the main gallery – and the book-stock is both dynamic and powerful. One integrating feature is the very bold lettering, within and without, designed by Winchester-based graphic design company, Peagreen, which works tremendously well, as can be seen in the shelf-end lettering.

There are three entrances. The first is through the main Corn Exchange portico which, like the entrance to the Stockholm Library, allows a view of a central staircase leading up into a circular room. The second is a side entrance from the car park, and there is also another main entrance through the new extension wing to the east, which is fronted by a small attractive café terrace, leading into the café, box office, gift shop and fiction section. In this double height wing, all the bookshelves are on castors, and can be moved to create a performance space with its own entrance, bar and catering.

The main library area is one large square hall with a central staircase leading up to a circular gallery (which in turn offers access to the main exhibition gallery, directly at the top of the staircase). There is also a specialist collection of over 10,000 books about railways – a regional interest – which attracts visitors from near and far. PCs are clustered in small islands, as well as distributed throughout the rest of the library. There are 27 PCs, though many users bring their own laptops and take advantage of the free Wi-Fi. Use of library computers is filtered so that, for example, under-15s cannot access social networking sites. The children's library is off-centre and freely accessible to all users, and is supervised by library staff acting as floor staff rather than sitting behind desks.

The Discovery Centre earns revenue through corporate bookings of the meeting rooms, performance hall and catering facilities, as well as through the hire of rooms on a regular basis to local educational and social organisations, arts and dance groups, and a number of employment clubs and careers advisory services. Events range from chamber music concerts, poetry readings, book-signings, theatre and dance performances, to fashion shows, craft fairs and touring exhibitions. Thus the building has created a vibrant arts and performance centre with a proper public library service at its heart. All facilities are fully accessible.

Figure 9.51 Grade I listed former Corn Exchange now refurbished as Winchester Discovery Centre (including library)

Figure 9.52 Well sign-posted lending library rotunda and stairs to upper library floor and gallery at Winchester Discovery Centre

Figure 9.53 Handsome extension to former Winchester Corn Exchange providing additional library space and café, designed by Hampshire County Council Architects

CHAPTER 10

Academic library case studies

Aberdeen: University of Aberdeen, University Library

Opening date: Autumn 2011
Client: University of Aberdeen
Architect: schmidt/hammer/lassen
Project description: university library, gallery, Special Collections centre, Glucksman Conservation Centre
Library size: 15,500 square metres
Cost: £57 million (including costs of demolition work, site clearance and landscaping)
Stock: 400,000 modern books, 200,000 rare books, 4,000 archive and manuscript collections
Visitor numbers: Up to 5,000 per day

This new library replaces two existing libraries: the Queen Mother Library and Special Libraries and Archives. The QML is to be demolished and was originally designed to cater for 5,000 students, but there are now 15,000 students on campus. SLA is the former location for the storage and research facilities for the collection of manuscripts, archives and rare books In fact Aberdeen University – one of the oldest universities in the world – also has 'one of the finest and rarest collections of books, prints, and manuscripts in existence,' according to its supporters, and these have to be properly conserved.

An international competition was held in 2005 to choose the architects for what was intended to be a building of international status. This attracted over 100 expressions of interest leading to 40 full submissions, from which a shortlist of six entries was made. The winning practice was schmidt/hammer/lassen, for whom libraries have become something of a speciality, with The Royal Danish Library (The 'Black Diamond') in Copenhagen, and libraries in Halmstad and Växjö (both in Sweden) to their credit during the past decade.

From the outside the building is a seven-storey high glazed cube, iridescent, but solid in form and appearance. 'A glittering building with resonances of the North,' the

University claims, no doubt referring to the green, blue and white striation of the glazing and irregular frame. Inside is another matter, with an atrium ('an architectural whirlwind' according to design critic Jonathan Glancey) created by an ascending series of irregular gallery floors reaching to a top skylight which, looking down from above, appear like a set of galleries in a surrealist opera house, and somewhat vertiginous as well. If the effect is dizzying, it is also spectacular and memorable, with each floor unique in its configuration, and, equally importantly, with sight-lines which run from one side to the other, with views to the North Sea to the east, and to the city to the west.

There are seven floors above ground, and two lower ground floors – where manuscripts, archives and rare book collections are kept in a highly controlled environment. The ground floor is largely taken up by a café area, reception desk, public gallery and concourse, while two 'IN' and 'OUT' electronic gates allow registered library users access to the lifts and to the library proper on the lower and upper floors. However, library use is not restricted only to university students, but is available to other members of the public on registration. For the library also sees its mission as making available its great collections and archives to the wider Scottish public for whom Aberdeen University has always enjoyed regional and national importance.

The building is mounted on a plinth and entered through a single entrance (with fully glazed revolving and manual doors) from a gently sloping ceremonial approach from the east which is where the main university campus is located. The external approach is paved with Caithness Stone, which is continued inside and constitutes the floor surface of the library at ground level (as well as the floor surface of the lifts). This is a terrific touch, grounding the library in an ancient stone of the region, and also evoking the reputation of Aberdeen as 'the granite city', where stone has a cultural resonance beyond its material qualities alone.

Thus there are six floors of open access library, with over 1200 study spaces, and hundreds of PCs and iMACs, including 13,000 kilometres of shelving. The atrium space is sensational. Looking upwards one looks through a series of randomly centred soft triangles, each one the balcony area of a new floor. The known problems associated with atria – noise levels, food smells, visual distraction from one floor to the next – are minimal here. As University Librarian, Chris Banks, told me: 'There's a tradition that the higher (or deeper) you go in a library the quieter it should be. We've done it differently. Each floor is designed to quieten down as you move from one side of the building to the other.' Thus the lifts are located to the north side of the building, on each floor, as are the photocopying machines, public access computers and other places where people gather or converse. As one moves across each floor – which are all roughly configured to the same floor-plan – the library shelves increase in density, baffling sound, and lead to a series of quiet spaces and study rooms effectively cut off from the busy areas of movement and congregation.

Although it is a public building, to which outsiders can secure quick registration and entry, it is governed by strong library protocols, into which students and other members are inducted. These range from the practical – 'no food or drink above the ground floor' – to respect for other users, along with induction for all users into understanding the principles of copyright, intellectual property rights, and the dangers of plagiarism (or simply copying material off the Internet). All public areas are Wi-Fi. The interior colour scheme is principally white, grey and black – the books and the people provide the colour, the architects have argued. Each floor is covered by CCTV as back-up for staff security should any problems arise.

The building has been certified as BREEAM Excellent, and incorporates rainwater harvesting for WC flushing; photo voltaic cells on library roof; hybrid ventilation systems, and energy capture from the high levels of glazing, along with high levels of natural light from the atrium roof-light.

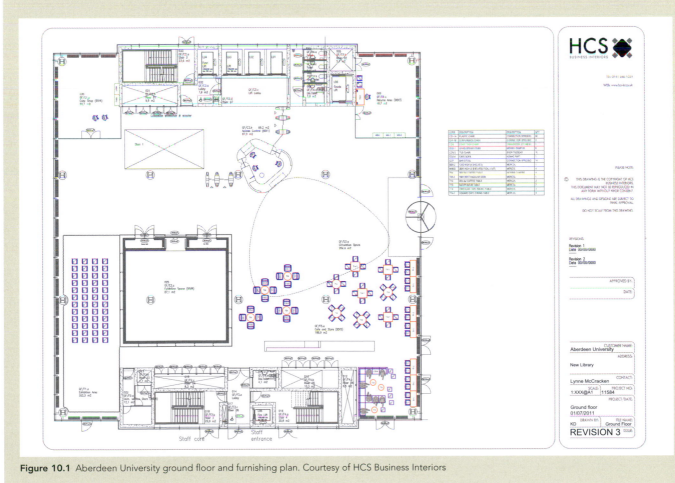

Figure 10.1 Aberdeen University ground floor and furnishing plan. Courtesy of HCS Business Interiors

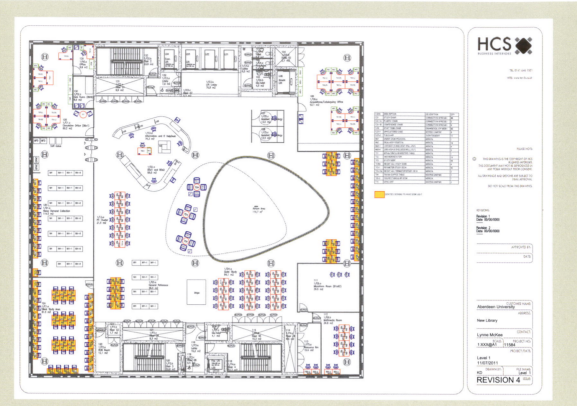

Figure 10.2 Aberdeen University first floor and furnishing plan. Courtesy of HCS Business Interiors

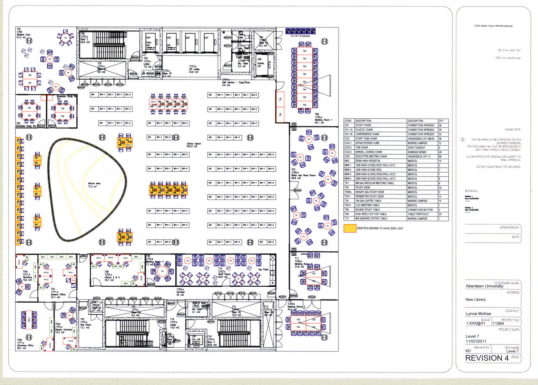

Figure 10.3 Aberdeen University seventh floor and furnishing plan. Courtesy of HCS Business Interiors

Figure 10.4 Aberdeen University Library by schmidt/hammer/lassen, opened in 2011

Figure 10.5 Main raised plaza entrance to Aberdeen University Library, reflecting older buidlings

Figure 10.6 Sculptural atrium balconies and library areas at Aberdeen University Library

Kings Norton Library: Cranfield University

Opened: 1992
Client: Cranfield University
Architect: Foster + Partners
Project description: university research library
Library size: 3,400 square metres
Cost: £7.5 million

Cranfield University (the former College of Aeronautics) is a post-graduate, research-based university specialising in aerospace and defence technology, engineering, applied science, healthcare and management. The University's Cranfield Campus is located on the perimeter of a still busy airfield in the rural Bedfordshire hinterland of Milton Keynes. The new library was the subject of a feasibility study first begun in 1986 which culminated in a competition won by Sir Norman Foster + Partners. The building was completed in 1992. Overall the library provides 3,400 square metres of floor space, with 266 seating places.

The Kings Norton Library, named after a former Chancellor, is essentially a three-storey glass-walled rectangle in four sections or bays, each given visual form by a distinctive scalloped or vaulted roof which overhangs on all sides to provide an arcade (as well as shading) at the front and sides. The elegant but nevertheless shed-like appearance matches the aircraft hangars close by. The library serves a somewhat sprawling campus made up of former aerodrome buildings and residential quarters, along with a lot of new buildings designed to cope with university expansion over the past four decades. One of the key ambitions of the library brief was to create a meeting place for the rather scattered community of post-graduate students, staff and researchers, and therefore it had to occupy a central position on the site, be easy to find,

enjoyable to use and as accessible for as much of the time as possible. While many students could equally access the material they need to use from personal computers in their rooms in halls of residence, today most choose to use the library as a more supportive and congenial space. In fact it opens from Monday to Friday from 8.30 to midnight, though at weekends opening hours are shorter. At night the building exudes a sense of drama and spectacle, illuminated from within.

The early design included lecture rooms and classrooms on the ground floor, though it was anticipated that later on these might be re-colonised for library storage and related use, and this has now happened. The ground floor also contains a refreshment area, now serviced by vending machines. The first floor is given over to the library proper, featuring open-plan welcome and information desks, self-issue and return book kiosks, and administration services grouped in a very informal manner, and the second, upper, floor is devoted to periodicals and quiet study areas. The building is triple-glazed for sound-proofing against the noise of the adjacent airfield. Central to the design brief was the idea that the library should employ minimal signage, be easy to understand at a glance, be light, open and welcoming. The building is essentially open access to anybody, though the library areas are security-screened at exit points for material taken out without being properly issued. The atmosphere is congenial and unbureaucratic.

On entering the library one enters a full-height atrium, with elegant, wide glass stairs inviting the visitor to see at a glance where everything is and how to get there. The colour scheme is mostly grey, with steel and glass accompaniment, and the interior feels engineered to perfection. It is a very

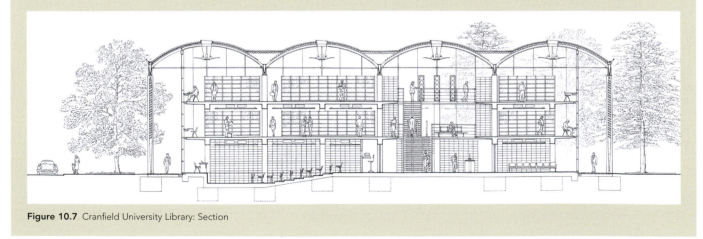

Figure 10.7 Cranfield University Library: Section

calm, beautiful space, and shows no sign of ageing even after twenty years of busy use – which is principally a testament to the quality of the materials used and the elegant simplicity of the design. At many points in between the bookshelves or in the more open areas, it is possible to see out of all four sides of the building, so there is enormous visual transparency to the scheme. Interestingly, a large proportion of the seats for readers are provided by a continuous desk-top which runs round the perimeter of the interior on first and second floors, looking out, with data, phone and power points every 800mm.

One problem which emerged early on was that the decision to allocate the ground floor to lecture theatres and seminar rooms meant that while students or conference attendees were gathering in the atrium to enter the rooms, the noise of their greetings and conversation intruded on library users on the two floors above. Fortunately this had always been designed as a temporary arrangement, and when the ground floor was regained for library purposes the problem disappeared. But it was a salutary lesson in the need to sound-insulate meeting spaces and study spaces in what may be desired as an open-plan setting – particularly those in which a public

staircase is a central feature of the interior. It is also soon evident that the spacing between the horizontal bars of the staircase supports and gallery balconies is wide enough for a child to slip through and would not be allowed in public buildings today, elegant though they certainly are. The figures on this page are reproduced by kind permission of Foster + Partners.

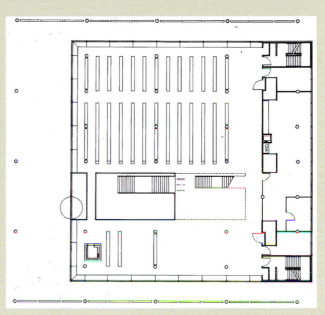

Figure 10.8 Cranfield University Library: Ground floor plan

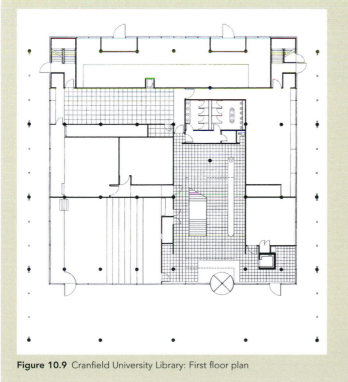

Figure 10.9 Cranfield University Library: First floor plan

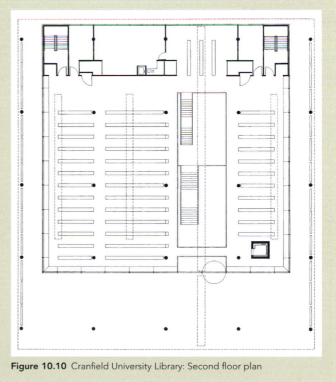

Figure 10.10 Cranfield University Library: Second floor plan

Figure 10.11 Scalloped overhang canopy at Cranfield University Library by Foster + Partners

Figure 10.12 Interior view of library atriums and galleries at Cranfield University Library

Figure 10.13 Library balconies and galleries at Cranfield University Library

University of Sheffield: The Information Commons

Opened: 2007
Client: University of Sheffield
Architect: RMJM
Project description: academic library
Library size: 11,500 square metres
Cost: £24m
Stock: 110,000 volumes
Visitor numbers: 1.5 million per annum

The Information Commons is a new library and information technology building on the University of Sheffield Campus designed by RMJM and opened in 2007. It complements the existing Western Bank Library – also detailed in these case studies – and is intended to provide nearly 1,400 study spaces primarily for undergraduate students. The new building contains a print collection of 110,000 volumes, 550 personal computers and a number of workstations, in a mix of open-plan and closed 'quiet rooms'. It also has 13 group study rooms, and 2 classrooms. On the ground floor adjacent to the entrance hall is a café. Entry is only accessible to those with swipe-cards, and in the foyer is a bank of overhead monitors which detail current vacant study spaces on every floor and in

every room. The building was conceived by – and is operated jointly by – the University Library and the University's IT service.

The IC (as it is called) is a seven-storey building in a rather monumental (indeed, monolithic) and dramatic style, clad in copper and grey terracotta tiles. At first sight this does not look anything like a library, and more like a great engine-room, but once inside the large four-floor central atrium – filled with natural light from side-windows oriented to the north which cannot be seen from the front of the building – is airy, bright, colourful and purposive. The high level of natural lighting in large open-plan spaces allows 'long-distance sight-lines for the majority of study spaces, enabling students to rest eyes during long study sessions.' Also, desks and shelves are served by highly localised task lighting.

The building is primarily constructed of a reinforced concrete frame with lightweight semi-precast floor slabs. The cladding is supported by a steel frame. As the building is sited at a very noisy location, with a busy traffic intersection

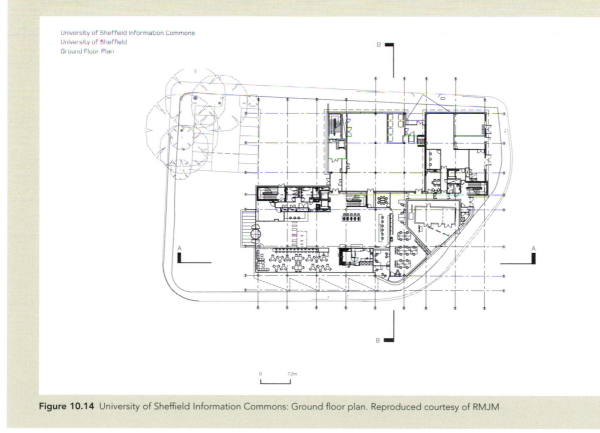

University of Sheffield Information Commons
University of Sheffield
Ground Floor Plan

0   7.2m

Figure 10.14 University of Sheffield Information Commons: Ground floor plan. Reproduced courtesy of RMJM

immediately adjacent, as well as a rapid transit tram system station, natural ventilation could not be considered, and the building is ventilated by chilled or heated air systems distributed through the floor void.

Senior library staff worked with RMJM to develop a typology of study spaces which should be made available in the IC, and ended up with nine distinct categories:

- Open-plan individual study desks (with PC or provision for users' laptops)

- Silent study space with individual study desks

- Open-plan group work tables

- Open-plan group work pods (semi-enclosed spaces)

- Informal soft seating (open plan and silent study)

- Enclosed group study rooms

- Flexi-space places with mobile furniture

- Classroom spaces

- Cybercafé places (wireless and kiosk-type workstations).

Individual study space has been generously designed to provide 4.2 square metres for each user, giving room for laptops, books and papers to be spread out. Shelving was widely spaced at 1.8 m centres to allow wheelchair users to turn in the aisles or pass other users, and shelving height was restricted to five shelves maximum to allow high levels of visibility (and light) across the open-plan floors. The whole building is wireless networked so that students can use laptops or smart phones wherever they are.

Access to the building is offered 24 hours a day, seven days a week with a concierge system operating when dedicated library staff are not at work in the building, which they are from 9am to 9pm weekdays and 9pm to 5pm at weekends. The café is also accessible 24 hours a day, but overnight food and drinks are only available from vending machines. Maximum occupancy is frequently achieved and the building is regarded as a great success not only with students and library managers, but has also won several architectural awards, and is visited by librarians from other parts of the UK and abroad to see how it operates. It has been estimated that the building alone has increased library use on the campus by as much as 50 per cent, confirming that the university library is still a major focal point of student life and learning.

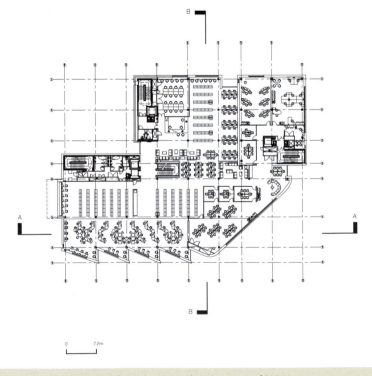

Figure 10.15 University of Sheffield Information Commons: First floor plan. Reproduced courtesy of RMJM

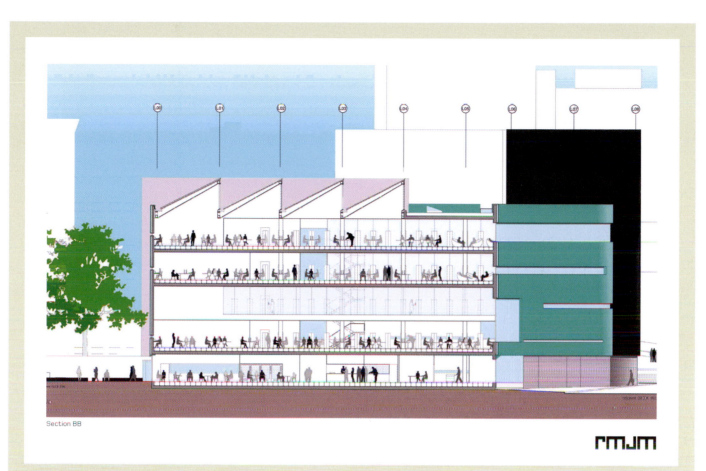

Section BB

Figure 10.16 University of Sheffield Information Commons: Section BB (Reproduced courtesy of RMJM)

Figure 10.17 External view of Sheffield University Information Commons by RMJM, opened in 2007

Figure 10.18 Informal reading room lounge at Sheffield University Information Commons

University of Sheffield: Western Bank Library

Opened: 1959, restored in 2009
Client: University of Sheffield
Architect: Gollins Melvin Ward and Partners, restored by Avanti Architects
Project description: academic library
Library size: 14,000 square metres
Cost of restoration: £3.4 million
Stock: over 1 million items
Visitor numbers: 400,000 per annum

The main university library at Sheffield – now called the Western Bank Library – was opened by poet T.S. Eliot in 1959 (when 75 per cent of the stock was in closed stacks). Designed by architects Gollins Melvin Ward and Partners it was described by Sir Nikolaus Pevsner as 'the best modern building in Sheffield.' This Grade II* listed building has recently been 'de-cluttered' and beautifully restored by Avanti Architects,

revealing just how wonderful the very best of modern movement architecture could be when done properly. It is *luxe, calme et volupté*, and yet cool and serene, as a serious library should be.

The best exterior view is from the rear, where the elegant low-slung building (with four floors of stacks below ground level) sits placidly in beautiful rising parkland, and the simple outline of a glazed rectangular box is clear to see. The main entrance is located in a paved piazza where it now has to compete with other buildings and distractions. Once inside, however, the wide hall and staircases immediately take the visitor into another world, and on the first floor there is the beautifully restored catalogue hall leading to the main reading room – one of 'the largest interiors in the city' according to critic Peter Blundell Jones – with vast windows looking out into the greensward behind.

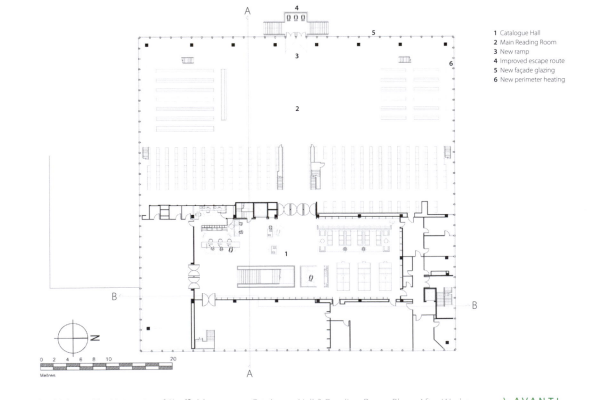

1 Catalogue Hall
2 Main Reading Room
3 New ramp
4 Improved escape route
5 New façade glazing
6 New perimeter heating

Western Bank Library, The University of Sheffield   Catalogue Hall & Reading Room Plan - After Works   AVANTI ARCHITECTS

Figure 10.19 Western Bank Library, The University of Sheffield. Catalogue Hall & Reading Room Plan – After Works. Reproduced with kind permission of Avanti Architects

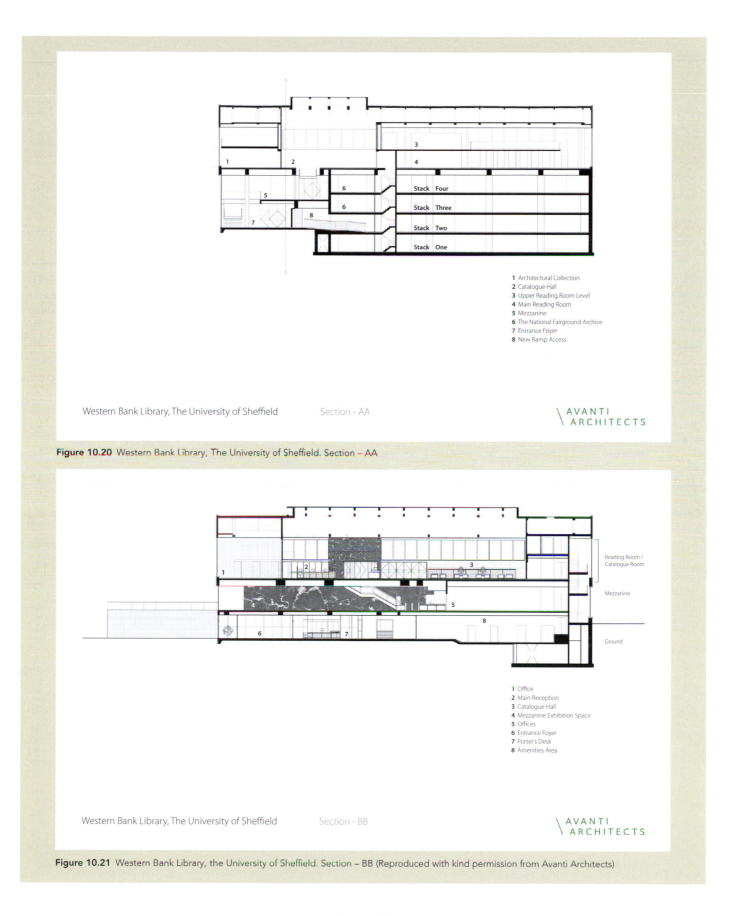

1 Architectural Collection
2 Catalogue Hall
3 Upper Reading Room Level
4 Main Reading Room
5 Mezzanine
6 The National Fairground Archive
7 Entrance Foyer
8 New Ramp Access

Western Bank Library, The University of Sheffield   Section - AA

\AVANTI
\ARCHITECTS

Figure 10.20 Western Bank Library, The University of Sheffield. Section – AA

1 Office
2 Main Reception
3 Catalogue Hall
4 Mezzanine Exhibition Space
5 Offices
6 Entrance Foyer
7 Porter's Desk
8 Amenities Area

Western Bank Library, The University of Sheffield   Section - BB

\AVANTI
\ARCHITECTS

Figure 10.21 Western Bank Library, the University of Sheffield. Section – BB (Reproduced with kind permission from Avanti Architects)

The architect John Allan of Avanti had been a student at the university, so brought a prior knowledge of the building, which he supplemented by extended research into the original plans and drawings. As Peter Blundell Jones has written:

> This led to a 'conservation plan with management guidelines' for both the library and the adjacent Arts Tower. The key conclusion was that the entry sequence had been lost by gradual encroachment of space and clumsy security measures, and therefore the major visual change to the building has been the clearing out of the entry corner, remaking of the mezzanine exhibition gallery and freeing-up of the main staircase. The catalogue hall, now the repository of the map collection and reference books, has had its ceiling restored and rooflights replaced, so daylight is again visible. In rearranging the security and admission arrangements new desks have been made for the librarians, designed by Avanti in a minimalist style that suits the Miesian aesthetic without following it slavishly.

(Jones, 2010: 18)

The environmental credentials of the restoration have been largely secured by the use of double glazing – without changing the visual appearance of the former glazed areas – together with improved lighting (relying on motion sensors to turn off unwanted lights when spaces are not in use), and more effective heating supplied by Sheffield's city district heating network. Library users, including those in wheelchairs, now have direct access to most of the book-stock, and reading conditions in the former basement stacks are much improved.

The Western Bank Library holds over 1 million volumes though specialist academic journals are increasingly available online through university subscription. As a building it possesses a renewed sense of purpose, confirming the view of Avanti Architects' principal, John Allan, that 'adding things rarely improves a building, whereas removing them almost always does'. The restoration was subsequently awarded a Royal Institute of British Architects White Rose Gold Award for Architecture.

Figure 10.22 Park view of Sheffield University Western Bank Library by Gollins Melvin Ward and Partners, restored by Avanti Architects

Figure 10.23 Restored first floor library reception hall at Sheffield Western Bank Library

University of Surrey: Library & Learning Centre

Opened: 2011
Client: University of Surrey
Architect: RMJM
Project description: university library and learning centre
Library size: 4950 square metres addition to existing building of 8308 square metres
Cost: £13.2 million
Stock: 540,000 printed books, 944 print journal subscriptions, 227,400 ebooks, 47,000 ejournal subscriptions

This new 'gold block' building sits tight in a crowded hillside campus and does so very effectively, with ground-floor entrances on opposite sides into a large foyer in which are located a café, bookshop and mini-market. The main library area occupies the first and second floors – the library entrance proper is on the first floor – with administrative offices on the third floor. The campus now serves over 15,000 students, and with the opening of the new building has been able to provide additional study space to cater for increased demand for place. It will be open 24 hours a day for 30 weeks of the year.

Architects RMJM were chosen in competition from a shortlist of five practices, on the basis of an hour-long presentation at which the contenders presented drawings, models and computer-generated images responding to a preliminary design brief. RMJM already had Sheffield University's Information Commons in their portfolio of past academic library projects. The design brief required the new building to achieve a high BREEAM rating, which it does, including a 10 KW photo-voltaic system generating 9,000 KW of renewable electricity per year, reducing carbon footprint and generating income from the government's Feed-In-Tariff (FIT) scheme. The gold exterior is achieved through the use of bronze anodised aluminium, and is both dramatic and uplifting, complementing the yellow brick of much of the surrounding campus buildings, as well as making a reference to the golden angel on the nearby

Guildford Cathedral with which it enjoys some common sight-lines (and was thus a major design constraint – or, perhaps, imperative).

In shape and structure the building is relatively conventional, with lift shaft and glazed stairwell at the centre providing access to all floors in a rectangular floor-plate. However the new library has also had to build bridges to two existing adjacent buildings, no mean feat, and create effective circulation routes connecting all three. Each floor mixes book stacks with a range of study areas and computer suites, thus avoiding a 'call centre' density of computer desks, with additional small breakout areas for private reading in comfortable chairs. There are a number of group study rooms – with floor to ceiling internal glazing – and several larger quiet study suites. In general though sound levels are subdued and the atmosphere is quiet and purposeful. The bold and clear signage was the result of a separate procurement, as was the provision of all the interior furniture and fittings.

All of the stock is RFID compliant, and thus all book issues and returns are done through self-service scanning machines.

Automatic sorting of returned books ensures that stock is back on the shelves quickly. The building is fully wireless enabled, and provides 300 additional study spaces and 180 additional PCs to the number provided previously. The decision to call the new building a library *and* learning centre reflects the more pro-active role of library staff in facilitating and helping students to become independent learners, and so staff in the library can assist those students with language problems, as well as helping Ph.D students work on their doctoral theses.

Interestingly the construction of the building itself became a teaching resource for students studying engineering at the university. The sequencing of construction works had to be meticulously planned in consultation with the client team, so that noise levels and other site disturbances and displacements did not affect the continuing life of the campus, especially at examination times – and this was regarded as a real success in client-constructor co-operation. The bold external articulation gives a real solidity to what internally is a series of discrete, transparent spaces of many shapes and sizes.

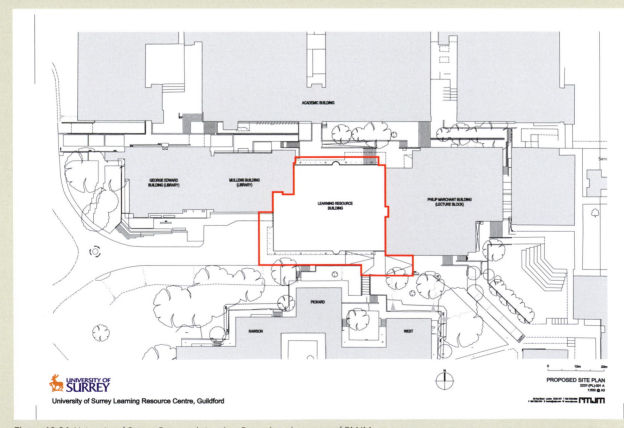

University of Surrey Learning Resource Centre, Guildford

Figure 10.24 University of Surrey: Proposed site plan. Reproduced courtesy of RMJM

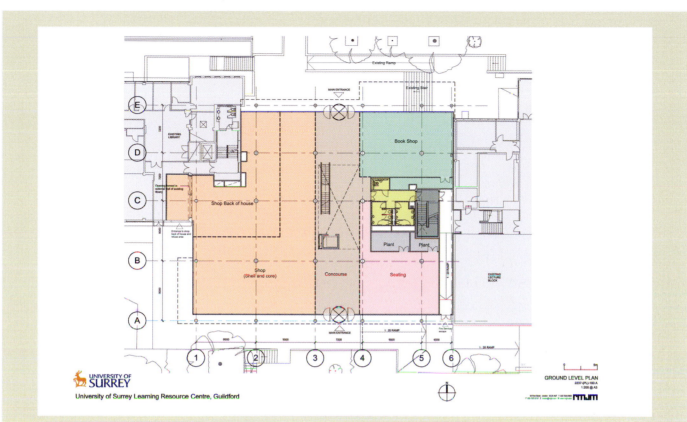

Figure 10.25 University of Surrey: Ground level plan. Reproduced courtesy of RMJM

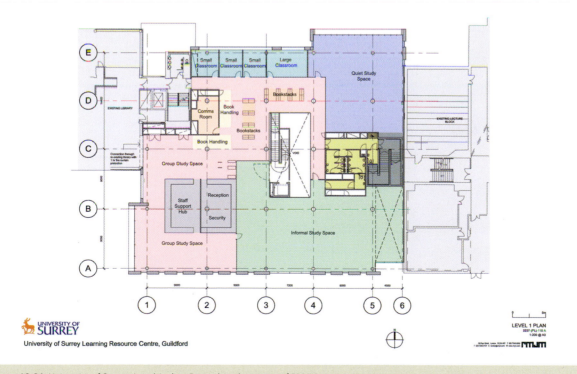

Figure 10.26 University of Surrey: Level 1 plan. Reproduced courtesy of RMJM

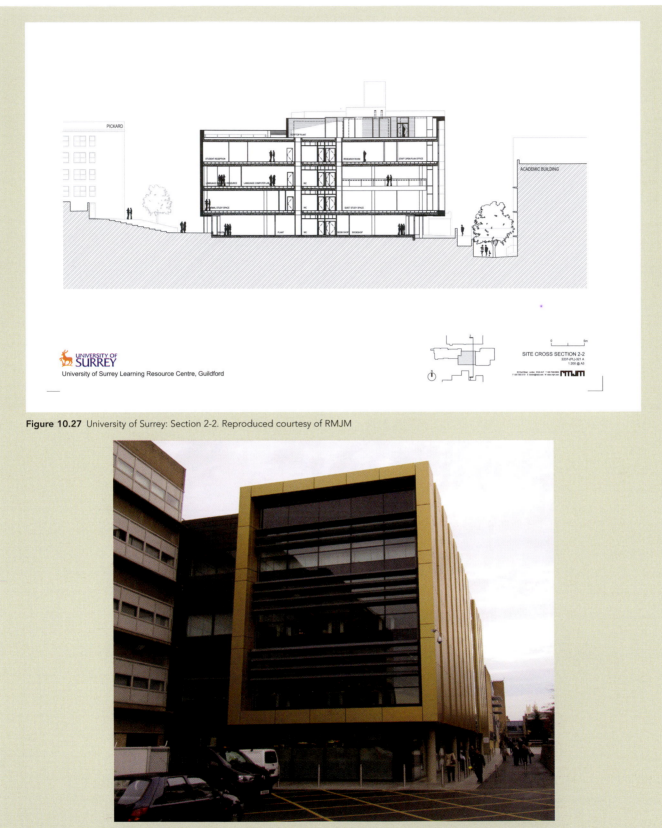

Figure 10.27 University of Surrey: Section 2-2. Reproduced courtesy of RMJM

Figure 10.28 New extension of Surrey University Library and Learning Centre by RMJM

Figure 10.29 Stairwell and study areas at Surrey University Library and Learning Centre

PART 5

Lessons for the future

Walkways, bridges, galleries and light-wells at the new Cardiff Central Library

CHAPTER 11

Lessons from the case studies and post-occupancy evaluation

A post-occupancy evaluation (POE) is a crucial stage in the overall assessment of how a new building fulfils the intentions of those who commissioned it, along with those responsible for its design. Thinking about this well in advance can aid the planning process from the outset. There are particular demands made on public buildings such as libraries – especially in terms of location, approach, public legibility, ease of access and sense of welcome – requiring special attention in the way they are accomplished. Inside, such buildings should provide clear signage and way-finding, expressing the diverse range of spaces and experiences on offer. They should also be self-evidently a place for children and families, offering amenities that support a longer and more enjoyable stay – not just be a drop-in facility. Provision for staff should also be of high-quality and fully integrated into – and of a piece with – the overall design. In turn architects and building managers have a right to expect staff to respect the original design intentions, and not undermine the overall effect by quickly filling the key public areas with clutter, or adding a proliferation of poorly executed signs and notices. An agreement about the post-occupancy maintenance regime and schedule should be part of the hand-over arrangements.

The moment of truth for any new building or refurbishment comes after a period of use, when the successes and failures of design come to the surface, or are revealed through everyday, repetitive use. This is the moment of the POE or post-occupancy evaluation, when the experiences of building users, visitors and the assessment of various engineering, environmental or design professionals come together in a jury verdict, testing Stuart Brand's observation, already cited, that 'All buildings are meeting predictions. All predictions are wrong' (Brand, 1997: 178)

In his standard American work, *Libraries Designed for Users*, Nolan Lushington suggests that any POE should include:

- A tracking study of user behaviour

- A focus group of library users

- A focus group of library staff

- A review of the building by the staff

- Behaviour mapping of seating types and comparative intensity of use

- A review of the building by an independent library consultant (not the consultant who wrote the original program) using the library program and plan review process

- A review of the building by a different architect (Lushington, 2002).

One might also suggest soliciting the views of passers-by as to whether the building adds interest and quality to the immediate townscape, as well as the now highly important evaluation for energy efficiency and other environmental impacts.

The post-occupancy evaluation of a whole building type genre is rare, though in 2002 academic Suzanne Enright undertook a survey of all current forms of evaluation of library buildings in the UK, sadly proving that the exception was the rule: they barely existed (Enright, 2002). Setting out by asking why they 'have been seldom done in a systematic way' she found that too many factors militated against their use, including inertia, lack of 'post-production' funds to carry them out, along with a reluctance to admit that the project might have got some, possibly a lot, of things wrong. Even The British Library had not then undertaken any POE, despite being the largest library building project ever. Nevertheless Enright applauds the various award schemes which apply to library design (The Library Association's Public Library Buildings Award, SCONUL Library Design Award), as well as architectural awards in general. When Peckham Library won the Stirling Prize in 2000, this was a major boost to library architecture, creating waves of public interest which continue to this day.

A good example of building on success has been evident at the Whitechapel Idea Store. Designed to acclaim by Adjaye Associates and opened in 2005, it was immediately popular and heavily used, so much so that over time it became clear that some re-adjustments to circulation patterns, entrances and exits, could only enhance the original vision. This was undertaken by architects and designers, mackenzie wheeler, in 2009 and is now in process. Regular reviews of how buildings are working or meeting changing demands has to be integral to the library service. This is 'how buildings learn'.

Enright suggests that post-occupancy evaluations can be used to:

- Introduce a culture of feedback and dissemination of expertise

- Identify and quantify value for money projects and cost-effectiveness

- Introduce appropriate record management and provide technical information

- Identify and quantify the need to improve building services and controls and evaluate performance issues such as energy performance

- Help address occupant dissatisfaction, thus contributing to better operation and management of the building

- Assess current occupancy in advance of any further alteration, refurbishment or new construction (Enright, 2002: 41).

The recent CABE Briefing (2008b) on Sure Start children's centres provides useful insight into some common problems, which might easily apply to new public libraries, especially those seeking to be family-friendly. That report included as the major areas of concern:

- Lack of external identity, poor approach and signage

- Insufficient storage throughout – with special problems being found with buggy storage and storage for flexible community spaces

- Poor quality spaces for staff (including community and training rooms)

- Absence of measures to make the building environmentally sustainable

- Excessive noise from hard surfaces

- Low rating for environmental comfort: bad thermal performance or conversely overheating and lack of cross-ventilation.

CABE's 2003 report on *Creating Excellent Buildings* concluded with a list of 'watch points' which signalled problems ahead if not addressed. In my experience the following are the ones which seem most to have occurred in recent library design and construction:

- Insufficient attention to the local context

- Insufficient site supervision on client's behalf

- Fit out and design poorly integrated, leading, for example, to inefficient use of space

- 'Behind the scenes' spaces overlooked, e.g. inadequate staff areas.

From the case studies which illustrate this book emerge a list of elements which characterise both the most successful new library buildings (principally in the UK), as well as highlighting those very same elements as areas where inattention to detail can cause problems in the years to come.

FIFTEEN QUESTIONS

It is important therefore to ask beforehand – and check during construction and post-occupancy evaluation – whether the following questions have been addressed. These are very general, and not all of them by any means peculiar to library buildings. But they help focus on the overall public effect of a completed project, and take account of the concerns of staff, users, managers, revenue budget-holders, and the wider public interest. For in the end, architecture is the most public of arts, and possesses the singular ability to inspire people and add something lasting to the quality of civic life, but, very occasionally, can fail to work any kind of magic at all, remaining earth-bound and utilitarian, and, at worst, an object of public and political regret.

Figure 11.1 Corner prow of Flushing Library, New York (Photo: Nick Darton)

Figure 11.2 Corner prow of Bournemouth Library providing a bold end-stop to the urban edge

Figure 11.3 The library at night: Barking Learning Centre (Library & Art Gallery)

Townscape

Does this new building or larger development add character and interest to the existing townscape, in the same way that traditional library architecture often achieved, creating a familiar and much-loved landmark? Can the library or library element be recognised as such by its design or the way it announces itself to the street? This is particularly true of those libraries which occupy corner sites – such as in Bournemouth, Canada Water, Dagenham, Newcastle, as well as in Flushing, New York – where buildings need to provide a focal point and strong visual presence to adjacent streets and street junctions.

The library at night

During winter months libraries will be open well into the hours of darkness, providing opportunities for adding light, warmth and colour to the street, becoming a beacon (literal as well as metaphorical) in the town or city. Has the library been designed to create this night-time effect? Some years ago the conversion of a utilities showroom in Lewisham into a public library was greatly enhanced by commissioning an artist to create a public lighting scheme for the building, which created a memorable block of colour at night.

Figure 11.4 The library at night: The Bridge Arts Centre, Easterhouse, Glasgow (Photo: Andrew Lee)

Figure 11.5 Lewisham Library at night

On the street or set-back?

The Idea Store in Whitechapel, like Rotterdam' great central library, is embedded in the life of the main street market, which surrounds these buildings like a crowded cathedral square. In Newcastle the ground-floor layout consciously continues the desire lines and street patterns of the adjacent area, thus continuing the public space network of the city. On the other hand, the library in March, Cambridgeshire, has taken advantage of an off-street site to create a welcoming public garden approach, which adds to a particular sense of escaping from the noise and bustle of the High Street to a calmer place. What is the intended relation of the library building to the life of the street – continuation or counterpoint?

Finding the door

Traditional library architecture often began with a building on a plinth or with the ground floor raised above street level, and an impressive flight of public stairs leading to a grand entrance. Today's libraries mostly continue the street level, which can create problems for some people in identifying the entrance doors, especially wholly glazed doors in a predominantly glazed building, such as are found in the design for the C.L.R. James Library at Dalston, or at Boscombe where neither the architecture nor signage help distinguish between entrance and exit. What has also been lost in this transition – which is wholly understandable in terms of easy physical access and the wider cause of urban democracy – has been the idea of the library steps or vestibule as a public

Figure 11.6 The Whitechapel Idea Store is firmly rooted in the street life of the busy market area

meeting place, as was famously the case at New York Public Library and in Birmingham's 1960s Central Library. For climate reasons, the entrance to the Jaume Fuster Library in Barcelona is contained within an overhanging canopy providing shade, as it is at Dagenham, though for different reasons, and where the overhang clearly marks the entrance, and is also used to boldly announce that this is the DAGENHAM LIBRARY. The new library in Cirencester does so similarly. What thought has been given to the way the library entrance announces itself to the street?

Libraries above ground floor

In a number of new libraries, the ground floor – predominantly a double-height space or even grander – acts principally as a foyer, information centre, meeting place and café, while the main lending and reading and study areas are located on higher floors. In the small library at Lewes what is essentially a large mezzanine second floor very effectively creates instant visual sight-lines between floors. What is going on in the entrance foyer sets the

tone of the building to its visitors. There are dangers that this can become a non-place, or dead space when quiet or empty, and therefore it is vital that sight-lines and/or sign-posted connections are made to the main library floors above. There are good reasons for locating short-time Internet access computers in these spaces, along with 'quick-read' fiction and non-fiction stock, with staff trained to be pro-active in meeting and greeting users as and when appropriate. It is interesting to see that while in most libraries café provision is located on the ground floor – almost as a street amenity – there are libraries such as those at Swiss Cottage and at the Whitechapel Idea Store, where the café is located at the top, as more of a club space or intimate space (as would be found, for example, in traditional department store cafés, always located on the top floor). How soon on entering is the new visitor told how much is on offer, where it is and how to get there? An unusual design for the public library at Essen in Germany put the library below ground, lit by a glazed roof structure. Both entrance and the view from immediately within are striking.

Figure 11.7 Bold corner presence of C.L.R. James Library, London Borough of Hackney, but entrance poorly evident

Figure 11.8 Confused arrangement and sign-posting of entrance and exit doors at Boscombe Library, Bournemouth

Signage and legibility

A beautifully designed and well-furnished library can be undermined and its effect negated by poor signage and way-finding legibility. All those entering the library for the first time should be able to see clearly what is on offer, especially where the traditional library desk or reception desk has been abandoned in favour of satellite information points. Already the bold entrance foyers and clear sight-lines of several new libraries have been compromised by staff arbitrarily filling the space with poor quality exhibition stands, free-standing tables of assorted types with leaflets or second-hand books for sale, corporate displays, and half-empty wheel-in shelving. In the signing off process there should be some compact between designers and library managers with regard to maintaining the integrity of the design, including a respect for its materials, and especially for

its circulation routes and sight-lines. The POE should not be just about identifying and correcting faults in the original design, but also about ensuring that staff and building managers work to maintain the original design intentions of the new building. Was there a distinct signage strategy for the library, who designed it, and is it being honoured in everyday use?

Shelving and flooring

The range of flooring used in libraries today is extensive, surprisingly so given the acoustic concerns which arise in this kind of public building. In Barcelona terrazzo tiles are used throughout. In Canada Water, parquet flooring is employed at ground level, and multi-coloured carpet tiles on the two upper floors. The Idea Store in Whitechapel uses studded bright red rubberised flooring, while at Clapham Library a very fine grain

Figure 11.9 The amphitheatre stairs outside Birmingham Central Library – a popular meeting place

Figure 11.10 Clear, well sign-posted entrance to the Library, Cirencester, new extension opened in 2008

Figure 11.11 Principal first floor library area at Bournemouth Library

Figure 11.12 Good connectivity between ground and first floors of Lewes Library

Figure 11.13 Bright glazed entrance vestibule to underground library at Essen in Germany

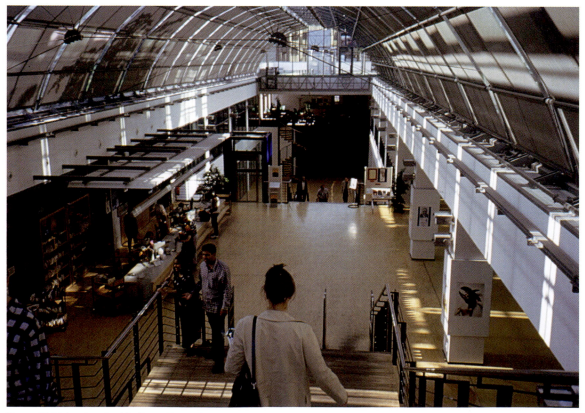

Figure 11.14 Interior of public library, Essen, Germany

Figure 11.15 Oval atrium with ceremonial staircase at Winchester Discovery Centre with excellent signage of shelving

parquet flooring is used, chosen so that its minimal patterning does not create a counter-grid to the wider design. The children's areas in many libraries employ different floor-coverings. Similar considerations apply to the shelving to be used, one of the most important decisions of all, but too often left as an afterthought. Aesthetics, durability and acoustic qualities all have to be balanced in choosing the floor coverings of a heavily used building such as a public library. What are the priorities in the choice of flooring materials and shelving – aesthetic, acoustic, sustainable, long-lasting? At what stage in the design are these vital decisions made?

A learning environment

The public library is as much a learning environment as it is a leisure centre or multi-media lending service. There is much to be said for integrating the book-stock, reading areas, with computer terminals and study spaces, so that learning, leisure and personal development are seen as a continuous and related set of activities (with one set of activities setting the tone for the other). The addition of study suites, seminar rooms, and homework centres, all add to this mix, though they also carry dangers of spatial compartmentalisation. How best to integrate browsing, reading, quiet study and computer use? When is a library side-room open or closed, available for public or private use, and how can other library users tell?

A meeting place (with coffee)

Libraries are now meeting places as well as study spaces and book-borrowing services. When users are asked what ancillary facilities they want to see in a new library, toilets and coffee shops are high priorities. The library café is now almost a distinctive genre of urban space, combining as it does proximity to reading and study, while offering a chance to meet fellow library users. Obviously a critical mass of users is needed to

Figure 11.16 Group Study Room at Surrey University Library: maximum transparency

Figure 11.17 Forest Gate interior

sustain a coffee bar commercially, and this can be a problem in some places. What does not work, however, is to substitute café space with vending machines, reducing the library to a filling station or a sports centre, another last redoubt of absentee municipal provision at its worst. Even a simple domestic coffee machine, as is found in some small community libraries, is preferable to a vending machine. It is clear at the Aberdeen and Surrey university campuses that the library café is a crucial meeting place both during the day and at night, and acts as a common ground for students from many disciplines, thus helping overcome the compartmentalisation of subject areas. The positioning of café facilities is a key decision in the library plan: at what stage in the design is it being considered as a substantive concern?

Quiet to loud (and back again)

Although traditionally places of silent reading, modern libraries also serve many other functions today, and careful design can be used to ensure that different spaces allow different sound levels without disturbing adjacent areas. Cafés, meeting rooms, children's areas, photocopier machines and computer suites are all gathering places where people need to talk and the spatial configuration of the library should be designed accordingly. This is especially the case where atria, light-wells or open voids are used in the design, increasing sight-lines and visual connectivity, but also potentially allowing sound to travel – or even become amplified – from one part of the building to another. Thus the new library should not only provide a range of different spaces but also a range of different library 'experiences', both individual and collective, private and sociable, educational and recreational. What is the best acoustic advice available to add into these problems of good and bad adjacencies?

Colour schemes and interior design

Post-modern architecture celebrated colour and shape to an almost exaggerated degree, and some library architects remain committed to creating a more playful effect in public buildings, none more especially than in the children's area. Internal steel columns no longer look intrusive if painted a bright red or cobalt blue, and lime green and pink armchairs can create a sense of luxury and fun for a younger generation who have grown up in a multi-media, consumer world of retailing and advertising. As several architects interviewed for this study observed, however, the books themselves and the people reading them provide plenty of colour – sometimes enough. They see the colour palette of interior design as providing a neutral setting, with minor outbursts of colour in the free-standing furniture. Who is making the key decisions about the colour scheme, and on what grounds?

Children should love libraries

The public library is a special place for children, and the modern library is becoming an even more important place for teenagers and young people. This makes it essential that the whole library should be child-friendly, not just the children's section. Today's children are often as media-savvy and computer-literate as the library staff themselves, and for them the whole building and its facilities – not just the children's section – should provide that special place in the city where they are fully enfranchised citizens and participants in life. In the best of the new libraries this is already evident, providing hope for the future that the public library remains a familiar but special place in an ever-changing and commercialised world. Are the needs of children and young people central to the library design brief, and who is representing their interests at the design stage?

Views out to the world

The classic design of the Victorian or Edwardian public library suggested entry into a closed world, and of separation from the life of the street and commerce. High shelves and high windows effectively shielded those inside from the outside world and thus became a place of retreat or sanctuary (including for some the possibility of a good sleep in a safe berth). But this was true of much public architecture until the arrival of new materials and a modernist aesthetic which promoted transparency and the interplay between indoor and outdoor spaces. The wonderful modernist circular library at Ewell in Surrey allows views onto parkland in most directions, including attractive terracing for sitting outside for those library users who so wish. Already a favourite space of library users are the window armchairs at the Canada Water Library, overlooking the ruffled and glinting waters of the former docks. It is a great thing for a town or city at night for passers-by to see people reading and studying in large numbers in a public space which they are also entitled to use. How can the need for strong visual connections between the library interior and the world outside be enhanced, without creating a goldfish bowl effect, or compromising a sense of sanctuary?

Quality of staff provision

The new model library is now managed with different objectives and outcomes in mind to the traditional library, and staff roles have also had to change, which has not always been a comfortable process. Library staff are no longer 'behind the desk' but often 'on the shop-floor', being more pro-active in dealing with users, young and old. The need for staff to retire somewhere quiet during tea-breaks and lunch-breaks is important, but in the

Figure 11.18 Café at the Library, Huntingdon Library, Cambridgeshire

Figure 11.19 Café and browsing area at Newcastle Central Library

Figure 11.20 Ground floor foyer and café area at Aberdeen University Library

past this has often been in spaces which have been improvised to provide tea-making and rest-room facilities, sometimes in inappropriate rooms and redundant stock-rooms. If library staff are to be proud of the new buildings they are now working in, then those spaces dedicated to their own working and resting conditions should share the same quality of design as the rest of the building. How much are staff needs taken into account in the design process, and how are their views represented?

Maintenance and cleaning

The post-occupancy evaluation should be a two-way process. Though most attention will be paid to whether the intentions of the architects and designers have been realised – and the degree to which these have fulfilled the requirements of the client and the building's users – in turn architects have a right to ask that their design ambitions are respected in the everyday management and maintenance of the building and its interior. In the case of some libraries visited, the bold and impressive effects achieved in design have already been seriously compromised by poor maintenance, inappropriate and amateurish signage, and the cluttering up of public spaces with random items of furniture, shelving, display cabinets and display stands, and other moveable items of kit. This invariably undermines the purpose of what the new building was intended to achieve: a dignified and modern setting that is memorable and a pleasure to use. Is there an agreement which commits the library maintenance and management regime to respecting the original architectural and design vision, or which supports a continuing relationship between architects and clients for a reasonable period after handover?

Figure 11.21 Informal meeting area for library users and local voluntary groups at The Bridge Arts Centre, Easterhouse, Glasgow

Figure 11.22 Colour can create a sense of luxury and fun: Cardiff Central Library

Figure 11.23 Transparency and interplay between indoor and outdoor spaces at Norwich Forum Library

Figure 11.24 Restored spiral staircase at Swiss Cottage Library

Figure 11.25 Open-plan and approachable staff area at Cranfield University Library

CHAPTER 12

Twenty-first century libraries: changing forms, changing functions

Do libraries have a future? There is no doubt they do, as the current wave of library-building across the world confirms. However, new designs for libraries will be much more site-specific in their future configurations, and their programme will be adapted to meet local social and demographic circumstances, along with the likelihood of more shared or co-located facilities and funding partners. In the USA the grand city library has become a focal point of urban renewal, and the same is true in the UK. These new libraries are no longer service-stations but destination buildings in their own right, and require architectural imagination to succeed. In an otherwise highly commercialised urban centre, the public library acts as a beacon of civility and will be increasingly valued as such.

Today people question whether libraries still have a future. This is the wrong question. More pertinent is to ask what kind of libraries are needed in tomorrow's world. This is the view of Stuart Hill, one of the project architects for schmidt/hammer/lassen's Aberdeen University Library, who has phrased the issue thus: 'One of the questions we were asked before we finalised the design was: why build a new library at all in this day and age? The answer is: we've been helping to build a new type of library.'

The days of the Carnegie and Passmore Edwards Free Public Libraries, when it was envisaged that every town should have at least one public library and that they would most likely be built to the same design and scale, irrespective of local need or particularities of interest, are gone. So too are the social and political conditions of post-war British local government, where every elected councillor wanted a library in his or her own electoral ward as a matter of right. The branch or community library is, as we have seen, in retreat. After a century of expansion during which a typical London borough or

medium-sized town in the UK might provide up to 20 or more branch libraries in addition to a central library, these are times of contraction or rationalisation. Even so, it is important to remember that since 1964 the provision of a 'comprehensive and efficient' library service has been – and remains – a local authority obligation imposed by parliament. It is also still the case that, as library historian Alistair Black has pointed out, there are three times as many public libraries in the UK as there are McDonald's food outlets. This public network remains at the heart of Britain's cultural infrastructure.

The reasons for the slimming down of a number of local authority branch networks are not all spurious. Book loans are down, visitor figures in many branch libraries are in decline, the Internet and e-books are providing a home-based, downloaded alternative to carrying and fetching real books from a distant building. What is being lost, however, is the small community library as a meeting place, particularly for those with young children, or the elderly, for whom frequent visits to their local library are combined with sometimes daily shopping trips by foot or on public transport as a way of keeping in touch with the world. For such reasons, in some areas, rather than closing small branch libraries, local authorities are handing them over to management by a community trust, or some such other not-for-profit arrangement, in which volunteer help is likely to play a significant role.

Yet there is also a counter-movement at work, and has been for some time, proclaiming the need for a renewed civic culture to arrest the drift to a wholly individualised, retail-based and digitised urbanity. Might there be more to life than shopping? Can we envisage or allow a world without libraries? Bob Usherwood (2007) cites the dystopian novelist, J.G. Ballard, on this matter, when Ballard describes a fictionalised modern London development in his 2006 novel, *Kingdom Come*, as,

> a place where it was impossible to borrow a book, attend a concert, say a prayer, consult a parish register or give to charity. In short, the town was an end state of consumerism.

There are already places like this in Britain unfortunately, especially in large new residential developments or town extensions, many devoid of any educational or cultural infrastructure, or even viable public transport connections. People are now realising, with some trepidation, that the public goods which David Marquand wrote about so eloquently, and whose views were cited at the beginning of this book, are under grave threat from the omnipresent cult of marketisation, now embraced by the main political parties at national level. This counter-movement at local level takes the form of the commissioning of new museums, new public spaces and, of course, new public libraries – all designed to restore balance to town centre life, providing amenities and facilities which cater for everybody, irrespective of wealth or lifestyle.

Shannon Mattern has already pointed out how it is the public library which holds centre-stage in programmes of urban renewal in the USA today, and the same is now true in Britain. But these new libraries are no longer financed and constructed to a pre-determined pattern. In almost all of the case studies provided in this book, it has been a bespoke programme of fund-raising, partnership-working and negotiated design which has been undertaken, so that every library is different, in scale, shape, design and programme, all tailored to a specific set of local circumstances and conditions, but each seeking to occupy a special place in the twenty-first century townscape. These are more in the 'long life, loose fit' architectural tradition: flexible spaces that can accommodate change as well as a widening variety of activities – unlike the formally arranged Victorian library with its strictly prescribed spaces and activities.

As such they are becoming 'destination buildings': places attractive in their own right, where visitors can browse, have a coffee, enjoy a talk by a visiting writer or book illustrator, take children, or spend hours in the family history archive. They are places to visit speculatively, which was not always the case with the formal libraries of the past. Within such terms the public library becomes a 'third place', somewhere free and open to all, between home and work, providing a breathing space in the modern urban terrain. Non-commercial and non-judgmental, public libraries are going to become even more important in the future as more people live alone, whether by choice or demographic circumstance. In the transition, in Morten Schmidt's phrase, 'from collection to connection', libraries are negotiating a new role in society. Schmidt has also enjoined librarians to ensure that every visit must not be a repetitive experience but a new experience, and here the skills of management and programming are vital, now that the spaces have been loosened up.

They are also buildings which embody public values in the way that Dutch architect Wiel Arets described: a place where one can be a private individual in a collective setting, combining the best of both worlds. It is important, furthermore, to remember that 'there is no typical library user any more', if there ever actually was. The conventional mythologies about libraries – as either settings for the leavening of working class life and culture, or as redoubts of the aspiring middle class and their children – are today redundant. They celebrate and enable individual choice and personal development within the context of a wider public good. It is surely right that libraries embrace the value of cultural pluralism, offering both the popular and the specialist texts, genre fiction as well as avant-garde literature, Hollywood films as well as wildlife documentaries. Remember, too, that the age of the book is not over. Far from it. According to Nielsen Books in the UK, 'The number of titles published over the last 10 years has grown steadily with a peak in 2009.' In 2011, 149,800 different titles were published in Britain, according to the company which specialises in publishing statistics (Nielsen, 2012). Most of these will find their way into libraries, and library users will find their way to them, by design or accident. This is the historic rendezvous of reader and writer in the serendipitous world of library browsing.

THE ARCHITECTURE OF DEMOCRACY

Has this anything to do with architecture? Surely it does. Good design embodies values above and beyond aesthetics or social function. A low-ceilinged room, harshly lit by fluorescent lighting, and containing row upon row of cheap steel shelving jammed tight with books, effectively denies the library user or staff member status or respect. This is welfare architecture and while cheap – though bad design is not necessarily cheaper – such a strategy is counter-productive. Bold, welcoming design can bring in people who have never thought of using libraries before, sometimes put off by the slightly intimidating institutional appearance of some library buildings. A recent national survey of non-users of libraries concluded that, 'For non-users, negative perceptions of libraries are fairly entrenched and there is a strong sense that libraries "are not for me"' (MLA, 2010b).

We know, however, that attractive buildings can win over hearts and minds. Architecture has the power to alter perceptions, sometimes almost effortlessly so. Yet it also needs to support the cultural values embodied in what public libraries offer to the world, historically as well as now. Central to this ideal is the concept of the library building as a place and a space for all, embodying a belief in the power of knowledge and education to allow individual capacities and opportunities to flourish, free of restriction and impartially provided.

Nowhere in my experience was this unique quality of the public library more evident than in Northern Ireland in the 1990s. It was the one institution that was above sectarian, political or religious affiliations, and open to all – and it was valued and used as such. This impartial ethos is still at work, even in the quietest of towns and cities, as much as it has been in war zones. As we have seen throughout history, attacks on library buildings and their contents are seen as attacks on the very essence of what stops societies descending into intolerance and communitarian division.

So we should take heart from the fact that many of the new libraries discussed in this book have been designed by some of the most inventive architectural practices today. The public library is moving into a new era of bespoke and original design, and has become a building type that many architects and designers aspire to work on, as it becomes the icon of a new kind of setting for civic democracy and public value. The new library is no longer modelled on prototypes taken from a standard neo-Gothic pattern book, nor is it just one element amongst many in 'design-and-build' developer-led regeneration programmes. It is *sui generis*, it has to create a sense of occasion, and it has to be adaptable in order to survive an unknown cultural future. Though many elements of these new buildings are familiar to type, they have been interpreted in new ways: the inviting public entrance, the circular reading room, the study carrels and quiet areas, the children's library, the high ceilings and the clerestory windows, the light-wells and roof-lanterns. All of these established library elements can still be detected in new configurations. When interviewed, architects Christophe Egret and Piers Gough both mentioned to me Asplund's great Stockholm City Library as being an inspiration for themselves and for all those interested in

library design, possibly for all time. And the same may be also said of Aalto's Viipuri Library.

The energetic and utopian designs in the 1960s for Swiss Cottage Library, by Sir Basil Spence, or Bourne Hall Library by A.G. Sheppard Fidler and Associates have not only lasted, but still feel generous and gracious inside, and convey a very strong sense of the power of the library building to change lives, and represent some of the brightest, unalloyed hopes of modernism. The architect's vision should be based on the very principle that space is an agent of change. The quality of space directly affects the experience and aspirations of its users. Library space is particularly important in this regard. It also allows people to feel that they are connected to a wider polis or democratic community, irrespective of their individual circumstances.

For young people this is especially important. Growing up in a consumer society, where lifestyles and social connections are shaped by brands and on-line social networks, rather than traditional political or cultural affiliations, public libraries are places where an older social ethos survives. What is encouraging about the new libraries, wherever they are being built, is that they have become gathering places for young people – places where a new generation can find a respect and an attention often denied them elsewhere in the public domain. Even so, young people live in a culture of fast and constant change, and the library programme has to keep up with technological and cultural innovation. Many of them are directly engaged in some form of further or higher education, or are working for themselves in the cultural industries, where keeping in touch with news and information networks is vital. In the modern city learning is now a moveable feast, and it is quite astonishing sometimes to see a library full of young people at their laptops, or at the banks of PCs provided, wholly absorbed in their own virtual worlds. They may be reading books, studying online, watching television or listening to music, but the cultural resources available to them are wider than those accessible to any generation before.

Penny-pinching politicians also need to be constantly reminded that public libraries are also places of work. More and more of the young people working at the PCs or on their laptops in today's academic and public libraries are adding value to society through their studies or productive and creative endeavours. For many writers, poets, philosophers, engineers, web-designers, bloggers, fashion-designers, musicians and artists, the public library is now 'the office' where they check-in daily to keep up with things and escape the confines of the private study or shared house.

What is undeniable is that for young people, architecture and design figure large in their lives. All the electronic devices they use have been designed with style and precision, as have the clothes they wear, the shops they frequent, the films they watch and the magazines they read. Their visual world is saturated with design. Today's generation have grown up in an era of consumer wealth, and are impatient with municipalism and functionalism: they are semiologists *avant la lettre*. They are walking style critics and want to visit or inhabit buildings which provide status and a sense of glamour to their users.

In this overview of new libraries, what has come across quite clearly is the renewed architectural interest in this most singular and inclusive of public buildings, which has endured through many different historical upheavals and social catastrophes, and yet which remains an abiding symbol of civility and the democratic intellect. Whether our nineteenth century forebears would recognise these twenty-first century libraries at first sight may be questionable – but once inside they would surely feel recognisably at home. The outside world is left behind and a space is created inside that is familiar across the ages – a combination of books, tables and chairs, private and public areas, all imbued with a general atmosphere of individual endeavour. The world inside the library has changed much less than the world outside it. Which is why the architect has so much to cherish, develop and re-interpret rather than invent anew. This is the challenge of library design in the twenty-first century.

Bibliography

Architectural Review (1998), 'Libraries', Volume CCIII, No 1216, June.

Arets, Wiel (2005), *Living Library*, Prestel, Munich & London.

Báez, Fernando (2008), *A Universal History of the Destruction of Books*, translated by Alfred MacAdam, Atlas & Co, New York.

Barcelona (2010) *The Futures of the Public Library*. Available online: http://elsfutursdelabibliotecapublica.wordpress.com

Battles, Matthew (2003), *Library: An Unquiet History*, Heinemann, London.

Bell, Leonie (2008), *Gareth Hoskins Architects 0–10 Years*, The Lighthouse Architecture Series, Glasgow.

Bevan, Robert (2006), *The Destruction of Memory: Architecture at War*, Reaktion Books, London.

Bing, Jon (2009), 'Does a library need a building?', *Scandinavian Public Library Quarterly*, 42(4), 16–17.

Black, Alistair (2000), *The Public Library in Britain 1914–2000*, The British Library, London.

Black, Alistair (2011a), '"New beauties": the design of British public library buildings in the 1960s' in *Library Design: From Past to Present, Library Trends*, edited by Alistair Black and Nan Dahlkild, 60(1), 71–111.

Black, Alistair (2011b), '"We don't do public libraries like we used to": attitudes to public library buildings in the UK at the start of the 21st century', *Journal of Librarianship and Information Sciences*, 43(1), 30–45.

Black, Alistair and Dahlkild, Nan (eds) (2011), *Library Design: From Past to Present, Library Trends*, 60(1), Summer, Illinois.

Black, Alistair, Pepper, Simon and Bagshaw, Kaye (2009), *Books, Buildings and Social Engineering: Early Public Libraries in Britain from Past to Present*, Ashgate, Farnham, Surrey.

Blagden, John (1994), 'Building for the future – Cranfield's new library', *New Library World*, 95(1111), 15–24.

Boddy, Trevor (2006), 'The library and the city', *The Architectural Review*, June, 44.

Bradbury, Dominic (2003), 'Read all about it', *Telegraph Magazine*, 16 March.

Brand, Stewart (1997), *How Buildings Learn*, Orion Books, London.

Brawne, Michael (ed.) (1997), *Library Builders*, Academy Editions, London.

Bryson, Jared, Usherwood, Bob and Proctor, Richard (2003), *Libraries Must Also Be Buildings? New Library Impact Study*, CPLIS, University of Sheffield.

CABE (2003), *Creating Excellent Buildings: A Guide for Clients*, CABE, London.

CABE & Resource (2003), *Better Public Libraries*, CABE, London.

CABE (2008a), *Inclusion by Design: Equality, Diversity and the Built Environment*, CABE, London.

CABE (2008b), *Sure Start Children's Centres: A Post-Occupancy Evalution*, CABE, London.

CABE (2010), *Liverpool Central Library: Design Review*. Available online: www.cabe.org.uk/design-review/liverpool-central-library

CABE & RIBA (2004), *21st Century Libraries: Changing Forms, Changing Futures*, CABE, London.

Clark, Jonathan (2009), 'Save the Lit & Phil', *Times Literary Supplement*, 6 March.

Cleef, Connie van (1999), 'Book bunker', *Architectural Review*, March, 120–214.

Coenen, Jo (2002), *Housing the Book: 7 Libraries by Jo Coenen*, Aedes, Berlin.

Cohn, David (2011), 'The death of the icon', *The Architectural Review*, November, 30–31.

Darnton, Robert (2012), 'In defense of the New York Public Library', *The New York Review of Books*, June 7.

Davey, Peter (1998), 'Malmo masterpieve – design of Malmo city library', *The Architectural Review*, June, 52–58.

DCMS (2010) *The Modernisation Review of Public Libraries: A Policy Statement*, Department of Culture, Media & Sport, London.

De Botton, Alain (2007), *The Architecture of Happiness*, Penguin Books, London.

DETR & CABE (2000), *By Design: Urban design in the Planning System – Towards Better Practice*. Available online: www.communities.gov.uk/publications/planningandbuilding/bydesignurban

Dewe, Michael (2006), *Planning Public Library Buildings*, Ashgate, Aldershot.

Edwards, Brian (2009) *Libraries and Learning Resource Centres*, Architectural Press, Oxford.

Edwards, Brian (2011), 'Sustainability as a driving force in contemporary library design' in *Library Trends: Library Design: From Past to Present*, 60(1), 190–214.

Egret, Christophe (2011), 'The heart of the matter', *RIBA Journal*, November, 55–56.

Enright, Suzanne (2002), 'Post-occupancy evaluation of UK library building projects: some examples of current activity', in *Liber Quarterly*, 12(1), 26–45.

Evans, Dean (2011), *Funding the Ladder: The Passmore Edwards Legacy*, Francis Boutle, London.

Evans, Graeme (2001), *Cultural Planning: An Urban Renaissance?*, Routledge, London.

Ezard, John (2003), 'Buy lattes and get online at Britain's first idea store', *The Guardian*, 15 February.

Glancey, Jonathan (2005), 'Sweet and lowdown', *The Guardian*, 28 February.

Glancey, Jonathan (2012), 'Swirl power: Aberdeen's new £57m university library', *The Guardian*, 8 January.

Glaeser, Edward (2011), *The Triumph of the City*, Macmillan, London.

Greenhalgh, Liz and Worpole, Ken, with Landry, Charles (1995), *Libraries in a World of Cultural Change*, UCL Press, London.

Gregory, Rob (2006), 'Between the lines', *The Architectural Review*, June, 56–63.

Hackett, Regina (2004), 'Cool house: a guide to Seattle Central Library', *Seattle Post-Intelligencer*, 28 May, Seattle.

Harrison, Dean (ed.) (1995), *Library Buildings in the United Kingdom 1990–1994*, Library Services Ltd., London.

Hodge, Margaret (2010), 'A vision for public libraries', *The Modernisation Review of Public Libraries: A Policy Statement*, Department of Media, Culture & Sport, London.

Hopkinson, Matthew (2011), 'The British high street: RIP', *The Guardian*, 22 January.

Jones, Peter Blundell (1979), 'State Library, Berlin', *Architectural Review*, June, 330–341.

Jones, Peter Blundell (1997), *Hans Scharoun*, Phaidon, London.

Jones, Peter Blundell (2010), 'A careful reading', *Building Design*, April, 14–20.

Jones, Theodore (1997), *Carnegie Libraries Across America*, John Wiley & Sons, New York.

Kelly, Thomas and Kelly, Edith (1977), *Books for the People*, Andre Deutsch, London.

Khan, Ayub (2009), *Better by Design: An Introduction to Planning and Designing a New Library Building*, Facet Publishing, London.

Klinenberg, Eric (2012), *Going Solo: The Extraordinary Rise and Surprising Appeal of Living Alone*, The Penguin Press, New York.

Kloos, Maarten (ed.) (1993), *Public Interiors*, Architecture & Natura Press, Amsterdam.

Krol, Jan and Koren, Marian (2003), *New Library Buildings in the Netherlands*, Netherlands Public Library Association, The Hague.

Larsen, Jonna Holmgaard (ed.) (2006), *Nordic Public Libraries in the Knowledge Society*, Danish National Library Authority, Copenhagen, Denmark.

Latimer, Karen (2011), 'Collections to connections: changing spaces and new challenges in academic library buildings', in *Library Design: From Past to Present, Library Trends*, 60(1), 112–133.

Lawson, Bryan (2001), *The Language of Space*, Architectural Press, London.

Lewis, Martin (2010), 'The University of Sheffield Library Information Commons: a case study', *Journal of Library Administration*, 50, 143–160.

Lushington, Nolan (2002), *Libraries Designed for Users*, Neal-Schuman Publishers, New York.

Lushington, Nolan (2008), *Libraries Designed for Kids*, Facet, London.

MacLeod, Roy (ed.) (2004), *The Library of Alexandria*, I.B. Tauris, London.

Markus, Thomas, A. (2004), *Buildings & Power: Freedom and Control in the Origin of Modern Building Types*, Routledge, London.

Marquand, David (2004) *Decline of the Public: The Hollowing-out of Citizenship*, Polity, Cambridge.

Martin, Hervé (1997), *Guide to Modern Architecture in Paris*, Éditions Alternatives, Paris.

Mattern, Shannon (2007), *The New Downtown Library*, University of Minneapolis Press, Minneapolis/London.

McKnight, Sue (ed.) (2010), *Envisioning Future Academic Libraries*, Facet Publishing, London.

McMenemy, David (2009), *The Public Library*, Facet Publishing, London.

McNicol, Sarah (2008), *Joint-use Libraries*, Chandos Press, Oxford.

Mehtonen, Pentti (2011), 'Public library buildings in Finland: an analysis of the architectural and librarianship discourses from 1945 to the present' in *Library Trends: Library Design: From Past to Present*, 60(1), 152–173.

MLA (November 2010b), *What Do the Public Want from Libraries? User and Non-user Research – Full Research Report*, Ipsos MORI Social Research Institute, London.

MLA (2010a), *Opening Up Spaces: Bringing New People into Museums, Libraries and Archives by Supporting Self-organised Learning*, MLA, London.

Moore, Rowan (2011), 'Canada Water Library – review', *The Observer*, 4 December.

Morrison, Catherine (2002), 'Between the lines', *The Guardian*, 30 April.

Niegaard, Hellen (2011), 'Library space and digital challenges' in *Library Trends: Library Design: From Past to Present*, 60(1), 174–189.

Nielsen Books (2012), *Press release*. Available at www.nag.org.uk/Nielsen_2011_book_production_figures_press_release_feb_2012_pdf

Oldenburg, Ray (1999), *The Great Good Place*, Marlowe & Company, New York.

Phethean, Ellen (ed.) (2009), *The Library Book: A History of the City Library in Newcastle*, City of Newcastle upon Tyne in association with Ryder Architecture, Newcastle upon Tyne.

Plummer, Henry (2009), *The Architecture of Natural Light*, Thames & Hudson, London.

Raven, Debby (2011), 'Drawing them in', *CILIP Update*, December, 33–36.

Reed, Henry Hope (1986), *The New York Public Library: Its Architecture and Decoration*, W.W. Norton & Company, New York.

Rees, Gwendolen (1924), *Libraries for Children*, Grafton & Co., London.

Resnais, Alain, *Tout la mémoire du monde*, 20 minute film exploring the interior of the Bibliothèque Nationale in Paris, 1956.

Revill, Don (1996), *Working Papers on Architects' Briefs*, SCONUL, London.

RIBA Journal (2011), *Read Between the Lines: Libraries for the Future*, 118(11), 1–98.

Rossiter, Ann (2011), *A Master Class in Library Design: Space Planning Visit to Leicester*, SCONUL, London (http://www.sconul.ac.uk/news/evolvinglibraries).

Sanin, Francisco (1994), *Münster City Library: Architekturbüro Bolles-Wilson + Partner*, Phaidon Press, London.

Sannwald, William W. (2001), *Checklist of Library Building Design Considerations*, American Library Association, Chicago.

Santi, Romero, *Library Architecture: Recommendations for a Comprehensive Research Project*, Col-legi d'Arquitectes de Catalunya, Barcelona, Spain.

Scandinavian Public Library Quarterly (2010 News item on Stockholm's subway libraries: 'Culture gets a prize in Stockholm', 43(4), 27.

Schlipf, Fred (2011), 'The dark side of library architecture: the persistence of dysfunctional designs' in *Library Trends: Library Design: From Past to Present*, 60(1), 227–255.

Schmidt, Morten, 2010, *On Library Architecture*, lecture at The Royal Academy, London, 19 April.

Shonfield, Katherine (2003), 'Reading room', *The Architects' Journal*, 20 March, 28–35.

Spens, Michael (1994), *Viipuri Library: Alvar Aalto*, Academy Editions, London.

Stauffacher, Jack W. (ed.) (2003), *Inscriptions at the Old Public Library in San Francisco*, The Book Club of California with the San Francisco Public Library, California.

Stonehouse, Roger and Stromberg, Gerhard (2004), *The Architecture of The British Library at St Pancras*, Spon Press, London.

Sudjic, Deyan (2006), *The Edifice Complex: How the Rich and Powerful Shape the World*, Penguin Books, London.

Swimmer, Laura (2004), *Process: Seattle Central Library*, Documentary Media, Seattle.

Thompson, Godfrey (1989), *Planning and Design of Library Buildings*, Butterworth Architecture, London.

Thorhauge, Jens (ed.) (2002), *Nordic Public Libraries*, Danish National Library Authority, Copenhagen.

Usherwood, Bob (2007), *Equity and Excellence in the Public Library*, Ashgate, Aldershot.

Wagner, Gulten S. (1992), *Public Libraries as Agents of Communication*, The Scarecrow Press, London.

Woodward, Jeanette, *Countdown to a New Library*, ALA, Chicago & London, 2000.

Worpole, Ken (1993), *Towns for People: Transforming Urban Life*, Open University Press, Milton Keynes.

Worpole, Ken (2000), *The Value of Architecture: Design, Economy and the Architectural Imagination*, RIBA Future Studies, London.

Yoshida, Yuko (2009), 'The public library as a space for informal learning', *Scandinavian Public Library Quarterly*, 42(2), 14–15.

Young, Eleanor (2011), 'Storeys with a twist', *RIBA Journal*, 118(11), 44–53.

WEBSITES

Academic Libraries of the Future www.futurelibraries.info

American Libraries Design showcase 2012 http://americanlibrariesmagazine.org/content/library-design-showcase-2012

Architectural Librarians Group www.arclib.org.uk

Cabe Design Library www.cabe.org.uk/library

Designing Libraries Database (UK) www.designinglibraries.org.uk

Library Design & Architecture – 2012 http://core.library.drake.edu/2012/04/18/library-design-architecture-2012-slideshow/

Library Journal (USA) http://lj.libraryjournal.com/about/lj-magazine-archive/

Libris Design (US) http://librisdesign.org

National Libraries Day http://nationallibrariesday.org.uk/

Sconul Library Design Awards www.sconul.ac.uk

Twentieth-Century Society www.c20society.org.uk

Further acknowledgements

In addition, the following people helped bring the project to fruition:

Zoinul Abidin, London Borough of Barking & Dagenham
John Allan, Avanti Architects
Chris Banks, University Librarian & Director, Library, Special Collections & Museums, University of Aberdeen
Sheri Besford, BDP Architects
Steve Beasant, Library Design Consultant, Demco Interiors
Alistair Black, Graduate School of Library & Information Services, University of Illinois
Medi Bernard, Services and Strategy Manager, Bournemouth Libraries, Information, Culture & Community Learning
Adam Blacker, BDP Architects
Gerald Blaikie, www.scotcities.com
Michelle Brennan, RMJM Architects
Graham Brown, Bournemouth Libraries, Information, Culture & Community Learning
Jane Bushell, Team Leader & Assistant Library Manager, London Borough Hammersmith & Fulham
Leonore Charlton, library design consultant
Chris Connolly, community activist
Richard Cowley, BDP
Karen Cunningham, Head of Libraries & Cultural Venues, Glasgow Life
Justin De Syllas, Avanti Architects
Sergio Dogliani, Deputy Head, Whitechapel Idea Store
Kevin Duff, Birmingham City Council
Tony Durcan, Newcastle City Council
Brian Edwards, Emeritus Professor, Edinburgh College of Art
Christophe Egret, Studio Egret West
David Fay, Newcastle City Council
Richard Flisher, CPMG Architects
Angela Foster, Newcastle City Council
Linda Foster, Area Manager, Library Services, London Borough of Southwark

Brian Gambles, Assistant Director – Culture, Directorate of Environment & Culture, Library & Archive Services, Birmingham City Council
Piers Gough, CZWG Architects
John Harrington, Head of Information Services, King's Norton Library, Cranfield University
Richard Hawkins, CILIP Library
Gareth Hoskins, Gareth Hoskins Architects
Yvonne Irvine, ArchitecturePLB
Oliver Key, University of Surrey Library
Lucas Lawrence, Studio Egret West
Martin Lewis, University of Sheffield
Josep Llinàs, Josep Llinàs Carmona, Barcelona
Nick Lomax, Managing Director, LCE Architects
Gayle Mault, Foster + Partners
Kate Millin, Asst Director, Libraries, Archives & Adult Learning, Dudley Council
Nathaniel Moore, Hopkins Architects
Anna Motture, CZWG Architects
Dawn Nash, Project Manager, Development Team, Cambridgeshire Libraries, Archives & Information
Michaela Newman, Royal London Borough of Kingston Upon Thames
Gemma Noakes, Studio Egret West
Graeme Pick, Centre Manager, Winchester Discovery Centre
Peter Reed, Epsom and Ewell Local & Family History Centre
Justine Rochester, Facilities Manager, Kier Services Limited, Brighton
Ann Rossiter, SCONUL
Kate Rouse, Jubilee and Central Services Manager, Brighton & Hove Council
Jane Savidge, Director of Library and Learning Support Services, University of Surrey
Mike Skilton, Architecture PLB
Roger Subirà, Josep Llinàs Carmona, Barcelona
Lee Taylor, Ryder Architecture

Vashti Thorne, London Borough of Barking & Dagenham
Catherine Tranmer, Architecture Information Consultant
Bob Usherwood, Emeritus Professor of Librarianship, University of Sheffield
Elizabeth Walker, Bennetts Associates
Jon Ward, London Borough of Sutton Library Services

Rupert Wheeler, mackenzie wheeler
Adrian Whittle, Head of Libraries, London Borough of Southwark
Valerie Wormald, mackenzie wheeler
Masha Zrncic, Consortium of the Centre De Cultura Contemporània De Barcelona

Index

Aberdeen, university library 8, 10, 13, 27, 54, 82, 146–149, 179, 181, 186

academic libraries 11, 94

agora 19, 24, 54

Amsterdam, life and culture 11, 56; city library 13, 55, 69, 99

Apeldoorn, library and cultural centre 73, 74, 75

architecture, competitions 26, 65, 66–68, 89, 114, 130, 146, 150, 159; and democracy 4, 5, 19, 49, 50, 54, 188, 189; library as building type 32, 38, 42, 49, 135, 167, 188; modernism 33, 49, 50, 188; neo-classical 13, 14, 32, 34, 42, 43, 49; signature 61; symbolic value 19, 32, 33, 41, 45, 50, 52, 56, 83

archives 16, 39, 40, 41, 120, 127, 146

ark, library as 33, 36, 114

art galleries in libraries 11, 69, 70, 73, 75, 83, 86, 87, 95, 121, 169

atrium 14, 17, 24, 25, 26, 27, 28, 46, 48, 81, 83, 86, 91, 95, 109, 112, 115, 119, 132, 134, 146, 147,149, 150, 151, 153, 177

Barcelona, Jaume Fuster Library 12, 38, 77, 79, 93, 94, 100, 104–106, 172, 173

Barking, learning centre and library 82, 86, 169

Belfast, Linen Hall Library 40

Berlin, state library 21, 91

Bibliothèque Nationale, Paris 8

Birmingham Central Library (1974) 15, 16, 43

Birmingham, new Library of Birmingham (2013) 11, 14, 15–18, 29, 33, 45, 53, 58, 62, 66, 73, 80, 174

bookshelves and book-stacks 14, 65, 94, 122, 144, 151

bookshops and libraries 19, 79

Boscombe, public library 39, 83, 87, 171, 173

Bourne Hall Library, Ewell, Surrey 46, 120–121, 188

Bournemouth, public library 8, 67, 69, 77, 84, 86, 95, 107–110, 169, 170

BREEAM rating 25, 62, 63, 86, 111, 147, 159

Brighton Jubilee Library 2, 8, 11, 63, 67, 69, 83, 90, 95, 101, 111–114

British Library 8, 9, 36, 44, 45, 63, 82, 130, 167

branch libraries 21, 39, 41, 76, 79, 186, 187

CABE 62, 63, 64, 66, 100, 130, 167, 168

cafés in libraries (other than in case studies) 6, 8, 9, 11, 14, 20, 21, 24, 48, 69, 73, 75, 80, 82, 86, 91, 94–96, 172, 177–181

Cambourne, public library 83, 85

campus libraries 8, 13

Canada Water, public library 13, 21, 36, 37, 46, 47, 56, 67, 77, 80, 82, 83, 92, 95, 96, 114–117, 170, 173, 179

Cardiff, city library 69, 79, 81, 95, 99, 165, 183

cathedrals, libraries and relationship to 32–34

Carnegie Libraries 49, 52, 63, 89, 186

car parking, provision for 7, 73, 76, 125, 144

children, libraries for 88, 98–101; infantilisation of design 98, 99, 100; child protection issues 41, 98, 101, 130; story-telling sessions 41, 123

circular plan in building type (other than in case studies) 19, 42, 45–48, 188

circulation 13, 14, 52, 62, 81, 88, 167, 173

citizenship, libraries and 33, 42, 98

Clapham, public library 13, 21, 22, 24–25, 46, 66, 83, 98, 173

collective and public memory, libraries as embodying 33, 37, 40

co-location, principle of 69, 83, 86; with health centres 22, 24, 46, 83, 85, 86; with housing 24, 83, 84, 118; with registry office 94

community libraries 21, 179

computer suites (other than in case studies) 13, 14, 17, 179

consultation (other than in case studies) 68, 73–74

Copenhagen, Krystalgade Library 26

Copenhagen, The Royal Danish National Library ('The Black Diamond') 37, 38, 69, 83, 146

Cranfield University, King's Norton Library 13, 34, 36, 55, 66, 68, 83, 94, 150–152, 185

Dagenham, public library 21, 22, 43, 69, 77, 83, 92, 93, 118–119, 170, 172

Dalston, C.L.R. James Library 21, 22, 83, 171

deep plan 14, 26, 63, 83

Delft, university library 13, 63, 83

design (other than in case studies), the design brief 33, 53, 62, 63, 64, 66, 67, 69, 77, 179; use of colour 26, 55, 63, 81, 82, 98, 99, 100, 120, 170, 173, 179, 183; inclusive design 62; interior design 53, 63, 65, 70, 80, 99, 179

destruction of libraries 39

disability access 14, 62, 66, 101
Discovery Centre, Winchester 84, 87, 95, 96, 97, 101, 143–145
domes, as part of library building type 14, 19, 34, 45–46, 48, 83, 90

education, higher 4, 8, 10, 61, 188
elevators and lifts (other than in case studies) 7, 14, 26, 27, 62, 81, 94
Enfield, public library and new extension 21, 23, 49, 81
English Heritage 16
entrances (other than in case studies) 2, 14, 31, 74, 77, 90, 95, 96 97, 167; basement 8; doors 36, 42, 171–174, 176; and facades 13, 34, 43, 49, 188; hall 39, 80, 83; plinths 8, 171; steps 14, 34, 42, 43, 45, 62 171
escalators 8, 14, 26, 27, 81

flooring 66, 82, 173, 177
Flushing, Queens, New York, public library 26, 168, 170
funding and funding partners 25, 63, 67, 68, 76, 77, 86, 186
furniture 14, 41, 62, 66, 179, 182

Glasgow, The Bridge Arts Centre and Library 122–124, 170, 182
Glasgow, The Mitchell Library 19–20, 41
glazing, darkened 36; public transparency 11, 48, 77, 81, 83, 99; stained glass 32, 37

Hook and Chessington, public library 84, 125–126
hubs and zones 14, 69
Huntingdon, public library and archives 67, 73, 76, 83, 91, 127–129, 180

icons, public buildings as 4, 5
ICT (information and communications technology) 19, 27, 28, 34, 38, 41, 42, 45, 52, 64, 69, 91, 99
Idea Store, Whitechapel 11, 69, 80, 92, 95–96, 139–142, 167, 171, 172, 173
inscription, as part of library design 4, 36

lighting, artificial 14, 38, 63; clerestory 14, 34, 83, 188; daylight and natural 14, 26, 61, 63, 8; night-time 15, 83, 124, 169, 170, 179; roof-lighting 83, 99; solar chimneys 14
life-cycle costings 63–64, 66, 82
living room in the city 4, 14, 26, 27, 64, 79–81
location 61, 64, 76–79, 80, 100, 166
LSE, university library 47

maintenance programmes 61, 63, 64, 82, 86, 166, 182
Malmö Library 13, 83
March, Cambridgeshire, public library 71–73, 83, 94, 96, 171
meeting rooms 62, 88, 95–96, 179
memorial, libraries as memorial buildings 37, 39

mezzanine floors 14, 21, 83, 172
Münster, city library 46, 52, 53

Newcastle, public library 11, 28, 66, 69, 73, 79, 83, 130–133, 170, 171, 180
new media formats 38, 69, 88, 93–94
New York Public Library 10, 37, 43, 172
noise 28, 40, 86, 167, 171
Norwich Millennium Library 11, 12, 13, 29, 43, 48, 56, 69, 79, 81, 91, 94, 95, 134–138, 183

opening hours 88, 90, 94, 95

Passmore Edwards Libraries 31, 49, 186
Peckham, public library 7, 13, 43, 44, 50, 94, 100, 167
performance spaces 54, 72, 76, 80, 84, 86, 95, 96
planning agreement 64, 67, 76, 77
pop-up library 63, 64, 65
post-occupancy evaluation 166–185
Private Finance Initiative (PFI) 63, 66, 67
project steering group 65–66

reading groups, provision for accommodating 41, 95, 99
reading rooms, in traditional library architecture 4, 33, 34, 39, 41, 42, 44, 45, 48, 49, 79, 80, 88, 89, 90, 91, 93, 188
Rotterdam, city library 28, 79, 171
rotunda, as traditional library element 14, 44, 45, 46

scenario planning 11–13
Seattle Public Library 4, 5–7, 11, 13, 21, 46, 63, 83, 93, 95
security 17, 39, 40, 61, 95, 101
self-service technology 14, 94, 95
Seven Kings, public library 65
shallow plan 14
Sheffield Information Commons, university library 83, 94, 153–155
Sheffield Western Bank Library, university library 82, 156–159
Shepherd's Bush, public library 11, 21, 23, 56, 77–78, 91, 95, 96, 101
signage and legibility 43, 62, 88, 93–94, 166, 167, 171, 173, 177, 182
silence, library as a place of 14, 38, 40, 48
space, defensive 14; domestic 41, 80, 99; exhibition 21, 32, 53, 54, 79, 84, 88, 91, 95, 96, 173; networked 14; open-plan 14, 26, 52, 88, 89, 185; public 4, 5, 8, 19, 28, 33, 43, 54, 55, 56, 96, 100, 101, 171, 179, 182, 187; sanctuary 11, 13, 27, 40, 64, 81, 179; shared 14, 99; universal 45, 63
staff roles and facilities (other than in case studies), key role in consultation of design 25, 55, 61, 64, 65, 66, 67, 68, 69, 90, 99, 167; public presence and satellite work-stations 28, 81, 95, 101, 172, 187; back-office facilities 96, 166, 168, 179–182
staircases, ceremonial 21, 34, 35, 36, 91, 177; spiral 46, 184

stock sections, lending library 11, 88, 90, 91, 94, 95, 101, 117, 172; reference library 10, 40, 41, 48, 88, 91, 93, 101

Stockholm, city library 34, 45, 46, 83, 188

storage, buggy space 101, 167; public lockers 73, 80, 101

Stratford, London, public library 54, 79, 80

study carrels 14, 188

Swiss Cottage, London, public library 34, 35, 51, 82, 95, 172, 184, 188

third place, library as a space between home and work 11, 12, 187

toilets 62, 73, 79, 88, 94, 95, 101, 177

townscape setting 54, 56, 79, 83, 89, 167, 170, 187

traditional library architecture, general schema 14

University of Surrey, library and learning centre 159–163, 178, 179

Uppsala, public library 50, 80

urban regeneration, library role in 5, 25, 43, 76, 186

Utrecht, university library 55, 56, 68

ventilation, air-conditioning 14; natural 167

Viipuri, public library 55, 83, 90, 99, 188

wayfinding 88, 93–94, 166, 173

Wi-fi provision 48, 91, 93